WHAT'S IN A RUSSIAN WORD?
From Sounds to Structures

Also available in the Russian Language series:

First Russian Vocabulary (key to the Russian Texts Series), Patrick Waddington
A Guide to Essay Writing in Russian, Svetlana and Stephen le Fleming
Modern Russian: An Advanced Grammar Course, Derek Offord
The New Russia: Readings on Russian Culture, Nijole White
Russian by Subjects (a classified vocabulary), Patrick Waddington
Russian for Business Studies, Svetlana le Fleming

WHAT'S IN A RUSSIAN WORD
From Sounds to Structures

IAN PRESS

Bristol Classical Press

First published in 2000 by
Bristol Classical Press
an imprint of
Gerald Duckworth & Co. Ltd
61 Frith Street
London W1D 3JL
e-mail: inquiries@duckworth-publishers.co.uk
Website: www.ducknet.co.uk

Reprinted 2001

A catalogue record for this book is available
from the British Library

ISBN 1-85399-615-7

Typeset by Ian Press

Contents

Preface

I hope here to provide a text which will help people interested in Russian develop their knowledge of its structure, particularly where this concerns the sound-system, the structure of Russian words, and the words themselves.

The book started off as a presentation exclusively of the structure of Russian words, the bits and pieces which can play a most useful part in helping build up vocabulary and making informed guesses about the meanings of words.

I reconsidered this original focus because existing presentations, particularly Charles E. Townsend's *Russian Word-Formation*, but also, for example, Andrews 1996, Cubberley 1994, and Gribble 1973, not to mention Unbegaun 1957, Ryazanova-Clarke/Wade 1999, and the considerable research done and being done in Russia, would have meant me reinventing the wheel. Instead I chose to offer, in a long chapter, a sequence of relatively informal explorations of a small number of Russian words, word-families, and connected topics. Some connections I make will be strictly 'wrong', but wrong connections (within reason) are valid and interesting in themselves. Russian is not my own language, so my intuitions will be different from those of a native speaker, but I still hope that they provide interesting reading and, more than anything, enhance the attractiveness and value of studying Russian. I've retained a certain amount of repetition and would beg the indulgence of more advanced readers for a certain informality and even 'clumsiness of expression' here and there.

While I am responsible for such deficiencies and shortcomings which remain, I gratefully acknowledge the help of many friends, colleagues, and students, among them (in no particular order) Donald Rayfield, Anna Pilkington, Lida Buravova, Neil Cornwell, Anthony Hippisley, Will Ryan, Michael Samilov, Harry Leeming, Tanya Filossofova, Charles Drage, Rachel Bass, Stefan Pugh, Anja Dempe, Oleg Grigorovich, Jamal Ouhalla, Albina Ozieva, Valentina Coe, John Sullivan, Noel Brackney, and particularly Craig Rollo and Lara Ryazanova-Clarke. The style is, I hope, accessible and casual. Some may feel I have overdone the latter, to the extent of the style being academically quite inappropriate; however, I feel comfortable with it as it is, and am assured, and sure, that that is all to the good, for various reasons. Finally, I have bound in the use made of scholarly literature, so that there are few actual references in the text. Everything, I trust, is to be found in the References. Most of all, I would hope that the book leaves space for the reader's imagination, expansion, and correction.

I have also to own up to the fact that, given precious guidance from Graham Douglas of BCP, I am responsible for the typesetting of the book. I reckon I've done a reasonable job, but I pray for your forbearance.

Ian Press

Walthamstow—Cupar—St Andrews, April 2000.

Introduction

Russian, almost everywhere it is learnt, is learnt in an accelerated fashion. This is a great pity, since it is languages such as Russian which are supremely important for all sorts of reasons but which somehow remain remote and exotic. Though the essentials of Russian grammar can be grasped quite quickly, familiarization with a useful chunk of Russian vocabulary, often composed of quite alien-looking words, presents real problems for many people. It is crucial to get down to reading continuous texts, exemplifying the best Russian, as soon as possible, but the most motivated learner can be rapidly disheartened by the constant need to look words up in a dictionary. Experience, both teaching dedicated courses and just dealing with the problems, not at all always with success, suggests that students not only enjoy courses in vocabulary and word-formation, but also advance by leaps and bounds in their learning of Russian once they know how to use dictionaries, how to make connections regarding the bits out of which words might be composed, and how to make *educated* guesses (these *educated* guesses are precisely that — they need to be educated).

None of this is to say that word-formation is a neglected area so far as books are concerned — the Preface should have made that clear. So I have tried to give my contribution a different bias, dwelling less on formal issues and more on actual words and groups of words. In other words (!), I aim to show how familiar Russian words often actually are, describing their structure, how they are derived and, to a much lesser extent, how they are inflected and relate to other words in the sentence. There is no pretension to any sort of 'truth'; that, so far as anyone knows what that is, is fudged. So much the better: this book is about learning, and we learn through mistakes, through exploration — I myself shall make mistakes in this book, but at least they will often be the type speakers make through popular etymology or hypercorrection, they will be mistakes which make some sort of sense — see Andrews 1996:17-24 for an illustration of this.

One area, however, where a reasonably comprehensible and accessible presentation seems needed is that of the sound system of Russian, its *phonology*. In English there are some wonderful, even renowned, technical presentations, and some excellent, down-to-earth, articles; here I offer one description of the sound-system of Russian, a description which in its generalities will help provide a bridge to the exploration of the structure of Russian words. I make only a few vague comments on the actual sounds, since they are in a considerable state of sociolinguistic flux and scholarly reassessment at the moment. It is for you, the reader, to get to real grips with them by listening to Russians.

As part of that bridge I shall look at just what Russian is. Such questions are socially among the most engaging of our times. Conversations with the most diverse people have indicated to me that what often interests people in languages is their history, and particularly the history of their words — doubtless another aspect of the interest in *roots*. This is because we are constantly looking for and selecting words, because more than anything else they are what we use to interpret, to make sense of, our experience — language reflects a small part of our struggle to communicate (or indeed to conceal our thoughts). More often than not we have the haziest, even the most wrong-headed, conception of what a word actually means, so we go for what seems best, most appropriate — we have a need to control our own and others' experience; that (mis)conception reflects our interpretation, our making sense, of the word.

It need not only be in individual words and families of words that this manifests itself: proverbs, sayings, idioms, set expressions, rhetoric, metaphor, silence — I could go on and on, even coming to the dreaded but fascinating *grammar* — all these come together within a language to build its own network, itself inseparable from the individual human being. Individual human beings *express themselves, reveal themselves*, very largely through language (the word *communicate* acquires a broader sense and implications here). Language is processed by speakers/writers, interlocutors/readers, and people who can't avoid processing what is said, written, or implied, in their own terms, and a reliable assessment of what is meant is a fiendishly difficult skill. Most good writers are susceptible of infinite analysis (as are bad writers and as is anyone's use of language, actually). Furthermore, language is part of the glue holding society, whatever that is, together, and varies for a mass of reasons: class, milieu, status of interlocutor, gender, dialect, etc. Language is hijacked by the (nation-)state to its own ends; to satisfy these the language is placed in the straitjacket of a standard, through normalization and occasionally *purification*, and may come over time to reflect the *identity* of a (nation-)state, to provide new, if shallower, roots. A language like English may now be used by more people than are actually native speakers; but for the foreseeable future the *native-speaker* Englishes will retain their sense of roots, and new ones will doubtless develop for the new varieties.

Your psychological makeup will affect what you do with your knowledge of Russian. You can get a long way if you have nothing but the gift of the gab, but knowing lots of words and how Russian words 'work', learning lots of idioms and 'sayings', and applying grammatical discipline and rigour, can arguably more than make up for not having that gift. And, I am most unfashionably convinced, if your aim is serious, then learn by becoming familiar with the best of the language, through voracious reading — familiarization with the language's realization, and through a good deal of regular practice, as if you were learning a musical instrument.

Chapter 1: Sounds and Spelling

1.1 Preamble

It was something of a twentieth-century commonplace that speech is primary and writing secondary; there is no problem taking on trust this rather obvious *prima facie* truth, so long as we remember that once languages started acquiring writing systems (and that happened a very long time ago) the original relationship between speech and writing started to change, with writing influencing speech.

The all-important tool with which Russian is written is the *Cyrillic alphabet*, as developed largely from the Greek majuscules in the tenth century. It is almost certainly secondary, having come quite hard on the heels of what is now known as *Glagolitic*, developed largely from the Greek minuscules by Constantine (subsequently St Cyril) in the ninth century. The application of these names to these alphabets is more recent than the alphabets themselves, with the name *Cyrillic* recognizing the creator of the first known Slavonic alphabet but not applied to that alphabet.

1.2 Transliteration and transcription

In western works on Russian and Slavonic linguistics, Russian may be transliterated using the Library of Congress (LC) system of transliteration (often without the extra marks of the full system). In linguistic works, the *International* system of transliteration is used. By *transliteration* is meant the replacement of one or more letters of one alphabet with one or more letters of another alphabet.

To represent the sounds or sound-structure of Russian, the *International Phonetic Alphabet* (IPA) is normally used. This is a *transcription*. It has nothing to do with spelling. Many Slavonic linguists use an adapted *International* system of transliteration for transcription (usually a very general transcription); justifications for this would include that it reduces the number of symbols required in the text, i.e. facilitates cross-referencing between transliteration and transcription, that it may be more generally accessible, and that it happens to be a reasonable guide to the system of sounds anyway.

Returning to transliteration, Cyrillic, plus the simplified LC and International transliterations of present-day Russian, are as follows (remember not to confuse transliteration with transcription, e.g. ы is transliterated as *y*, but transcribed in most instances as [ɨ], while IPA [y] corresponds to French *u*, German *ü*):

а	б	в	г	д	е	ё	ж	з	и	й	к	л	м	н	о	п
a	b	v	g	d	e	ë	zh	z	i	i	k	l	m	n	o	p
a	b	v	g	d	e	ë	ž	z	i	j	k	l	m	n	o	p

1

р	с	т	у	ф	х	ц	ч	ш	щ	ъ	ы	ь	э	ю	я
r	s	t	u	f	kh	ts	ch	sh	shch	"	y	'	è	iu	ia
r	s	t	u	f	x/ch	c	č	š	šč	"	y	'	é/è	ju	ja

We might mention the *International* transliteration of certain letters which are either, for ъ and ь, now used differently, or are no longer used (those with a subscript denote original nasals, ǫ and ę becoming respectively *u* and *ja* in the immediate ancestor of Russian):

ѣ	ѵ	ѳ	i	ь	ъ	w	ѭ	ѩ	ꙗ	ѧ	ѫ	ꙃ	ѱ	оу
ě	i	f/t	i	ь	ъ	o	jǫ	ję	ja	ę	ǫ	ks	ps	u

1.3 The sound-system of Russian

1.3.1 General presentation

Phonetics might be defined as the general description and classification of speech sounds, without reference to any specific language. It traditionally comprises three branches, namely *articulatory phonetics* (how our organs of speech produce the sounds), *acoustic phonetics* (how the sounds are transmitted through, usually, the air), and *auditory phonetics* (how the sounds are received by the ear and decoded by the brain). The approach here is through articulatory phonetics.

Phonology is traditionally the study of the *system* of the sounds of a particular language, partly through the application of phonetic data, partly through the formulation of hypotheses.

The aim here is to provide a very simple description of the phonology of Russian. Phonology ideally covers all the data of the language, but this is impossible because, for instance, language is creative (i.e. the data are infinite), and it is difficult precisely to define the limits of the admissible data, i.e. do we include absolutely everything — but how do we know what 'everything' is?

Phonetics will take a back seat here, both because the sounds of Russian are currently in a state of considerable, and most interesting, flux and because a considerable amount of reassessment of the description of Russian is underway.

What is the minimum we need to know? Well, we can start with the division into *vowels* (no articulatory obstruction) and *consonants*, the latter sub-dividing into *sonorants* (or *resonants*), which have both vocalic and consonantal features and where there is some small measure of obstruction, and *obstruents*, where there is more to considerable obstruction. Bear in mind that vowels and sonorants tend to be *voiced-only*, and that the latter may behave as if vowels, i.e. they may form syllables, e.g. *-en* in German *haben*, *r* in Czech *Brno*. We conventionally see the vowels as *a, e, i, o, u,* and the sonorants as *l, r, m, n, j* (as in *yacht*), and *w* (which may become *v* in certain languages, e.g. Russian) —

the last two are often referred to as *glides*. The consonants may be divided, on the basis of their place of articulation, into *labial* (*p, b, m*), *labio-dental* (*f, v*), *interdental* (English *th*), *dental* (*t, d, s, z, c* (= *ts*), *l, n, r*), *palatal* (*š, ž, č, šč, j*), and *velar* (*k, g, x*). On the basis of their manner or mode of articulation they may be divided into *stops/plosives* (consonants where the expulsion of air is momentarily totally blocked, e.g. *p, b, t, d, k, g, m, n*),[1] *fricatives* (consonants where the passage of air is considerably constricted, e.g. *f, s, l, r*), and *affricates* (consonants where a total blockage is released slowly, creating a stop which becomes a fricative during articulation, e.g. the dental affricate *č*, i.e. *t* becoming *sh*). Let's put this into Cyrillic:

Vowels:	а я э е ы и о ё у ю
Consonants:	
Sonorants:	л р м н й (в)
Obstruents:	all the others, thus...
Labial:	п б and the sonorant м
Labio-dental:	ф в
Dental:	т д с з ц and the sonorants н л р
Palatal:	ж ч ш щ and the sonorant й
Velar:	к г х

In Russian most of these consonants can be paired phonemically (= phonologically, systematically) according to whether they are *voiceless* or *voiced*, e.g. *t — d, k — g*, or *non-palatalized/hard* or *palatalized/soft*, e.g. the *b*'s in быть 'to be' — бить 'to beat' The sonorants and affricates do not participate in the phonological voice pairing in Russian (from the point of view of phonemes[2]), and the dental affricate (ц), the palatals, and to some extent the velars, do not participate in the palatalization pairing. The following lists are restricted to what is conveyed by the individual Cyrillic letters:

---

[1] In the case of the last two the mouth is simply blocked, the air emerging through the nose — explore what happens when you have a cold and your nose is blocked.

[2] A phoneme is a distinctive, abstract unit, which may be likened to an actual sound or characterized (in a somewhat circular fashion) by its difference from other phonemes. It is essentially a group of very similar sounds each of which occurs automatically in a particular phonetic context (they are thus all in 'complementary distribution'), but which are never, as a rule, confused with other such groups of sounds (they thus guarantee semantic differences). The phoneme is often seen as somewhat 'old-hat' as a concept, but it does, from the point of view of many European *spelling systems*, seem to reflect a psychological reality, given that they are devised by speakers.

Voiced/Voiceless:	п-б ф-в т-д с-з ш-ж к-г
Hard/Soft:	none

For a language with a claimed extensive pairing of distinctive hard and soft consonants, the last line in the box above comes as a surprise. How are these pairs represented? Well, Russian arguably has five distinctive vowels, but ten vowel letters.[3] These letters, when they *immediately* follow a consonant in the spelling, tell you whether the consonant immediately preceding is hard or soft. For those consonants which do not participate in the hard-soft pairing, the spelling is by historical convention rather than based on the pronunciation, except, arguably, in the case of velars, where the hard-soft distinction is largely automatic, i.e. there are few cases where meaning distinctions hinge on whether the velar is hard or soft. When the 'soft-series vowel letters' (see below) follow a hard or soft sign, or follow another vowel, or come at the very beginning of a word, they stand for two sounds, viz. the consonant *j* + one of the vowels *a*, *e*, *o*, *u* (*i* is omitted, since the *j* most often seems absorbed into the *i*-sound, though it might be kept in mind from the point of view of word-formation). Do remember that the letter й represents a consonant (*j*), and that this consonant may be spelt either with й or 'understood' as the first component of the soft-series vowel letter. So, first vowel-letters:

а э ы о у:	hard-series vowel letters (*not* hard vowels!)
я е и ё ю:	soft-series vowel letters (*not* soft vowels!)

Secondly, distinctive hard-soft pairs of consonants:

б в д з к л м н п р с т ф + а э ы о у	— hard consonant
б в д з к л м н п р с т ф + я е и ё ю	— soft consonant

And thirdly, other consonant letters (spelling by historical convention):

ж ш + а е и ё/о у (ь):	hard consonant
ч щ + а е и ё/о у (ь):	soft consonant
ц + а е и/ы о у:	hard consonant
к г х + а о у:	hard consonant
к г х + е и:	soft consonant
я е (и) ё ю:	absolute word-initially and after a vowel = йа йэ (йи) йо йу
я е и ё ю:	after a hard or soft sign = йа йэ йи йо йу[4]

---

[3]There are compelling arguments for a sixth distinctive vowel, informally that partly represented by the letter ы, but let us exploit the neat 5:10 pairing here.

[4]Since the use of й in these combinations can sometimes confuse because it suggests actual spelling, it can be helpful to substitute j, giving ja jэ jи jo jy. You might feel

So, the pairs of vowel letters in the first of the three boxes above are an efficient way of representing one set of five vowels but at least twenty-six (the second box) distinctive consonants. The actual usage of the five pairs is not equal: the э-е pair is barely exploited, since palatalizable consonants occurring before an *e*-sound in all but recent borrowings are automatically palatalized. Note too that the two *i*-sounds, different though they may appear to most ears, seem to be paired: и occurs absolute word-initially and after *soft* consonants, while ы occurs after *hard* consonants. It is interesting that the two vowels, *i* and *e*, palatal or front vowels (the two you might dare to call 'soft'), which in many languages *automatically* cause some degree of palatalization, are the ones which 'upset' the system. Current research is beginning to clarify this.

What can be said to clarify why there are conventions here in the third box? To start with, would it not make more sense to have the following little system?

| ша шэ шы шо шу жа жэ жы жо жу | (because hard-only) |
| чя че чи чё чю щя ще щи щё щю | (because soft-only) |

The answer (needed because some people often argue for such spellings as чя) is quite simply 'no'. Such a 'solution' would be phonetic. Given that the hardness or softness of the sounds represented by these letters, and of ц, is phonologically irrelevant, the orthography as it has emerged over the years is, while imperfect, completely tolerable.

There are a few exceptions for ж ш ч щ, e.g. borrowings such as жюри 'jury', парашют 'parachute'. Originally all four represented soft sounds. The choice of ё or о (i.e. only under stress) after all four is quite tricky, and has no effect on the pronunciation. We can start by suggesting that о is used where the stress never ever moves from that vowel. But what does 'never ever' mean? Thus, in шёпот 'whisper(ing)' the stress is fixed in the noun, but the verb is шептáть 'to whisper', 'justifying' the ё. But then we have поджóг 'arson' with о as against жгла 'she/it burnt', жечь 'to burn', and жёг 'he/it burnt', with no vowel, phonetic *e* and phonetic *o* respectively. Moreover, in шептáть we have, among other forms, ты шéпчешь 'you whisper', with phonetic, stressed *e*. Perhaps шёпот is more 'verbal' than поджóг (and also the other nouns, all with о, with the 'burn' root, e.g. изжóга 'heartburn', ожóг 'a burn (injury)'). Formerly one *did* encounter шóпот (just as with other 'major' languages, Russian was refreshingly variable until codified and standardized — and, of course, it *essentially* still is!). Overall, however, the rule works: thus we have жёлтый 'yellow' 'because of' the feminine short form желтá, but чóпорный 'staid, strait-laced' because the stress never moves — note, by the way, for example, the 'infernal' spelling in Blok's «В соседнем дóме óкна жóлты.» (*Фáбрика*, 1903). It might be asked why we have ё in печёшь 'you bake'. After all, the stress is fixed. Well, here perhaps you

---

it would be theoretically neater to have jы rather than jи (i.e. to use the hard-series vowels only), though that might not reflect what we hear. See 1.3.4.

go outside the verb печь 'to bake'. First, in мо́чь 'to be able, can', there is ты мо́жешь 'you can' (the stress is therefore *not* fixed from a conjugational point of view); and secondly, where the consonant before the ё is one paired for hardness and softness, since the underlying vowel is *e*, you must have ё in order to reflect the softness, thus ты идёшь you are going/walking', ты дрéмлешь 'you doze'.

So it might be a case of gradation, starting with strict o where stress is fixed on the o, then shading from where the whole family of words linked to a particular root is felt to belong together, to word nests which are looser, and finally to inflectional endings, where the rule will be affected by influences from outside the word family, and also most susceptible to stress variation. All this is somewhat undermined by the apparent fact that щ is never followed by o, and occurs in several words and word families where the [o] is always stressed, e.g. щёлкать 'to crack', щётка 'brush'. Such examples even demolish the idea that o is to be found in nominal forms and ё in verbal ones. But some justification for the argument can be clawed back because on a closer look що in fact *does* occur, in stressed endings, e.g. плащо́м, instrumental singular of masculine плащ 'raincoat' (there are about twelve such nouns) and the single мощо́й, instrumental singular of epicene моща́ 'a very thin person' (there are no neuters), and at least in the suffix of the diminutive борщо́к 'borshch'.

The consonant ц is hard, but its rules of combinability with a following vowel are slightly different from those for the other unpaired hard consonants, ж and ш. For a start, цё is not found at all — it is always цо́ (the reason for this is that the language overwhelmingly only has це́, where e is actually a different type of *e*, which doesn't as a rule become o — more about ѣ *jat'* (ě) below — and, of course, it has unstressed це, alternating with це́, e.g., це́лый — цела́ 'whole' and with цо́, e.g., па́льцев — отцо́в 'fingers. — fathers (gen.pl.)'. Secondly, цы is restricted to endings, e.g. отцы́ 'fathers', длиннолúцый 'long-faced', and to a very few roots, e.g. на цы́почках 'on tiptoe', цыга́не 'gipsies', цыплёнок 'chick(en)'. In this connection, you may have wondered why an *e*-type letter may be used in Russian to denote an o. Well, the reason is that *e* became *o* at a certain, quite early, period in the history of the language, but at a time when the spelling system was more or less in place; since then, efforts have been made to devise a new letter, but no generally accepted solution has ever been found (and there remains the fact that the e pronounced *o* is often actually pronounced *e* in other forms in a single word family (as seen above), so that keeping e may be simpler all round). Basically, *e* became *o* in Russian when it was stressed and at the same time *either* immediately preceded a hard consonant *or* immediately preceded silence. The change must have been underway when ж and ш became hard, since we have идёшь, etc. (the soft sign here is purely historical and conventional); but what of купéц 'merchant', отéц 'father'? The answer would have to be that the *c*-sound hardened later, when the change of *e* to *o* had ceased to be 'alive' or 'productive'. This can be confirmed by relatively recent borrowings, e.g. газéта 'newspaper', билéт 'ticket', which are certainly never ⁺газёта, ⁺билёт.

In this connection, you will notice words where, given what has just been said, you would expect the e to be pronounced o, e.g. лес 'forest', бéлый 'white', and нéбо 'sky', житиé 'life of a saint', where the e's are stressed and followed by a hard consonant or silence. Here two factors are to be borne in mind. The first two examples, looked up in a pre-1918 dictionary, would be found as лѣсъ, бѣлый (and you might have difficulty finding them at first, as ѣ *jat'* comes much later in the alphabet than e); this quite different letter reflects what was originally another e, phonetically quite different (there is still no consensus as to exactly how it sounded, though probably [ie] or like the é in French *porté* 'carried' or even closer, supported by the fact that original stressed e before a soft consonant, which doesn't change to o, is actually pronounced like that; there is also evidence for its having been an a-sound). For the last two examples, both with original e (i.e. not *jat'*), the hint comes out clearest in the second: these are Church Slavonic words, and the change to o tended not to happen in such words. This is reflected in the different semantic nuances of нéбо 'roof of the mouth, palate' and житьё 'everyday life'. We'll return to this, particularly in Chapter 3.

Last, note that the distribution of к, г, х before the vowel letters is neat and complementary. Consequently, though hard and soft *k, g, x* are indeed found, they are entirely predictable (more later). In the thirteen *paired* consonants this is *not* the case: they can in principle all contrast before all five vowels, at the end of words, and immediately before other consonants. The situation with *k, g, x* is complicated by only a very few words within what might be called 'core Russian' (there will always be exceptions in exotic words, e.g. non-Russian place-names). Thus: э́то ткёт 'weaves this' — э́тот кот 'this cat' (if the words are pronounced together, which is reasonably normal, the significant difference is between the two *k*'s; see Hamilton 1980), берегя́ 'keeping, saving' (a disputed imperfective gerund of берéчь) — берегá 'banks, shores' (the only difference is in the two *g*'s), and a surname such as Лукья́нов, where there is a soft (or, optionally, hard) *k* before the consonant *y*. Another instance where there is a soft velar before a soft consonant is where both consonants are velars, e.g. in мя́гкий 'soft', лёгкий 'light, easy' (the г here is most often pronounced as a soft х).

All other consonants may be followed by both series of vowels and by both the hard sign and the soft sign. The *hard series* indicates that

> the preceding consonant is hard
> *or* there is no consonant before the vowel when the vowel is absolute word-initial
> *or* when, rarely, another vowel immediately precedes

The *soft series* indicates that

> the preceding consonant is soft
> *or* there is a й-sound, i.e. the consonant [j] (jot/yod), before the vowel
> when it is absolute word-initial or immediately preceded by another
> vowel (exceptions = loan words, e.g. район)

A soft or hard sign *preceded by a consonant and followed by a soft-series vowel* makes the vowel behave as if it were absolute word-initial; for the consonant see 1.3.4.1.2.

1.3.2 Stress

Russian is often regarded as having 'free stress' — this is not the case, as the stress is simply mobile in a regular, though still complex, fashion. The fact is that there is no single rule as to where the stress falls in a word. The stressed vowel of Russian is characterized by its force and even loudness; it is not distinguished by, for instance, length.

Russian spelling is historical. The changes in vowels ('reduction') when they are unstressed are almost certainly more recent, so the fact that the unstressed vowels in Russian are not pronounced as might be expected from the spelling need not worry us too much in a book about words. Just to realize how lucky we are with this spelling policy in Russian, compare two words and some of their forms in, respectively, Russian and Belarusian, where the reformers made the decision to adopt a partially phonetic spelling system:

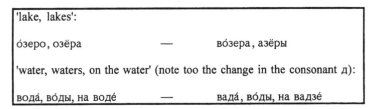

'lake, lakes':		
óзеро, озёра	—	вóзера, азёры
'water, waters, on the water' (note too the change in the consonant д):		
водá, вóды, на водé	—	вадá, вóды, на вадзé

A good deal of work is being done at the moment in the area of Russian unstressed vowels, and intriguing changes are happening, or phenomena are being noted or explored for the first time. Russian may be becoming more 'sing-song', the vowels may be becoming more 'open', and vowels immediately preceding the stressed vowel (always a rather special position in Russian) may lengthen. We have to leave that alone here, so 1.3.3 is rather conventional.

1.3.3 More on the vowels

The approximate vowels of Russian are as follows, using the IPA:

(a) *stressed*:	i		u	(b) *unstressed*:	ɪ		ɯ
		ɛ	ɔ			ʌ/ə	
		a					

The diagrams take a left profile of the mouth and, very approximately, reflect the position of the highest point of the tongue. The *i*- and *e*-type vowels are front, *a*-type vowels are central, and the *u*- and *o*-type vowels are back (note that it is typically the front, i.e., palatal, vowels, which soften immediately preceding consonants in languages); the top line contains the close(d) vowels, the next line down the mid vowels, and the bottom line the open vowel. The five stressed vowels are the phonetic symbols for the five distinctive vowels. Do bear in mind that the 'front' vowels, namely /i/ and /ɛ/, are articulated below the hard palate and are further apart than the 'back', or 'velar' or 'rounded', vowels /u/ and /ɔ/ (/a/ comes somewhat in between).[5]

Are the unstressed vowels to be interpreted as separate phonemes (= distinctive sounds, i.e. sounds which have to be differentiated from other distinctive sounds)? This is suggested by the fact that there is no straight matching between stressed and unstressed vowels in Russian. From the box below we note that unstressed *o* and unstressed *a*, and unstressed *e* and *i*, on the whole coalesce, so that it cannot be predicted from an unstressed *o* or *a* whether the stressed 'form' is *o* or *a* (we can only predict from a stressed vowel to an unstressed one, and even then not in all circumstances), i.e. we only know the correct spelling of the first two vowels of карандáш if we have learnt how to spell it, and the Russian vernacular may have such forms as third person singular non-past[6] он плóтит 'he pays' (instead of 'correct' он плáтит 'he pays') from платúть 'to pay'. This suggests that the unstressed vowels have a certain autonomy, i.e. distinctiveness. The consequence of this is that stress itself is not distinctive. Alternatively, if we see stress as distinctive in Russian (and consequently standing on its own, not attached to any individual vowel), then we simply have the five vowels *i, e, a, o, u*, i.e. stress is independent of the vowels, and the 'stressed' ones may unambiguously represent the 'unstressed' ones when no stress mark accompanies them in the transcription.

---

[5]The slants indicate phonemes.

[6]Far better to refer to what is often thought of as 'present' or 'perfective future' as the non-past; that way we don't have to keep differentiating imperfectives from perfectives, and present and future overlap semantically as well as morphologically anyway. Once you refer to the first person singular, etc., you don't even need to specify the non-past, as the past is morphologically specified by gender and number, not by person and number.

We can argue that the actual variation in the pronunciation of the unstressed vowels reduces their potential distinctive status, favouring the five-vowel system plus distinctive stress.

So, a possible system of the Russian vowels, noting approximate phonetic realizations, is as follows:

Phonemes	Chief Allophones	Allophones (Stressed)	Allophones (Unstressed)
/u/	[u]	SC+[ü]+SC	[ɷ]
/ɛ/	[ɛ]	[e]+SC	[ι], [ɨ]
/i/	[i]	HC+[ɨ]	[ι], [ɨ]
/ɔ/	[ɔ]	SC+[ö]+SC	[ʌ]-, [ʌ‘], [ə]
/a/	[a]	SC+[æ]+SC	[ʌ]-, [ʌ‘], [ə]

Key:

(i)   By convention the chief allophone (an allophone is basically a sound, one of the 'family of sounds' which makes up the phoneme), i.e. the sound found in a majority of environments, represents the phoneme;

(ii) SC = 'soft (palatalized) consonant', HC = 'hard (non-palatalized) consonant';

(iii) '-' = beginning of word if the hyphen follows, end of word if it precedes;

(iv) apostrophe = stress (here in the syllable immediately after the allophone);

(v)   The allophones are enclosed in square brackets, the phonemes in slants.

1.3.4 More on the consonants

The consonantal phonemes may be presented as in the box on the following page (another convention for conveying a soft consonant is to add a line-level hook to the right of or underneath the symbol, e.g. [ḅ] and not as here, where the most recent IPA method is used[7]). Look at the table on thenext page, then come back to the text.

Remember that, essentially, the soft consonants are pronounced accompanied by a simultaneous, so far as is possible, palatal, i.e. *y*, element.[8] The *t* of British English *tune* provides an approximation. Different consonants will realize softness in different ways; in other words, different consonants will soften more or less easily. Or, put even another way, the *y*-sound will be the more perceptible the more difficult the particular consonant is to palatalize — it all comes down to

---

[7]This has the disadvantage of suggesting that the palatal element follows, when the point is that it is a synchronous component of the articulation. In books on Slavonic linguistics palatalization is indicated by an apostrophe.

[8]This becomes more convincing when we recall that soft consonants occur at the very end of words, e.g., мать 'mother' and before other consonants, e.g., только 'only'.

anatomy.[9] Other consonants will be easier, e.g. *t*, or, as in British English the automatic contrast between soft *l* in *leak*, and hard *l* in *look*. But do beware of comparisons with other languages.

So, keep in mind that some Russian consonants are paired for hardness and softness. This is a phonological feature, true of all but six Russian consonants. The exceptions, again, are /ʒ/, /ʃ/, /ts/ (≈ ж, ш, ц: hard-only), /tʃʲ/, /ʃʲː/, /j/ (≈ ч, щ, й: soft-only). In other words, there are three *hard* unpaired consonants and three *soft* unpaired consonants.

PLACE→ MODE ↓		LABIAL vs	vd	LABIO-DENTAL vs	vd	DENTAL vs	vd	PALATAL vs	vd	VELAR vs	vd
STOP	h	p	b	-	-	t	d	-	-	k	g
	s	pʲ	bʲ	-	-	tʲ	dʲ	-	-	kʲ	(gʲ)
AFFR	h	-	-	-	-	ts	-	-	-	-	-
	s	-	-	-	-	-	-	tʃʲ	-	-	-
FRIC	h	-	-	f	v	s	z	ʃ	ʒ	x	(ɣ)
	s	-	-	fʲ	vʲ	sʲ	zʲ	ʃʲː	ʒʲː	(xʲ)	(ɣʲ)
SON	h	-	m	-	-	-	n	-	-	-	-
	s	-	mʲ	-	-	-	nʲ	-	-	-	ŋʲ
	h	-	-	-	-	-	l	-	-	-	-
	s	-	-	-	-	-	lʲ	-	-	-	-
	h	-	-	-	-	-	r	-	-	-	-
	s	-	-	-	-	-	rʲ	-	-	-	-
		-	-	-	-	-	-	-	j	-	-

Key:

The *horizontal axis* gives the place of articulation. The *vertical axis* gives the manner/mode of articulation, respectively *stops, affricates, fricatives*, and *sonorants* or *resonants*. In historical Slavonic linguistics *l* and *r* are often referred to as *liquids*.. The abbreviations 'h' and 's' = 'hard' (or 'non-palatalized') and = 'soft' (or 'palatalized'), and 'vs' and 'vd' = respectively 'voiceless' and 'voiced'.

Now let's come to the velars, where the spelling rules reflect the actual pronunciation: on the one hand ки, ке (automatically soft), and on the other hand ка, ко, and ку (automatically hard) — see the table below.

---

[9] Labials are difficult to palatalize, and the *y*-sound may be very salient when they are soft (from comparison with other languages one concludes that this *is* the case, though native speaker assertions and even practice make one feel the situation in Russian is indeed rather special; the sense of absence of the *y*-element may be psychological in native speakers).

But, since there are generally accepted exceptions indicating /k/-/kʲ/ (киоскёр 'kiosk-holder', etc.), there is a need to split this natural, i.e. *velar*, class (there may be no examples of /x/-/xʲ/, and the most often cited pair for /g/-/gʲ/ is controversial, i.e. берегá /bʲɛrʲɛ'ga/ 'banks, shores' — берегя́ /bʲɛrʲɛ'gʲa/ 'saving, protecting').

Let us summarize the hard-soft opposition as realized after consonants in the following way, taking /t/-/tʲ/ as an example of a paired consonant (i), /k/ as an example of a velar (ii), and /ʒ/ as an example of one of the six unpaired consonants (iii):

(i)	[tʲɛ]	[tʲa]	[tʲi]	[tʲɔ]	[tʲu]	=	/tʲ/
	◊	◊	◊	◊	◊		
	([tɛ])	[ta]	[ti]	[tɔ]	[tu]	=	/t/
(ii)	[kʲɛ]	—	[kʲi]	—	—		
	—	[ka]	—	[kɔ]	[ku]	=	/k/
or	[kʲɛ]	—	[kʲi]	[kʲɔ]	—	=	/kʲ/
				◊			
	—	[ka]	—	[kɔ]	[ku]	=	/k/
or	[kʲɛ]	—	[kʲi]	[kʲɔ]	—	=	/kʲ/
			◊	◊			
	—	[ka]	[ki]	[kɔ]	[ku]	=	/k/
(iii)	[ʒɛ]	[ʒa]	[ʒi]	[ʒɔ]	[ʒu]	=	/ʒ/
	—	—	—	—	—		

The presence of a contrast before a single vowel (= '◊') recommends a hard-soft phonemic opposition. Don't see this as a linguist's 'obsession with tidiness'; it's rather a reflection of the dynamically 'ordered' nature of a language.

For the paired consonants recall that palatalization of a consonant before /ɛ/ is the norm or default; it is for this reason that [tɛ] has been placed in parentheses. For the velars note that three possibilities are proposed. The first is perhaps the standard interpretation, which does not admit marginal data — here there is no contrast at all. The second is the interpretation admitted for /k/-/kʲ/, and which enjoys a certain acceptance. The third has not so far been considered, and in fact is mainly relevant to the argument for a phoneme /i/, in other words, the idea that there might be a sixth Russian vowel, achieved by asserting the independent status of the sound mainly conveyed by the letter ы.

To illustrate this case, recall that Russian words beginning in и-, to which a prefix is added, retain the hardness of the final consonant of the prefix and rewrite the и- as ы, thus игрáть 'to play' and the perfective сыгрáть (prefix с-) 'to have a game'. This suggests that [i] and [i] are in complementary distribution.

What, however, of the case of the preposition к followed by a word beginning in и-?[10] If we reject the *preposition + X* sequence as forming a single unit (see 1.3.4.1.1), then we have /ɨ/, since absolute word-initial и is now revealed as [ɨ] (or, unstressed, [ɪ]), and [i] (and [ɪ]) are restricted to the position after soft consonants. If, however, we accept the sequence *preposition + X* as a single unit, then the /k/-/kʲ/ opposition is strengthened by one more opposition, as given in the third interpretation, viz. к Ире 'to Ira' has a hard *k* before *i*.[11] The latter seems the theoretically less costly option, in that one more consonant joins the already strongly represented hard-soft opposition, and we retain the neat five-vowel system. However, one argument against the *preposition + X* sequence being a unit would be that it is a relatively fluid affair, viz. a pause could easily intervene. We may counter that we should not bear in mind non-phonological considerations, i.e. the interposition of a pause; prepositions are normally clitics (words without their own stress) and, in the rare situations where they *do* bear the stress, the immediately following 'word' is unstressed. In other words, *preposition + word* behaves like a unit. The usual minimal pair proposed is:

к Ире	['kɨrʲɪ]	—	Кире	['kʲirʲɪ]
'to Ira'			'to Kira'	

The only other disputed areas in the table concern, first, the status of /ɣ/. Since it and the suggested /ɣʲ/ seem non-distinctive for hardness-softness, like /x/, we can rule out /ɣʲ/. But there is nothing to stop /ɣ/ existing as a phoneme, unless it is considered too marginal in Russian, because it is:

(i)   lexically highly restricted, e.g. the interjections ага́, ого́, угу́, and бухга́лтер 'accountant', where it is often the pronunciation of the group хг: [bʊˈɣaltʲɪr];

(ii) replaceable with /g/ in words where it occurs, e.g. Бóгом 'God' (instr.sg. of Бог, i.e. when non-final), and the interjection Го́споди! [ˈɣɔspədʲɪ] (formerly vocative case of госпо́дь 'Lord');

(iii) positionally restricted, e.g. дух был [ˈdʊɣ͡bɨl], where the voiceless velar fricative is voiced because it precedes a voiced consonant without a pause. Note that ч and ц may voice too when followed without a pause by a voiced consonant, e.g. пала́ч дал 'the executioner gave', отéц был 'father was'.

---

[10]There is the same situation with other prepositions ending in a hard consonant, e.g., в избе́ 'in the hut/izba'. The и here is definitely pronounced [ɨ], and the *v* is hard, but the issue of the distinctive status of both hard and soft *v* is not an issue.

[11]In this particular position [g] will never occur, as it will always behave *as if* absolute word-final and devoice to [k].

Secondly, there are the long soft palatal fricatives, viz. /ʃʲ:/, /ʒʲ:/ (orthographically щ, сч, зч, and жж, зж, less (if at all) сж, respectively, and some жд for both). The *voiced* soft palatal fricative is arguably disappearing in its palatalized form. Though phonetically they are long, there is generally in Russian no *long-short* phonological opposition; since, also, there are no short soft palatal fricatives, it seems to be a useful generalization to posit /ʃʲ/, /ʒʲ/ instead, giving us two more consonants paired for palatalization, viz. /ʃ/-/ʃʲ/, /ʒ/-/ʒʲ/. We might, of course, prefer to use the phonetically more correct, i.e. with length indicated, symbol in a phonetic transcription. There remains, connected with this, the problem of [ʃtʃʲ], the alternative pronunciation of [ʃʲ:]. Should it be considered a phoneme, at least in the speech of those people who use it? Or should it be seen as a sequence of /ʃ/ (or /ʃʲ/) and /tʃʲ/? In favour of the former might be that it alternates with the single /t/, e.g., as in посетить — посещу. (It is worth recalling that the unpaired phonemes are only phonologically unpaired; it is perfectly normal that they should have subsidiary allophones. Thus /tʃʲ/ might be seen as having a hard allophone in the stem лучш- ['lutʃʃ] 'better, best'.)

All this set aside, the orthographic-phonetic-phonological mapping of the Russian consonants is on the whole quite straightforward.

1.3.4.1 Groups of consonants

What happens in the pronunciation of groups of consonants is not central to our progression from the sound system to the structure of Russian words, so only a very selective presentation is given here. Groups, however, may often be the locus of meeting-places between different components of words.

1.3.4.1.1 Voicing assimilation

This does not exclusively concern groups of consonants, but might be considered here. There are essentially three rules of voicing assimilation:[12]

(i) voiced obstruents devoice at the end of a word before a pause and, without a pause, before words beginning in a vowel, a sonorant, or *v* followed by a vowel or sonorant (this also applies to the particles ведь and уж and to the prepositions без, близ, в , вглубь, вокруг, вслед, из, из-под, над, напротив, перед, под, против, and сквозь):

сад ['sat]	глаз ['glas]
сад Ольги, сад Маши, сад Володи, сад Владимира	= ['sat]
ведь Ольга, ведь Маша, ведь Володя, ведь Владимир	= [vʲɪtʲ]
без Ольги, без Маши, без Володи, без Владимира	= [bʲɪs]

---

[12]Kalenčuk/Kasatkina 1997: 13-14.

(ii) voiced obstruents devoice before voiceless consonants (including between words without a pause):

нóжка ['nɔʃkə]	скóльзко ['skɔlʲskə]	вод крáсных ['vɔt]

(iii) voiceless consonants voice before voiced obstruents and, without a pause, before words beginning in a voiced obstruent or in *v* followed by a voiced obstruent (this also applies to the particle вот and the prepositions повéрх, сверх, за счёт, к, на предмéт, насчёт, поперёк, and с):

сбóрник	['zbornʲɩk]
тáкже	['tagʒɪ]
сбóрник Глéба, сбóрник вдовы́	['zbɔrnʲɩg]
вот Глеб, вот вдовá	['vɔd]
к Глéбу, к вдовé	[g]

1.3.4.1.2 Palatalization assimilation

A soft consonant may soften an immediately preceding hard consonant, something which in the past was rather prevalent. However, in almost all positions and combinations this assimilation seems now to be at most optional. So, let's say the first consonant is generally hard or optionally hard, as suggested by the spelling, except for several pairs and positions where the second *does* tend to soften the first (there are, of course, individual exceptions).

First we have 'long' consonants. These are very often encountered in loan words, written as a sequence of two identical consonants. If they come between vowels and the stress immediately precedes them (there *are* exceptions), they are pronounced as a long consonant — and if the circumstances are appropriate, they are soft: в прогрáмме, в клáссе, о грýппе (if the sequence is of two labials, i.e., пп, бб, мм the consonant may be rather geminate than long). Two asides here are the patterns exemplified by тури́стский, where the group of four consonants simplifies to [sːkʲ] or [skʲ], and past passive participles and adjectives in -нн(ый), where one has [nː] if the stress immediately precedes — this latter pattern may provide examples of palatalization assimilation, viz. определённее 'more definitely'.

Now, note that given that we have not yet begun analysing the makeup of words, what follows is rather inexact and unavoidably clumsily expressed, but should serve for the moment.

First, where the two consonants are different, the first tends to soften by assimilation to the second in the main part or root of relatively common 'native' words, but not at the very beginning of the words, in the following sequences:

hard	+	soft	examples
с з		т д н	мо́стик, везде́, усни́
т д		н	пя́тница, на дне́
н		т д	банди́т
н		ч	ко́нчик

In the same type of words, in the sequence н + щ, crossing a boundary within a word, н softens, thus же́нщина (in other words, we have жена́ expanded by -щина, a suffix).

Secondly, the sequence гк, where the к is soft, has the pronunciation [xʲkʲ], as in лёгкий, already mentioned

Thirdly, and particularly interesting, is where a consonant precedes *jot*. Essentially this environment concerns where a soft or hard sign comes after a consonant before a soft-series vowel. Here the tendencies towards assimilation are as follows:

			examples
stress	п б м ф в	jot	се́мьи, но́вью
	с з т д н л р	jot	обезья́на, льёт

In those examples the sequences are within the main part or root of the word. The second of the above two assimilations also happens where the main part of a word is expanded by a suffix, e.g., ко́зья 'goat's (nom.sg.fem.)'.

Hard signs, remember, indicate that what precedes them is *outside* the main part of the word. If с or з precede the hard sign, as with съ-, разъ-, взъ-, e.g. съе́хать, assimilation is optional. The same goes for т and д, e.g., отъе́хать, подъём, but assimilation seems to be becoming rarer.

In the case of a preposition ending in a consonant preceding a word beginning with a soft-series vowel, then assimilation is only optional, and only in the case of с and з, e.g. с я́хты, из Екатеринбу́рга.

For fuller information see Kalenčuk/Kasatkina 1997:14-39.

Chapter 2: Bridging the Gap

2.1 From sounds and spelling through to the words themselves

2.1.1 Consonantal alternations

The construction of words by combining 'bits' may cause adjustments in the sounds making up the components.[1] Knowing these adjustments, and about them, can be very helpful in building up vocabulary. A major adjustment is known as the *consonantal alternations*; once we know these we can dramatically reduce, for example, the number of 'irregular verbs' in Russian. The most generally pervasive involve, essentially, the adaptation (various manifestations of palatalization) of consonants by a historically immediately following *y*-sound (*yod* or *jot* as referred to already) and are as follows (do note that the superscript jot in the second column merely indicates that the л is palatalized or softened and not present in the pronunciation of the actual word, where softness is conveyed in the spelling by the appropriate soft-series vowel):

Labials	П	ПЛ^j	купи́ть - куплю́ - ку́пят 'to buy'
			ка́пать - ка́плю - ка́плют 'to drip'
	Б	БЛ^j	люби́ть - люблю́ - лю́бят 'to love't
			колеба́ться - колеблю́сь - коле́блются 'to waver' (Note the first person sg stress.)
	М	МЛ^j	корми́ть - кормлю́ - ко́рмят 'to feed'
			дрема́ть - дремлю́ - дре́млют 'to doze'
	Ф	ФЛ^j	графи́ть - графлю́ - графя́т 'to rule'
	В	ВЛ^j	лови́ть - ловлю́ - ло́вят 'to catch'

Dentals	Т^1	Ч	встре́тить - встреча́ть 'to meet'
			плати́ть - плачу́ - пла́тят 'to pay'
	Т^2	Щ	посети́ть - посеща́ть 'to visit'
			посети́ть - посещу́ - посетя́т 'to visit'
	Д^1	Ж	ходи́ть - хожу́ - хо́дят 'to walk'
			суди́ть - сужу́ - су́дят 'to judge'
	Д^2	ЖД	суди́ть - сужде́ние 'judgement'

---

[1]Linguistic terminology is to some extent held back from the presentation, but it is eventually crucial to 'making sense'. The terms do simplify things, and later on terms such as 'morphemes', 'roots', 'affixes', 'prefixes', 'suffixes', 'particles', and 'endings' or 'desinences' will be used. For the moment 'bits', 'elements', and 'components' will do.

	С	Ш	писа́ть - пишу́ - пи́шут 'to write'
			носи́ть - ношу́ - но́сят 'to carry'
	З	Ж	ре́зать - ре́жу - ре́жут 'to cut'
			вози́ть - вожу́ - во́зят 'to convey'

Velars	К	Ч	пла́кать - пла́чу - пла́чут 'to weep'
	Г	Ж	дви́гать- дви́жу- дви́жут 'to move'
	Х	Ш	паха́ть - пашу́ - па́шут 'to plough'

Groups	СТ	Щ	прости́ться - проща́ться 'to say goodbye'
	СК	Щ	иска́ть - ищу́ - и́щут 'to seek'
	ЗГ	ЗЖ	визг - визжа́ть 'to squeal'
	ТВ	ЩВЛ^j	умертви́ть - умерщвлю́ 'to kill, deaden'

Looking through these examples, can you see when they occur? First look, then read on.

In the first place, all the examples but one focus on verbal forms. In the second place, the alternations are present in the non-past (there are, partially, three more exceptions in the list). In the third place, there seems to be a difference between the first conjugation (*e/o*) and the second conjugation (*i*): the former has the alternations throughout, and the latter has them only in the first person singular. If we look beyond the verb, as in the case of сужде́ние, then the observation is that the alternation also takes place in the verbal noun and, if we now adduce the related verb осуди́ть 'to condemn', the same thing is noted for the past passive participle, namely осуждённый 'condemned'. You will have noticed that the three partial exceptions are imperfective infinitives; and here the alternation is, of course, present throughout their non-past.

From this it might be assumed that the alternation does not occur when, historically, a *jot* was absent. And this will be absolutely correct, though it is an accident of Russian's faithfulness to linguistic history. In the case of many first-conjugation verbs, it seems entirely regular to have a *jot* throughout the non-past: a verb such as чита́ть is just like писа́ть, except that in the latter the *jot* immediately followed the consonant — though they both 'start off' from ЧИТ and ПИС, ЧИТ is expanded by a suffix -a- before the *jot* comes onto the scene. But the second-conjugation verbs seem odd in having the alternation only in the first person singular. So does the alternation take place before a *non-front* vowel, here the [u] of this ending? What, however, of the third person plural, with *its* non-front vowel, [a], e.g. лю́бят? Well, of the other Slavonic languages Ukrainian, to take one example, found this odd as well, and for the verbs whose base ends in a labial actually introduced the alternation into the third person plural, thus роби́ти 'to do' — я роблю́ 'I do' — ти ро́биш 'you do' — вони́ ро́бл̲я̲ть 'they do'.

Incidentally, why the alternation, after all the characteristic of these verbs is *i*, not *j*? Well, at an earlier period, in every person but the first person singular, there was an *i* between the final consonant of the base and the first consonant of the ending; so the *i* survived (no *jot* developed) — it would have been a real phonetic complication for anything else to have happened. But it's still not clear: the third person plural doesn't look like that! Well, the ancient third person plural ending was, simplifying a little, something like *-nt-*; if we put *i* in front, we have the sequence *-int-* after the root, so the *i* actually *is* between consonants. The sequence *in* would, in front of a consonant (the *t*), have yielded a nasal vowel in late Common Slavonic, namely *ę* (perhaps pronounced something like French *in* in *fin*); in the ancestor of Russian this became *a* preceded by a soft consonant around the tenth century — in other words, there never *was* a *jot* there, so there wasn't any consonantal alternation. The Cyrillic letter for this sound was ꙗ, which probably eventually took on the shape я.

As for the first person singular, here the *i* came up against an ending beginning in a vowel (*i-ǫ*), so the *i*, between a consonant and a vowel, changed into *jot* as an easing of pronunciation, here a reduction of hiatus — this must have happened early enough for it to behave like a real *jot* and cause the alternation. For the labials the 'intrusive *l*' probably came in throughout Slavonic — so must have been early, but later it dropped out (barring a few exceptions) on the boundary between bits of words in West Slavonic (Polish, Czech, Slovak, Upper and Lower Sorbian), and the South Slavonic Bulgarian and Macedonian (but not Serbo-Croatian or Slovene). This may be demonstrated using the verb 'to spit', where the alternation is in the base and present everywhere: Russian я плюю — Polish *pluję* — Bulgarian плувам, and the noun 'land', where the alternation is on the boundary: Russian земля (think of подзе́мный 'underground', with no *l* because there wasn't a *jot* in that form) — Polish *ziemia* — Bulgarian земя. You can see that what happens on the boundary between bits can be rather special. By the way, note that we just used another noun for an explanation: the alternations aren't confined to verbs.

While I'm at it, let's note two other things. First, there seem to be two results of the alternation for *t* and *d*. The first of the two for each reflects the 'Native Russian' alternation, while the second reflects the 'Church Slavonic' alternation (dressed up in an East Slavonic disguise). Church Slavonic is a major component of the Russian standard or literary language (I don't want to spend time on the differences between a standard and a literary language), and some scholars even consider it to be its basic building block — more will be said about this in the next chapter, and throughout the rest of the book. Such alternative forms have played a vital part in creating the richness of the Russian vocabulary; the particular process may seem to have gone hand-in-hand with the emergence of the political and cultural independence of Muscovy, since neither Ukrainian nor Belarusian has this Church Slavonic component in any significant measure. Secondly, note that the alternation can jump over [v], as in умерщвлю from умертви́ть 'to mortify'. Recall that *v* is a sonorant, a sound which has consonantal and vocalic features. It would seem to present a weak barrier to sound changes. Note this with other sonorants, e.g. посла́ть 'to send' — я пошлю́ 'I'll send', and the verb умудри́ть 'to make wise', which formerly could have, for

19

instance, the past participle passive умуждрённый (now умудрённый) and the imperfective умуждрять (now умудрять — you can see how Jotation also played, and still plays, a part in imperfective derivation: оста́вить 'to leave, abandon' gives imperfective оставля́ть; in Old Church Slavonic the first person singular was, simplifying the spelling slightly, умж ждрж).

I might mention certain other alternations which look similar, yet have different origins and are restricted to the velar consonants. These are what are traditionally known as the *Three Slavonic Palatalizations of Velars*.[2] They are called 'Slavonic' because they are seen as applying to all the Slavonic languages, i.e. they happened at a time when the dialectal division of Slavonic was still only slight — as recently as during the first millennium. The first palatalization is without doubt general throughout Slavonic and hence almost certainly was the first to occur (it probably overlapped with Jotation, given that it and the Jotation of the velars give the same results); the second and third coincide in the changes they cause in the velars, but occurred in different and not entirely clear circumstances; moreover, the East Slavonic and the South Slavonic languages coincide in what they yield, while West Slavonic is slightly different, and indeed there is some divergence within this group.

The second palatalization is generally reckoned to have come second, though it doubtless overlapped with the third; the third seems to have needed reference to following as well as preceding vowels in order to take place, which suggests lateness, given that things in Common Slavonic tended to happen within the environment *consonant + vowel* (the *open syllable*); this is also suggested by its application to certain words borrowed only relatively late.[3] What seems reasonably certain is that the second applied throughout Slavonic within roots, but possibly not across component boundaries in at least a part of East Slavonic (underlying certain Russian dialects), perhaps a reflection of the remoteness of these dialects or the influence of local non-Slavonic speakers assimilated to the Slavs. The third palatalization is often held also to be a Church Slavonic feature of Russian, but there are complications (which might be considered expected in the case of something happening late, at a time of migration, of loss of contact, not to mention changes in syllabic structure). What happened is, roughly:

I:	*k, *g, *x became *$\check{c}$, *$\check{z}$, *$\check{s}$ (all palatalized as well as palatal; immediately before primary, i.e. original Slavonic front vowels, at the time probably long and short *e and *i);
II:	*k, *g, *x became *c, *$(d)z$, *s (all palatalized; before new front vowels arising from monophthongized diphthongs with a first non-front component, namely *aj/oj, which gave new versions of *$\check{e}$ and *i);

[2] See Appendices 1 and 2.

[3] It may have happened very early, before the open syllable acquired an important status, though this is difficult to substantiate. Alternatively, one could question the importance of open syllables, useful and valid though they appear to be.

III: *k*, *g*, *x* became *c*, *(d)z*, *s* (all palatalized; when preceded by high front vowels, namely *i*, *ь*, *ę*, so long as not immediately followed by a high back vowel, namely *u*, *y*, *ъ*).

Useful to bear in mind here are (i) the relation between the originals and what they became remains, as with Jotation, important and visible in word families; (ii) the reflexes of the first palatalization and at least *c* of the other two gave *new* sounds in Slavonic, so that when we encounter them it is good strategy to think of *k*, *g*, and *x*.

Remember, examples of the last two palatalizations are rather restricted in Russian, and the last is often seen as a feature of Church Slavonic. We have a reflection of the second in the plural forms друзья́, etc. 'friends'. Now consider a few examples:

I:	к/ч	рука́ - ру́чка - ручно́й	'hand —handle — hand-'
	г/ж	нога́ - но́жка	'foot — (table-)leg'
	х/ш	у́хо - нау́шники	'ear — earphones'
II:	к/ц	ка́яться - цена́	'repent — price'
	г/з	дру́г - друзья́	'friend — friends'
	х/с	у́хо - серьга́	'ear — earring' (this pairing is arguable)
III:	к/ц	накли́кать - восклица́ть	'to conjure up — exclaim'
	г/з	княги́ня - князь	'prince's wife — prince'

If you put the examples together with the account given regarding in what circumstances these palatalizations occur, you will be quite right in wondering what is going on. Let's take the examples palatalization by palatalization.

For the first set, there are no front vowels after ч, ж, ш. This can be tackled in two ways. First, recall that above it was mentioned that in Common Slavonic there was a tendency to have things happening in the context *consonant + vowel*. All the while bearing in mind that the three examples given may not actually have existed in Common Slavonic, we would expect there to be a vowel between ч/ж/ш and the following consonant; perhaps there was, and it was lost later — indeed, there must have been one there to have had the palatalization! Secondly, do any of the four words with the palatalization ever occur without -а, -ной, -ник-? Well, we do have the genitive plurals of ру́чка and но́жка, namely ру́чек and но́жек. Now, if you know French, ask yourself how you would pronounce *je le vois*, which, taken word by word, would be [ʒə] [lə] [vwa]. If your answer is that you pronounce no vowel in *le*, but do have an *about* sound in *je*, then there you have it: where you have a sequence of *about* sounds ([ʒə] + [lə]), in the syllable immediately before a syllable with a 'full' vowel ([vwa]), you have nothing, and before that nothing you have something, thus [ʒəlvwa] (you might even consider the *l* to be a vowel)! But why is *le* spelt *l* + *e*? Well, because there used to be something there (and, of course, there often still *is* something there, but we don't want to go into the horrors of French phonology).

So, in ру́чка and но́жка, and in all the others, there used to be something there. Now look at по́лька 'Polish woman' and its genitive-accusative plural по́лек, just like the others. A quirk of the linguistic history of Russian has retained the 'something' between the consonants there in the form of the soft sign, indicating the softness of *l*. This is something which was on the whole lost when consonants came together, but that soft sign reveals the vowel which was originally there: the soft sign itself actually represented a vowel, originally a short *i* (thus quite appropriate to cause the first palatalization), subsequently an extremely short *i*, or alternatively an *about* sound with a preceding soft(ish) consonant, at least in part of Slavonic. In other words, the base РУК when followed by a suffix ьк became ручк-. And we can assume the same for the other examples: РУК + ьн-, на + УХ + ьн + ик-.[4] *Now* you know why the short forms of adjectives in -ный have -ен in the masculine (don't ask about по́лон from по́лный 'full' — that will be tackled in good time — but you can see for a start that there's no soft sign!). At least you now have an inkling of how the mobile vowel(s) of Russian started out.

How about the examples of the second palatalization? Well, the first of them is tied up with those open syllables too. Given that in *repenting* we are *redeeming* our sins, *taking/buying* them back (i.e. *paying* for them — look up *redimo* in a Latin dictionary, or just look back to *redeem*), we can see the semantic link between the two words. Now, note that ка́яться looks like it might have a base КАЙ, in other words it has a diphthong *aj* which might have monophthongized to a new **ě*. So why didn't it? Well, it *did* in цена́, which used to be цѣна, and in Lithuanian (almost always wonderfully useful for earlier forms) the modern word for 'price' is *kainà*. But it *didn't* monophthongize in the verb. Well, again, first — common sense: it would create an awkward hiatus to create a vowel immediately in front of another vowel: *\+cěa-* (on top of it, note, the **k* would have palatalized). Now, remember that Common Slavonic liked the *consonant + vowel* (= CV) unit (in other words, it liked 'open syllables', something languages tend to aim for now and then). Now let's rewrite the verb without the troublesome soft-series vowels: кайатьсьа. That looks horrendous, so let's try transliteration: *kajat'sja* (or, closer to transcription, *kajat's'a*). Now take that back to an earlier form, appropriate to the era of open syllables: **kajati sę*. Now split up the first word into CV units: *ka ja ti*. In other words, in order to maintain the CV structure diphthongs didn't monophongize before vowels (the **j* was transferred to the next syllable, i.e. to before the **a*), — but in front of a consonant a transfer was not possible, so the diphthong monophongized, as is clear from цена́, and the palatalization took place. In the case of друзья́, we have the original nominative plural, друзи (second palatalization, the *i* being a monophthongization), with the ending replaced by the collective suffix + ending

---

[4]The bases, as I call them here, I give in capital letters.

-ьj- + -a (simplifying slightly), something quite widespread in Russian plurals: брáтья 'brothers', сыновья 'sons', стýлья 'chairs'. Is there a zero ending in the accusative-genitive plural друзéй? Well, yes, though you can't absolutely rule out influence from the genitive plural ending -ей in, say, костéй 'bones', повестéй 'stories'. Why 'yes'? Well, if we delete -*a*, we are left with -ьj- (= -ьй- minus -*a*, as concealed in -ья); and the mobile vowel, given a zero ending, pops up: -ей. In серьгá, though the etymology is controversial, it is so tempting to see an earlier усѣ 'ears' + a Slavonic verson of *ring*, from Germanic and losing the *n*.

As for the third palatalization examples, the first is straightforward. The second, however, confuses at first because of the и after г; well, after *g* we would actually have had *y* at the time (otherwise there would have been a palatalization), so there is nothing odd about the phonetics of the word for a prince's wife. The real problem is the з in князь. Why? Well, *before* palatalization the final vowel would have been -ъ, which as a high back vowel would have blocked the palatalization. The solution is probably that the palatalization happened in a case form, such as the genitive, where there was no high back vowel, and spread from there. Alternatively, or along with that, we might bear in mind that this is a borrowing from Germanic, reflected in modern Swedish as *k(on)ung* 'king' (see the connection between that and English?) and, as a borrowing from Germanic, in Finnish *kuningas* — it is impossible to be sure about the phonetic perception of loanwords.

There are other consonantal alternations caused by ancient sound changes. Rather important ones, since they are to be found in a number of very common verbs, are as follows:

Infinitive	Non-past	Past	Alternation
грести	гребу́ - гребёшь - гребу́т	грёб - гребла́	бт > ст - б - б
жить	живу́ - живёшь - живу́т	жил - жила́...	вт > т - в - л
плести	плету́ - плетёшь - плету́т	плёл - плела́...	тт > ст - т - л
вести	веду́ - ведёшь - веду́т	вёл - вела́...	дт > тт > ст - д - л
нести	несу́ - несёшь - несу́т	нёс - несла́...	ст > ст - с - с
везти	везу́ - везёшь - везу́т	вёз - везла́...	зт > зт [sⁱtⁱ] - з - з
печь	пеку́ - печёшь - пеку́т	пёк - пекла́...	кт > ч - к/ч - к
мочь	могу́ - мо́жешь - мо́гут	мог - могла́...	гт > кт > ч - г/ж - г

(Meanings, in order: 'to row (boating)', 'to live', 'to plait', 'to lead (on foot)', 'to carry (on foot)', 'to carry/convey (by transport)', 'to bake', 'to be able ("can").')

These reflect certain early simplifications of consonantal groups. Basically, in each case (and there are more examples of such verbs) we would originally have had the consonant occurring before the non-past ending also before the other endings, thus (achronologically using modern Russian bits):

ГРЕБ + -ТЬ	ГРЕБ + -у...	ГРЕБ + -л-
ЖИВ + -ТЬ	ЖИВ + -у...	ЖИВ + -л-
ПЛЕТ + -ТЬ	ПЛЕТ + -у...	ПЛЕТ + -л-
ВЕД + -ТЬ	ВЕД + -у...	ВЕД + -л-
НЕС + -ТЬ	НЕС + -у...	НЕС + -л-
ВЕЗ + -ТЬ	ВЕЗ + -у...	ВЕЗ + -л-
ПЕК + -ТЬ	ПЕК + -у...	ПЕК + -л-
МОГ + -ТЬ	МОГ + -у...	МОГ + -л-

In case this gives you the impression that sequences of *d* or *t* followed by *l* do not occur in Russian, note тлеть 'to rot, putrefy; smoulder', дно 'bottom' (think of Dostoevskij's тлетво́рный дух 'the odour of corruption' (in Magarshack's translation) in *Бра́тья Карама́зовы The Brothers Karamazov*, and Gor'kij's play *На дне The Lower Depths*). Can you imagine why these groups are found here? Well, the plural of дно is до́нья; rather more obscure, тлеть may be related to Lithuanian *tylḗti* 'to be silent' (when we're dead and putrefying, we are, we hope, silent; a colleague suggests a possible relationship with *tilth* 'soft, ploughed earth', which is very tempting). Both share what? Well, a vowel between the two consonants. So this modern consonantal group wasn't originally a group, or at least it wasn't when the group was simplified. There was a soft sign between the consonants in тло (it doesn't have to be a soft sign, but the Lithuanian *y* (a long *i*) suggests that, and we do in any case find early incidences of the word with a soft sign there), and the о of до́нья indicates an earlier hard sign. Why does the hard sign appear as о here? After all, there is a vowel in the next syllable. Well, because the structure is: ДЪН + -ьй- + -а, in other words, the suffix -ьй- itself actually contained a vowel, so the hard sign, before the soft sign (remember the two *about*'s in *je le vois*) becomes a full vowel. A nice line is Blok's Жизнь пуста́, безу́мна и бездо́нна! 'Life is empty, insane, and bottomless!', which, coming as it does from his incomparable poem *Шаги́ командо́ра* 'The Comendador's Steps', might, for the last adjective, be taken to suggest 'without a *donna*' (setting aside grammar, and bearing in mind that the word до́нна is used several times in the poem. Well, why not?). Coming back to the business in hand, why is the о there? Let's break the word up into its components: без- + ДЪН + -ьн- + -а — note the sequence of hard and soft signs (together they are often referred to as the *jers*). So the hard sign, which was much more in evidence in earlier Russian spelling, is behind the mobile vowel(s) too. Later it will be a task to work out how many mobile vowels Russian has, and whether they always come from the *jers*.

2.1.2 Vocalic alternations[5]

2.1.2.1 'Lengthening' of the root vowel

Of these the -o-/-a- alternation in aspect pairs of verbs, e.g. устрóить > устрáивать 'to arrange, suit', договори́ться > догова́риваться 'to come to an agreement', сбрóсить > сбра́сывать 'to cast off', спроси́ть > спра́шивать 'to ask' (note for now the oddity of an *s* in сбра́сывать and a *š* in спра́шивать, likely to be an instance of Jotation), and many others, is productive. It is referred to as 'lengthening', presumably because it is reckoned to reflect a Common Slavonic long *o*, as against the short *o* which is found in the simple imperfective verb or prefixed perfective (more precisely, there was a long vowel and a short vowel, the long one eventually becoming *a* and the short one eventually *o*). It doesn't always happen, but what we *can* say is that the stress is always on the vowel preceding the -ыв-/-ив- suffix.

It is not certain just how early this lengthening happened, but we can definitely see similar developments in other pairs. For instance, from звать 'to call' can be derived назва́ть 'to name'; the imperfective verb meaning 'to name' is называ́ть. Now, at first glance this seems to go against the stress rule just given, but after a careful second look we note that there is already a в in the perfective (and in the basic verb звать), so in fact there is no suffix -ыв- here, and the stress rule, whatever it's ultimately based on, doesn't apply.

Now, going back to звать, one notes that the non-past is зову́, зовёшь, ... зову́т (and there are nouns such as вы́зов 'call; challenge'). Looking at early texts, there is often a hard sign in place of o. A hard sign is historically a short *ŭ*, and ы, which we have in называ́ть, is a *long* *ŭ*. So here there is lengthening too. We would have the same thing with брать — беру́, берёшь, ... беру́т 'take', and собра́ть 'to gather, collect', imperfective собира́ть. The е hints at an earlier soft sign in бр; the soft sign historically was a short *ĭ*, and и, as in собира́ть, is the continuation of a long *ĭ*. The stress is on the a, which is consistently the case in derived imperfectives other than those with the suffix -ыв-/-ив-.

Coming back to -o-/-a-, this doesn't happen where the perfective has -ева́ть (where the е is an underlying *o*) or -ова́ть: истолкова́ть 'to interpret' > истолкóвывать, зева́ть 'to yawn' > позева́ть 'to yawn a little' > позёвывать 'to yawn a little now and then' (interesting here is that the е is historically ѣ, *jat'*, which does not normally become *o*; so there may either be analogy or the derivation can be recent, i.e. after *jat'* merged with *e*). Verbs in -ова́ть/-ева́ть with -ýю/-ю́ю, etc. in the non-past are, by the way, quite interesting. If the -ов- /-ев- is part of the root, then it doesn't disappear: здорóваться 'to greet' — здорóваюсь; from this point of view сомнева́ться 'to doubt' — сомнева́юсь

---

[5]An alternative term, particularly as regards the pre-Slavonic period and which I occasionally use, is *ablaut*.

is initially rather mysterious — essentially there is a relationship with a verb *тьнěti*, suggesting the stressed suffix -вá-, which makes us think that only the -о-/-е- might need to be part of the root. What, though, of основáть 'to found' where we have оснóва 'foundation, basis'? The non-past, surprisingly, is осную́, оснуёшь, ... осну́ют. Here we may have a link with сновáть, сную́, etc. 'to warp (in weaving)' and, given Slavonic forms suggesting an alternative infinitive снуть (modernized), perhaps there is something else in the background. This might be suggested by клевáть 'to peck', non-past клюю́, клюёшь, ... клюю́т, with earlier *klьvati* and плевáть 'to spit', non-past плюю́, плюёшь, ... плюю́т, with earlier *plьvati*. Might we have *osnьvati*? Anyway, you can see how complex things are, and in any event note, for instance, the imperfective сплёвывать 'to spit (out)' (imperf. of сплю́нуть). Note, by the way, the stress pattern in -овáть verbs proper and in a verb such as основáть.

2.1.2.2 Alternation involving *e* and *o*

The preceding section already referred to the change of an *e* to an *o*. Within Russian an *e* coming historically from Common Slavonic *e* or *ь* becomes *o* (hence ё) when stressed before a hard consonant or silence. Exceptions are Church Slavonic or recent borrowings. If the change occurs before a soft consonant, then it is usually a case of analogy, e.g. несёте because of несёшь (the spelling with a soft sign is purely historical here; *š* was hard by the time the change began to take place), несёт, несём 'carry'. And if *jat'* (*ě*) becomes *o*, it is also usually analogy. Note a few examples showing the variation: чéрти — чёрт 'devils — devil' (perhaps the *r* was soft, or the softness of the *t* in the nominative plural passed over the sonorant), весéлье — весёлый 'happiness — happy', жéнщина — жéнский — жёны 'woman — female — wives' (the first two must have had a soft sign after the *n*), ель — ёлка 'fir/spruce', лечь — лёг 'to lie down — (he) lay down', дешёвый — дешéвле 'cheap — cheaper' (the *v* was originally soft, via Jotation).

Much more ancient are examples indicated by the spelling of related words such as нести́ — носи́ть 'to carry', стелю́ — стол 'I lay/spread — table', тебя́ — тобóй 'you (acc./gen. — instr.)'. These are unproductive, and have to be learnt. Do note that the fact that the *o* comes after a hard consonant, notably one which *could* be softened, marks it out as different. Rather old too is мелю́ — молóть 'I grind — to grind', though it belongs to Common Slavonic rather than reflects the pre-Slavonic alternation in at least the first two of the others.

Worth mentioning here, and in fact taking up one of our examples in the preceding paragraph, is an additional complication (thankfully, rather restricted). Note that the verb лечь 'to lie down', in addition to having a past tense лёг has, in the non-past, ля́гу, ля́жешь... ля́гут. Recall that the letter я often reflects an earlier nasal vowel, and it does indeed here. There is something identical in сесть 'to sit down', with its past tense сел (not сёл, because the е here is from *jat'*) and non-past ся́ду, ся́дешь... ся́дут. We lie down, sit down, and stand up, so, slightly different (but still the semantic and formal similarity): стать — стáну — стал, with the nasal consonant quite visible — you can probably work out why (it's because it comes immediately before a vowel, not a consonant, as in the others). It doesn't quite work for 'hanging', where one verb is вúснуть, which is imperfective, the н probably being of another origin. A different sort of nasal insertion is present in быть 'to be', with its future бýду 'I'll be', where the first y, within the verb, was originally a back nasal (think, perhaps, of *moribund*, where you might imagine *bund* having a sense of the future). The y in the ending goes back to a back nasal too, but that's another story.

2.1.2.3 Alternation with a nasal consonant

Earlier we had the example собрáть — собирáть 'to collect'. At the time it was tempting to adduce an example such as начáть — начнý, but that would have introduced the complication of explaining where the *n* was in начáть. Here it can just be illustrated, without going into details:

начáть - начнý - начинáть 'to begin (perf.) / I'll begin / to begin (imperf.)'
снять - снимý - снимáть 'to take off (perf.) / I'll take off / to take off (imperf.)'
взять - возьмý 'to take (perf.) / I'll take'
жать - жму - пожимáть 'to squeeze (simple verb) / I squeeze / to squeeze (imperf.)'
жать - жну - пожинáть 'to reap (simple verb) / I reap / to reap (imperf.)'

The last two are fascinating, since the infinitives of the two simple verbs are identical. Perhaps you can try to work out what is going on. Look at взять (something about that verb gives a hint, and if you've taken in the spelling conventions of Russian you'll have no problem), note when the *n* or *m* occurs, and recall кáяться — ценá 'to repent — price'. Regarding начнý, ask yourself where ч comes from, then ask yourself about that consonant and н, and think about related meanings. Perhaps that's a bit obscure, but it will be explored later.

2.1.2.4 Alternation involving mid and high back vowels (*o, u, y*)

The examples aren't plentiful, but overall this is worth bearing in mind. Basically they all boil down to modern reflexes of (i) earlier short and long *u*, (ii) *u* as the *w*, closing or tautosyllabic (work *that* word out) component, of a diphthong (which ultimately gave *u*), and (iii) the back nasal. Remember that short *u* would give a back jer (as a letter the hard sign), which could disappear or become *o*. Long *u* would give *y* (ы). And *u* would reflect a *w*-diphthong or could be the reflex of a back nasal. Thus:

сóхнуть - сухóй 'to become dry (imperf) / dry'
ковáть - кую́ 'to forge (imperf) / I forge'
дух - вздыхáть - вздох - дóхнуть 'spirit — to sigh (imperf.) / a sigh / to die'
(in neutral style the last refers to an animal and is imperf.; with the stress on the ý it means 'to give a gasp/sigh' and is perfective)
слýшать - слы́шать 'to listen to — to hear'
губи́ть - ги́бнуть 'to destroy — to be destroyed/ perish'

In the first pair we probably start with a stressed hard sign, which became o, contrasted with, in the second, a dipththong in $*w$, reflected in Lithuanian *saũsas* 'dry'; in the second there is something odd, as in клевáть 'to peck', etc. mentioned above — basically it's a diphthong as in сухóй; note Lithuanian *káuti* 'to forge', but with ковáть we have a possible restructuring on the basis of кую́. In the next there is a w diphthong, a long $*u$, a short $*u$ (thus hard sign), and another stressed hard sign. In слýшать — слы́шать it is, respectively, a w diphthong (note the related Lithuanian *klausýti* 'to listen, obey') and a long $*u$. And in the last pair in the box we have the same. But we can't, it's и in ги́бнуть! Well, of course, it isn't: it's ы (coming from long $*u$) after $*g$ — ы came to be written и, reflecting the pronunciation, after г, and к and х.

There are many other traces of ancient, often Proto-Indo-European, alternations in Russian. They tend to seem weird because what was once quite regular has been obscured by change over the years. A quick example might be provided by words for 'hanging' and 'weighing'. In Russian висéть/ви́снуть 'to hang' (both imperfective) and вéсить 'to weigh (+ weight)' (also imperfective) look similar, and indeed if we group together the most common verbs in the family we see that they seem to overlap, to the potential confusion of learners, e.g. вéшать, perf. повéсить 'to hang (something)' ('to weigh (something)' = взвéшивать, perf. взвéсить, which may also be used figuratively 'to weigh up, consider, ponder', the last English rendering recalling the French verbs *penser* 'to think' and *peser* 'to weigh', related to each other and to 'ponder'). Could they actually belong together? Well, it's likely, given that to weigh something we often still suspend it in the air on scales. So вес/вис are, though the etymologies remain shrouded in darkness, likely to be related. Since the e of вес is historically a *jat'* (ѣ), we might suspect a *j*-diphthong ($*oj/*aj$), which would fit in nicely with another *j*-diphthong ($*ej$) which would give вис (see Appendix 1). And recall that our temples, on the head, are виски́ (from висóк), possibly referring to locks of hair hanging down there. Not to be confused with ви́ски! (By the way, is indeclinable ви́ски singular or plural in Russian, and what gender?)

2.1.2.5 Alternations linked to the relationship between the Church Slavonic and Native Russian components of Russian.

The history of the Russian language and the relationship between 'Native Russian' and 'Church Slavonic' will be presented tentatively, with examples, in Chapter 3. Below just one of these features is mentioned, as an appetizer.

Well, one of the most problematic (for reasons to do with prosody, i.e., accent, stress, intonation) concerns the behaviour of *jers* in front of *j*. This 'alternation' also shows that many of these features are not simply 'Russian' vs. 'Church Slavonic', since it seems more like a case of Russian vs. all the other Slavonic languages. And it might be argued that Russian is 'regular' here, while the other Slavonic languages (and this includes East Slavonic Ukrainian and Belarusian) do something strange. Thus, Russian treats the *jers* more or less as expected, while elsewhere the combination of a front *jer* with *j* gives *i* and that of a back *jer* with *j* gives *y* — this particular type of *jer*, if that is what it is, is traditionally referred to as a 'tense *jer*'. This is reflected in the relationship between Russian and Church Slavonic, notably in certain forms of the long adjective and in neuter nouns in -ие. When an adjective is ending-stressed, the final component is -о́й (this doesn't apply to soft adjectives); all other adjectives have -ый or -ий. This doesn't seem to make sense — why such a discrepancy? (When first learning the language, this is one of many things we somehow just accept.)

Well, the Old Moscow pronunciation of -ый (this may not apply to -ий, because of *ikańje*) was 'as if we had unstressed -ой. In other words, the regularity was there, though hidden, as still now, by the spelling, and that spelling is Church Slavonic. Recall that the adjective in Russian occurs in short and long forms; alternative names for these are, respectively, indefinite and definite, and nominal and pronominal. The last pair of names is most helpful here, in that it indicates that the short adjective declined like a noun and the long one declines like a pronoun. Actually, at first there was a double-declension here (think of -ая, -ую, -ое, etc.), which was reduced by contraction of the two and, in Russian, eventual installation of the endings to be found in such pronouns as тот 'that' and он 'he'. This ending, in the nominative and inanimate accusative singular masculine, was *-ъ + *jь and *-ь + *jь. The second component is actually the original nominative of the third-person and demonstrative pronoun, replaced in Russian by the nominative of another pronoun, familiar to us as он, она́, etc. In Russian we would expect the endings -ой and -ей, whether stressed or not, but the unstressed endings are replaced by the Church Slavonic spelling, and in the modern language simply do not occur for the soft adjective, unless we accept such forms as the adverb сам-трете́й 'one person with two others' (it's interesting that it's not трете́й, by analogy with худо́й, etc.) and, capped off with an extra suffix, трете́йский суд 'court of arbitration'. As for the neuter nouns, we can contrast воскресе́ние 'resurrection' with воскресе́нье 'Sunday' and варе́ние 'cooking' with варе́нье 'jam'. Outside such examples we find this Russian peculiarity (or should it be a peculiarity of the other Slavonic languages?) in such forms as пить - пью - пей 'drink' (the last two on a base *pьj*-; extendable to лить 'to flow, pour', шить 'to sew', вить 'to wind', бить 'to beat'), verbs in -ыть (thus покрою 'I'll cover', мою 'I wash', etc.; taking the latter to provide an example, there is a base **mъj*-), the verb брить 'to shave' (брею, thus a base *brьj*-), and a word such as шея 'neck' (this 'should' be шья; perhaps we have the influence of — the general technical term is *analogy*, another case form). Attempts to explain the realizations in Russian usually founder: why брею rather than the 'expected' [+]брю (since the *jer* would be weak)? Stress may have played a part.

2.2 'Word-Formation'

For quite a while now the discussion has been within the area of 'word-formation'. This is conventionally seen as one of the two components of morphology, the study of the forms which go to make up a language. Knowing about word-formation is crucial to accumulating vocabulary.[6] The other component of morphology is to do with inflection: the bits, often endings, which are attached to words in order to help them relate to other words in the sentence or utterance — in some languages this component of the morphology is rather meagre (English is an example of that), while in others (and here Russian comes in) it is extremely rich. Now and then attempts are made to show that in some respects or senses derivational or lexical morphology (= 'word-formation')[7] and inflexional morphology, are one and the same thing, ultimately. There may be something in that, in that most inflexions may well at some stage be separate words, which fuse with other words to create synthetic structures. On the whole, however, we might stay with derivational and inflexional morphology as the two components of morphology.

So, in morphological study we analyse the makeup of words, isolating the smallest meaning-bearing units, or *morphemes*. Some morphemes, e.g. endings, are grammatical, telling us the word is in such and such a case or person — these are the bits and pieces of inflexional morphology, which on the whole will be left in peace here. (Do bear in mind, by the way, that they are not always endings; they can come elsewhere in the word. Ask yourself, and do try to forget the spelling, how the persons, tenses, and numbers of the French verb are conveyed.)

The other morphemes are the lexical ones, conveying the dictionary meaning of a word. So, having set aside the 'ending', we have what is usually referred to as the *stem*. The stem is made up of a root, and to the root prefixes and suffixes may

---

[6] I'll avoid trying to define *word*: is a word marked by where you go back to if you make a mistake, is it determined accentually, is it that thing which has spaces or punctuation around it in a text?

[7]'Derivation' may sometimes be held to exclude prefixation, though the tendency in this work is to let 'derivation' cover all word-formation.

be added, often modifying the basic meaning of the stem. Remember that prefixes (in front of the root/stem) and suffixes (after the root/stem) *may* be added. They don't have to be, so if neither is added the root and the stem are identical. Let's take the following Russian word: in сотру́дник 'collaborator' the root is труд: the affixes are со- (prefix) and -/ник (suffix) (the slash indicates a potential alternation of a vowel with zero, compare тру́дный and masculine short form тру́ден). In сотру́дник there may be an invisible component, namely the zero-ending, and this arguably tells us the case, gender, and number of the word, i.e. it provides us with the syntactic information needed for agreement. (We can take this further and argue that words without a visible suffix actually have a zero-suffix (and the same goes for those without a prefix) — by arguing in this way we can justify the *potentiality* for affixes.) By the way, it is important to distinguish a root from an actual word. Quite often it will be 'identical' with a real word, but their theoretic statuses are different, so in books the root is often placed in capital letters, even with a square root sign in front. So the root of сотру́дник is √ТРУД. And there is an actual word труд 'labour', though there doesn't have to be. English provides a fine example of one which does not occur alone (a *portmanteau* form) in the root √TAIN, as in *contain, maintain, sustain*, etc.. A little thought, e.g. French *tenir* 'to hold' (where the *ten* corresponds to *tain*), will reveal that this root is a Latinate equivalent to √HOLD, which *can* stand on its own: *uphold, withhold*, and *hold*. In Russian we have √ЯТЬ or √ЬМ 'take' as an example of a *portmanteau* form.[8]

When morphemes together create words, there is greater or lesser fusion. Some of these 'fusions' may be very ancient and no longer active in the language — they are unproductive or dead (indeed, such apparently composite words may behave as if they were roots themselves, e.g. сказ-, actually с/-+КАЗ — more about this later); others are active in the language — such changes are productive, e.g. -/н-, -ов- creating adjectives, -ов(а)- creating verbs.

So, each Russian word has a structure, the core of which is a *root*. One or more *prefixes* may be placed before the root, and one or more *suffixes* may be placed after it — *prefixes* and *suffixes* may together be referred to as *affixes*. Some people add a third type of *affix*, namely an *infix*. On the whole, however, *infixes* may be regarded as *suffixes* — exceptions in Russian may seem to be the nasal elements in the non-past of лечь, сесть, стать. Altogether these make up the *stem*. An *ending*, also known as a *desinence* and central to inflexion, and finally *particles,* may be placed after the *stem*. And these components are known as *morphemes*, definable as 'minimal meaning-bearing grammatical elements' of words. Some morphemes give basic, core lexical information, others adapt this lexical information (prefixes, suffixes, arguably particles), and others provide syntactic information (inflexional endings: case, number, gender, person, tense). To illustrate, starting with the basic element at the bottom:

---

[8] From here on the square-root sign is left out, capitals being seen as sufficient to indicate that reference is to a root.

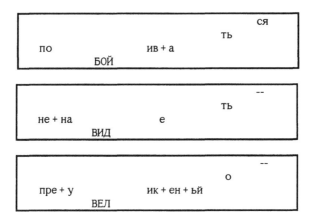

The root, plus or minus the prefix(es) and suffix(es), forms the stem. We might argue for inclusion of the particle, typically the reflexive particle -ся/-сь and arguably the imperative formant -те too, in the stem, giving a discontinuous stem (= ROOT + suffix + ending + suffix) — if that were accepted, 'particle' would appear on the same tier as 'prefix(es)' and 'suffix(es)'.

Here are a few examples: побáиваться 'to be "chairy"', ненавúдеть 'to hate', and преувеличéние 'exaggeration':

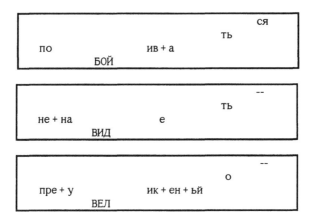

Explanation as to how the components come together will emerge gradually. For the moment, note (i) how the о of the root БОЙ becomes а (that lengthening which may ultimately be ancient) before the suffix ив/ыв, (ii) how we might reasonably expect ВЕЛИК to be a root (can you think of any words with the component ВЕЛ in a sense of 'big, great'? The answer to that will be found in a good dictionary or, but resist it for a moment, in the footnote[9]), (iii) how the к changes, (iv) the at first sight strange suffix ьй — a 'tense *jer*', see 3.3.9), and (v) the unexpected (see 2.5.1) ending о.

Words that have endings, i.e. almost all words, practically always have only one ending (but see the example at the end of this paragraph). There is no such limitation on prefixes and suffixes, although in reality words tend to have an upper limit of three prefixes or suffixes — -/ник- in сотрýдник above is actually two suffixes, -/н- and -ик-. Depending on how the particle is defined, words may

---

[9]Try вельмóжа 'eminent, rich man, "bigwig"', and the ironic and antiquated велеречúвый 'pompous; eloquent'.

have up to two of *them*. In fact, we might suggest that the sequence of two particles is limited to the вы-form of the inclusive imperative: Оде́нем<u>тесь</u>! 'Let's get dressed!' We might argue that -те here is a second ending (the first is -м) rather than a particle. In some Slavonic languages even the inclusive 'ending' seems as if it may be a particle in certain paradigms, e.g. Ukrainian чита́й 'read', with plural/formal чита́йте and inclusive чита́ймо, with -мо tacked on to чита́й.

2.3   Productive and unproductive affixes

A distinction to bear in mind is that between productive affixes and unproductive ones. Verbal -ова- and adjectival -/н- are productive, while nominal -/ба- and -зн- are unproductive, and there are the very important verbal -е- and -и-: торгова́ть, а́томный, сва́дьба, неприя́знь, беле́ть, бели́ть. 'Productive' means that the formants are being used currently to form new words, while 'unproductive' means that the formants have ceased being used to form new words, i.e. you can actually *list* the instances. The usual conclusion is that productive affixes are more useful. In many ways they are, but many elements of core vocabulary often reflect unproductive affixes and morphological processes.

2.4   Securing the bridge

Note that in word-formation some of the core 'rules' of Russian phonology are broken, e.g.:

(i)	the opposition of hard and soft consonants
(ii)	the opposition of voiced and voiceless consonants

Examples:

(i)	знал	зна́ли
	стол	сто́лик
(ii)	вода́	во́дка

The sort of transcription which comes in useful when bridging the gap between the phonology and the morphology is one which reflects what is often known as a systematic phonemic or morphonological analysis. Basically, it uses the phoneme symbols but does not convey the consequences of consonantal assimilations of voice and palatalization, and assimilations in consonantal groups. It employs many of the symbols used in the *International* transliteration system, conveys palatalization (where distinctive) and the soft sign by an apostrophe, and inserts a jot before the soft-series vowels (see the next sentence) when they are initial or follow a hard sign, a soft sign, or a vowel. Since exceptions are rare and assumed to be listable, convention has it that jot and the apostrophe are not used before *e*, since the palatalization of immediately preceding distinctively soft consonants is the default situation, but one might go against this, for the former, in order to note etymological *j* (though the devil is very present in the detail) and, for the latter, in the interests of generalizing the pattern to all the vowels and because there are more and more instances of hard consonants before *e*. In the case of *ё*, this symbol may be preferred if there is an underlying *ё*, i.e. it could be *o* in another form either of the word or of the morpheme in which it is found. A problem might arise with *i*, when it occurs after a vowel and initially; in the former case one might allow variation for when the *i* is on the morpheme boundary, between the stem and an ending, since there is most often an etymological jot here (e.g. читáешь), and in the latter case, given that ы hardly ever occurs initially, one might dispense with the jot, even though one may be heard and one may be etymologically justified (e.g. их) — this skirts the very real issue of the phonemic status of the sound represented, partly, by ы.

Rules, too, would be needed to account for where hard consonants in consonantal groups emerge as soft when the group is broken up, as in, for instance, the masculine short form of adjectives with the suffix -/н-: прекрáсный — прекрáсен *prekrásnij* — *prekrás'en* (better: *prekrás'ën*, because of умён, хитёр, etc.).

Observe the examples in the next few boxes below, in which there is reference to verb classes. These follow the Leskien classification, for more details of which you might consult Kiparsky 1967. In a very few words, however: there are five classes, based on the non-past stem and each of these subdivided according to the infinitive/past stem. Except in the case of the fifth class, each stem ends in a theme, respectively *-e-*, *-ne-*, *-je-*, and *-i-*. The fifth class is 'theme-less', or *athematic*, with endings attached directly to the root, and included at least the ancient verbs for 'to be', 'to give', 'to eat', and 'to know' — the non-pasts of the first three (быть, дать, есть) survive as non-pasts residually; otherwise, the class now comprises oddities, e.g. спать, бежáть, ревéть. The fourth class is represented by second-conjugation verbs, namely most verbs in -ить, e.g. носи́ть, черни́ть, a good number of verbs in -еть, e.g. смотрéть, ви́деть, болéть, the two verbs in -оять, and many verbs in a husher plus -ать, e.g. молчáть, визжáть, лежáть. The third class comprises verbs with a *jot* before the ending, e.g. читáть, торговáть, болéть (not the same as the fourth-class verb), чернéть, пить, откры́ть, бри́ть, гнить, and those where the jot has jotated a preceding consonant, e.g. писáть, дремáть. The second class comprises verbs whose infinitive is in -нуть (there are two types of these verbs), e.g. рискнýть, сóхнуть, and perhaps also стать. And the first class comprises verbs in -у, -ешь, ... -ут, where the consonant preceding -у- has always been hard, e.g., идти́, мочь, жить, начáть, нести́. Work this out for yourself by checking the non-pasts of the verbs just given.

(i) the First Slavonic Palatalization of Velars and Jotation — /k, g, x - č, ž, š/:

рука́ — ру́чка	нога́ — но́жка	му́ха — му́шка	(fem. dim.)
ruká — rúčka	*nogá — nóžka*	*múka — múška*	
гро́мко — гро́мче	до́рого — доро́же	ти́хо — ти́ше	(short comp.)
grómko — grómče	*dórogo — doróže*	*t'íxo — t'íše*	
пеку́ — печёшь	берегу́ — бережёшь	могу́ — мо́жешь	(Class I verbs)
p'ekú — p'ečёš'	*b'er'egú — b'er'ežёš'*	*mogú — móžёš'*	
пла́кал — пла́чешь	дви́гал — дви́жешь	маха́л — ма́шешь	(Class III verbs)
plákal — pláčёš'	*dv'ígal — dv'ížё š'*	*maxál — máš̌ёš'*	
бегу́ — бежа́л			(Class V verb)
b'egú — b'ežál			

And some examples bringing in the Third Slavonic Palatalization of Velars:

/k/	/c/	/č/
(об)лик	лицо́	ли́чный
(ób)l'ik	*l'icó*	*l'íčnij*
	пти́ца	пти́чий
	pt'íca	*pt'íčij*
	оте́ц	оте́чество
	ot'éc	*ot'éčestvo*

Thus: adjectives in -/н-, possessive adjectives, and the suffix -ество.

And now Jotation, namely

/d - ž, t - č, z - ž, s - š, sk - šč, st - šč, zg - žž, zd' - žž, b - bʲ, p - pʲ, v - vʲ, f - fʲ, m - mʲ/

As indicated, these alternations were caused by the presence originally of a /j/ after the consonant on the left of each pair. They occur in aspect formation, in the first person singular of the non-past of second-conjugation verbs (and in the formation of their past participle passive), throughout the non-past of many common first-conjugation verbs, and, for instance, in the noun, e.g. дух - душа́ *dux — dušá* 'spirit — soul'. Thus:

замеча́ть — заме́тить	отвеча́ть — отве́тить
zam'ečát' — zam'étit'	*otv'ečát' — otv'étit'*
укра́сить — украша́ть	угости́ть — угоща́ть
ukrásit' — ukrašát'	*ugostít' — ugoščát'*
употреби́ть — употребля́ть	
upotr'ebít' — upotr'ebl'át'	
ходи́ть — хожу́	свети́ть — свечу́
xodít' — xožú	*sv'etít' — sv'ečú*
прости́ть — прощу́	
prostít' — proščú	

простить — прощённый	купить — купленный
prostít' — proščénnij	*kupít' — kúpl'énnij*

The change is not productive in verbs like писа́ть (forming part of the first conjugation), where as mentioned the change occurs throughout the present tense:

пла́кать — пла́чу	писа́ть — пишу́	иска́ть — ищу́
plákat' — pláču	*pisát' — pišú*	*iskát' — iščú*

or in short comparatives:

бли́зко — бли́же	бога́тый — бога́че
bl'ízko — bl'íže	*bogátij — bogáče*

Nor are they productive where the change is due to the influence on Russian of Church Slavonic (where the alternation is /t - šč, d - žd/). Thus:

клевета́ть — клевещу́	посети́ть — посещу́
kl'ev'etát' — kl'ev'eščú	*pos'et'ít' — pos'eščú*
убеди́ть — убеждённый	ходи́ть — хожде́ние
ub'ed'ít' — ub'ežd'énnij	*xod'ít' — xožd'én'ijë*

Other unproductive alternations are as follows:

/t, d - s/:	веду́ - вести́, мету́ - мести́
/d, t - ø/:	веду́ - вёл, мету́ - мёл
/b, p, d, t, g, k - ø/:	сгиба́ть - согну́ть, утопа́ть - утону́ть, кида́ть - ки́нуть, гляде́ть - гля́нуть, тро́гать - тро́нуть. But: поги́бнуть, хлебну́ть, то́пнуть, сту́кнуть, метну́ть...
/v - ø/:	обо́з, обо́д, оборо́ти́ться. But: обвини́ть, обвести́...
Isolated:	лик - лицо́ (ли́чный), восклиќнуть - восклица́ть, грек - Гре́ция (гре́ческий), пусти́ть - пуска́ть, блеск - блесте́ть, паути́на - пау́к, друг - друзья́ (дру́жеский), княги́ня - князь (княжна́). For the /t - k/ alternation, think of French *tabac - tabatière*.

Try to formulate just when these alternations occur, i.e. which forms are affected.

2.5 A few links to inflexion

If we adopt the above morphonological approach to the vowels, it is soon realized that the morphology of Russian is much simpler than thought; it's often a question of seeing through, and understanding and accepting, the spelling system (much of what follows is not strictly to do with word-formation, as it looks at endings). And if you know other Slavonic languages, or intend to learn them, such an approach becomes very enlightening.

2.5.1 The noun:

Think of жена́ 'wife' as жёна́ *žёná*, because of the plural (жёны, etc.), where the root vowel is stressed — in other words, the stressed vowel is accepted as more basic. Do the same for по́ле 'field', thus *pól'ё*. Within declension, note that the *hard* — *soft* declension opposition fades once we understand the spelling of vowels.[10]

стола́ - коня́	(both = -a)	*stolá — kon'á*
жёна́ - земля́; - а́рмия	(all = -a)	*žёná — z'eml'á — árm'ija*
ле́то - сёло́ - по́лё - бельё̈	(all = -o)	*l'éto — sёló — pól'ё — bel'jё̈*

In the dative and prepositional singular of а́рмия *árm'ija* 'army' there is the odd ending а́рмии *ármiji*, but if we think of the pronunciation, and the (on the whole) identical pronunciation of unstressed и and е, then it turns out to be regular — the pronunciation has levelled the *hard* and the *soft* declensions. In this particular instance, we might note that the ending -и actually was originally that of the *soft* declension. Note too that odd-looking forms like а́рмий *árm'ij* (gen.pl.) are simply the orthography's way of rendering a quite regular *zero ending* (denoted as 'ø'), cf. кни́га — книг *kn'íga — kn'ig*; after all, й is a consonant which happens to be spelt as part of я, е, и, ё, ю after a vowel or a soft or hard sign.

кни́га / «книг-а»	а́рмия / «армий-а»
книг / «книг-ø»	а́рмий / «армий-ø»

Similarly, why стате́й in the genitive plural of статья́ 'article'? The й marks the zero ending; but why -e-! Well, that is the fill (or 'zero-alternating', or 'fleeting', or 'mobile') vowel, which we find in де́нь — дня 'day', кни́жек — кни́жка 'book'. Another example: соловей — соловья 'nightingale'. If you want a real test, then ask yourself about це́рк<u>о</u>вью 'church (instr.sg.)'. The -o- remains, and yet there's an ending. The answer is that there is a zero where the ь is, so the vowel appears before the zero, just as in де́нь, кни́жек. From the point of view of the modern language there is the initial oddity of the ending in це́рковью beginning in a consonant; but the history of the language says otherwise. The zero here, by the way, is one of those special *jers* before a *j*.

---

[10]What I don't convey consistently in these examples, where I'm focussing on the modern language, is the incidence of an etymological *j*. Could you justify, by the way, *zёml'á*?

2.5.2 The pronoun:

Try to see нáшего, вáшего, моегó, егó, etc. as нáшёго, вáшёго, моёгó, ёгó. Like тогó, какóго.

2.5.3 The adjective:

As already mentioned, a disappearing pronunciation, and the history of the language, reveal that the ending -ый is -ой; it is usually found only in 'hard' adjectives under stress, e.g. худóй 'thin'. Through an adjective such as плохóй bad' we realize that this applies to an adjective such as тихий 'quiet', and to рýсский 'Russian', упрýгий 'taut', too, i.e. after velars. Following the familiar pattern of reducing the hard-soft opposition, this can be applied to сйний 'blue' as well (remember that unstressed и may correspond to e, e.g., dat./prep.sg. áрмии (see above), and that e may conceal o, e.g., nom.-acc.sg. пóлё (also above)). Some Muscovites still pronounce дóбрый and рýсский as if they were written дóброй, рýсской. And peer closely at the first stanza of Lermontov's *Пáрус*: «Белéет пáрус одинóкий / В тумáне мóря голубóм. / Что йщет он в странé далёкой? / Что кйнул он в краю роднóм?»

2.5.4 The verb:

Here we learn, by applying the stress rule, that in fact the *two* Russian verb conjugations are -*o*- and -*i*-, not -*e*- and -*i* (though the -*e*- isn't pronounced like an unstressed o and is always preceded by a soft or historically soft consonant, except in a few isolated or former present participle actives, e.g. искóмое 'unknown (maths)'). Furthermore, note from the Old Moscow pronunciation that -и- verbs like носйть 'to carry' had a pronunciation нóсют in the third person plural (for нóсят) — and we often still hear it, even in the speech of relatively young Muscovites. Bearing in mind the -o- conjugation's ведýт 'they lead', плáчут 'they weep', this suggests that -и- conjugation verbs not stressed on the ending could have crossed over into the -o- conjugation. You might look into this more carefully, to see how the conjugation system might have been repatterned — don't forget the past tense (but is it relevant here?). This transfer has, in fact, been stopped by, among other things, the influence of the spelling.

And now let's continue the bridge with Russian and Church Slavonic.

Chapter 3: Just what is Russian?

After setting the scene of the system of sounds and how they begin to interact with the forms, it seems appropriate to admit an aside on the character of the Russian language before looking at a few actual 'word-families'. See Appendices 1 and 2 for an outline of the development of the Russian sound system.

3.1 The Emergence of the Russian Literary Language

Given Proto-Indo-European, then probably Balto-Slavonic, then Proto- or Common Slavonic, there is a shading, towards the end of the first millennium A.D., to what might be called 'Proto-East Slavonic'.[1] There would have been many dialects, existing alongside Baltic, Germanic (mainly Norse), Uralic (mainly Balto-Finnic), and Turkic dialects.

From the late tenth century, and with the first texts from the mid-eleventh century, there is the beginning of the centuries-long influence of Church Slavonic, which almost certainly provided the first written language. It was Vladimir the Great of Kiev's conversion to Greek-Orthodox christianity in 988 which started this process, but it also reflected a conversion process already underway and brought Old Church Slavonic (OChS) from the south, the Balkans, to Rus'. Before then, and indeed long after, there was an East Slavonic (ES) oral tradition, manifested in poetic, legal, and commercial language, and indeed there is evidence for a written tradition, as manifested in, for example, the *birch-bark documents*, but Old Church Slavonic, doubtless gradually penetrated by East Slavonic elements, became established as the state and church language. The seal on this was probably set during the reign of Jaroslav the Wise (effectively 1036-54), a time of learning and of many translations from Greek, comparable with the reign of Alfonso X el Sabio in the Iberian Peninsula. Thus the local 'language' and a secular tradition found themselves with a new written language, very similar, yet different and imported. The precise nature of the relationship between the two (essentially and inevitably more than two), from the eleventh to the end of the eighteenth century, has aroused considerable debate. Is Russian basically East Slavonic or basically the originally South Slavonic Old Church Slavonic? Were East Slavonic and (Old) Church Slavonic two separate languages, giving a

---

[1] Just before this one might insert 'Late Common Slavonic', as the common linguistic ancestor of the Slavonic languages in its form immediately before the breakup into the 'ancestors' of the individual Slavonic languages. The earliest extant writings from the East Slavonic area are referred to as being in the 'Old Rus' language' or in 'Common East Slavonic'. The East Slavonic languages are Belarusian, Russian, Ukrainian, and (a new addition) Rusyn.

bilingual situation, or was there one language with two principal and complementary functional variants, giving a state of diglossia? Needless to say, such questions are probably badly posed, and it has to be that such a dichotomy is a simplification. The situation, even as regards formal communication, would have been more complex, and yet it may be felt that during the eleventh-early fourteenth centuries Rus' was linguistically relatively homogeneous: Kiev was the linguistic, political, economic, and cultural centre. Communication was through a sort of *koiné*: Church Slavonic embraced culture, not just the liturgy. It was, too, supra-national, linking the East Slavs with the Byzantine cultural world. Local varieties of East Slavonic were the means of everyday (including written) communication, the law, and administration. The two influenced each other, Church Slavonic taking on East Slavonic characteristics and East Slavonic adopting Church Slavonic expressive means, some of which it would eventually assimilate completely, with many shadings. It is in this context that some argue that the basis of standard Russian is not East Slavonic, but the originally South Slavonic Old Church Slavonic, however originally localized, artificial, and 'Greek' it may have been. Bear in mind that for this early period the local dialects for the geographical area now, very approximately, covered by Russian, Ukrainian, and Belarusian — and at least Rusyn, are probably best referred to together as 'East Slavonic'.

Remember: the two 'languages', East Slavonic and Old Church Slavonic, were very similar, just caught in a 'relationship' at a time when the Slavonic linguistic world was, whatever the details, fragmenting. Perhaps their differences, and the later 'reintroduction' of a very 'archaic', or really just 'out of step', Church Slavonic in the fourteenth-fifteenth centuries, contributed to the special character of the relationship between Russian and Church Slavonic. The influence of Church Slavonic is perceptible principally in the sphere of word-formation — but syntax may be rather significant, and the language was to some extent ultimately shaped by Greek, which provided the bulk of the texts translated. What probably happened in Kievan Rus' was that Church Slavonic was very early 'East-Slavonicized', notably in pronunciation, e.g. the pronunciation of *št'* as *šč*. Little by little the influence of the local language must have spread also into the way Church Slavonic was written — there was mutual linguistic enrichment and insecurity. At this early stage there was uncertainty as to how to speak and write, rather than the *bilingualism* or *diglossia* which is often claimed for the linguistic situation in Kievan Rus'. There is nothing particularly surprising or unique in this — codified and eventually standardized languages are a recent phenomenon, dating from the Renaissance onwards even in the Western European tradition. Writing was predominantly Church Slavonic, so the establishment of writing patterns was at first the establishment of Church Slavonic patterns.

Subsequently, alongside East-Slavonification and, eventually, Russification, there was in progress a gradual evolution of the grammatical structure of Church Slavonic — the language changed, quite naturally, and was not exactly 'living' in an East Slavonic context. And East Slavonic itself changed — how else could things have been? Clerics were not unaware of this 'lowering of the tone' of their language — it was really just the passing of time, plus a naturalization, a linguistic assimilation.

And around the mid-fourteenth to fifteenth centuries Church Slavonic was revived, though in an archaicizing and artificial way, by the 'Second South Slavonic Influence', when clerics came to Muscovy from the Balkans after the fall of Byzantium. This opened up a rift or, perhaps better, brought out into relief the rift between Church Slavonic and Russian, something which might *now* be described as *bilingualism* or *diglossia*. And one must remember that Russian is not a naturally developed ES dialect (whatever that means), but an ES dialect considerably enriched by the wealth of expressive power of tenth-century OChS and by what OChS developed into in contact with East Slavonic over the tenth-fourteenth centuries.

By this, however, the position of Church Slavonic was weakened — it stood out more, its range of usage was more clearly delineated, something which was aggravated by the opening up of Muscovy to Western European influence through Poland. There would have been what might now be termed Russification of many features of the language, as if the native element was resurfacing from everyday informal communication and folk literature and a western component was being grafted on thanks to a new taste, especially on the part of the merchant class, for literature which entertained. There would also have been a growth in self-confidence stemming from political developments. At the end of the seventeenth century H.W. Ludolf (Unbegaun 1959) may well have written that in Russia people wrote Slavonic and spoke Russian, but this does not have to mean a dichotomy between Church Slavonic and Native Russian. Centuries had passed since such an interpretation might be put on the two; things were changing, with 'Slavonic' as Church Slavonic having its functions narrowed as those of Russian expanded. Ludolf cannot reasonably be expected to have had anything but an approximate idea of what was happening. And will we ever have a really precise understanding?

With Peter the Great Church Slavonic was finally cut down to its rôle as the language of the church — the final functional narrowing took place. The foundation of the modern Russian language was slowly worked out during the eighteenth century, with something close to the language we now learn emerging in the poetry and prose of Puškin and of contemporary journalists and literary critics in the first half of the nineteenth century — indeed, whatever the rôle of journalists and literary critics, the crucial position of Puškin in the Russian mind and heart in connection with the final emergence of a Russian literary language and, somehow, the real 'coming-of-age' of Russia, cannot even begin to be denied. Since then there has been stabilization — until now, that is, with a new linguistic revolution, involving some return to the pre-revolutionary past and a massive revamping of all aspects of the language under the influence of English.[2]

3.2 Contemporary Standard Russian

Contemporary Standard Russian (CSR) is a blend of the urban dialect of Moscow (in the Central Russian band of dialects) and Church Slavonic (perhaps more precisely, Russian Church Slavonic, the Russian recension of Old Church Slavonic). As already noted in 3.1, there may have been writing in the East Slavonic area (the geographical area from which CSR sprang) before the christianization of Rus' in 988, but it is generally accepted that East Slavonic became a regular written medium of communication only after christianization. Remember: this was not 'Russian' — the main centre was Kiev, which is now the capital of Ukraine. Moscow only emerged much later (the first mention of it is in 1147, so it must have existed before then), and Novgorod, though important, did not rival Kiev as a centre of learning.

There follows a list of elements which can be allocated, more or less reliably, to Russian or Church Slavonic — try to bear in mind that the overall picture as given is largely peculiar to the Russian situation (if it were not contextualized in that way, I might give the misleading impression that, say, Polish had certain Church Slavonic features). Overall, note that the written Church Slavonic base was straight away subject to the influence of East Slavonic pronunciation, so that what was written in a Church Slavonic way would so far as is known have been pronounced in an East Slavonic way. Over the years Church Slavonic was in this respect East Slavonicized, then Russified.

Church Slavonic has remained an essential element of Russian in the extent to which it provides parts of words, rather than entire words. The influence in the sense of 'loanwords' was restricted to the earliest period and to religious or learned words.

---

[2]Research over the last two centuries, but particularly since the 1950s and since recent developments in sociolinguistics and historical linguistics, has led to an extensive literature investigating the precise processes involved in the emergence of standard Russian. The actual relationship between dialects at the beginning of East Slavonic literacy and particularly over the centuries since then is highly complex. Notable scholars in this area include R. Auty, V.I. Borkovskij, I.A. Bulakhovskij, R. Cleminson, D.E. Collins, C.L. Drage, A.I. Gorškov, G. Hüttl-Worth, A. Issatschenko, V.V. Ivanov, V. Kiparsky, A.N. Kozin, P.S. Kuznecov, V.D. Levin, H.G. Lunt, W.K. Matthews, S.P. Obnorskij, A. Pennington, R. Picchio, M.L. Remněva, A.M. Schenker, G.Y. Shevelov, S. Signorini, A.I. Sobolevskij, G.S. Stone, A.A. Šachmatov, B.O. Unbegaun, B.A. Uspenskij, W. Vermeer, Ch.J. Veyrenc, V.V. Vinogradov, G. Vinokur, and A.P. Vlasto. The situation remains controversial.

3.3 The Native Russian and Church Slavonic Elements of Russian[3]

In what follows the Church Slavonic forms are given on the left where the columns are contrastive. If you examine the examples given, you will find that several could be given as examples of other features. Try, too, to think of more examples; and in any event be on the lookout for examples in your reading.

3.3.1 Metathesis and pleophony

брань 'abuse'	оборо́на 'defence'
безбре́жный 'boundless'	бе́рег 'bank, shore'
загла́вие book 'title'	заголо́вок newspaper 'headline'
граждани́н 'citizen'	горожа́нин 'town dweller'
кра́ткий 'brief'	коро́ткий 'short'
Мле́чный пу́ть 'Milky Way'	молоко́ 'milk'
бре́мя 'burden'	бере́менная 'pregnant'
хладоте́хника 'refrigeration science'	холоди́льник 'refrigerator'

And many, many others. An indication of the influence of ES pronunciation on the Church Slavonic forms here is that in a word such as безбре́жный the е would have been written ѣ in Old Church Slavonic; however, ѣ had a different pronunciation in that dialect of South Slavonic, and East Slavonic substituted its own е, which seemed correct in the context of the related, native, word бе́рег (the closeness of East Slavonic and Church Slavonic is revealed in this East Slav awareness that these words were 'dialectal variants').[4]

In the grossest terms, where between consonants Russian has -ра-, -ла-, -ре-, -ле- in some words and in others respectively -оро-, -оло-, -ере-, -оло-, the former reflect Church Slavonic. The pleophonic form -оло- contrasting with Church Slavonic -ле- is a special development; the expected -еле- is present in a very few words, e.g. се́лезень 'drake'; and there may be -ело- after hushing

---

[3]It is worth noting that the only real *Church Slavonicisms* might be the *whole words* borrowed into East Slavonic from around the end of the tenth century until the fall of Kiev in 1240. Examples include алта́рь 'altar', ад 'hell, hades', ами́нь 'amen', благода́ть 'abundance; grace (fem.)', диа́кон 'deacon', е́ресь 'heresy (fem.)', ико́на 'icon', ла́вра 'monastery', па́сха 'Easter'. Church Slavonic elements in Russian word formation are often referred to as *Neoslavonicisms* — these are what is interesting and important from a sociolinguistic point of view. A few whole words which look Church Slavonic might be seen as *Pseudo-Slavonic*, e.g. ю́бка 'skirt', юбиле́й 'jubilee' (see 3.3.6). Words with Church Slavonic features are typically seen as higher style, figurative, technical, abstract; but occasionally they come 'down in the world' or have optional less lofty usages and, more interestingly, become an integral part of 'Native Russian'.

[4]It would be possible to write at some length on the various complications of many of these features and issues.

consonants, e.g. ошеломи́ть 'to astonish, astound', related to Church Slavonic шлем '(safety/crash) helmet'. Note that:

(i)	one or the other form may be absent, e.g. there is no extant native, i.e. pleophonic, form corresponding to вре́мя 'time';
(ii)	not all words with an apparently appropriate shape are evidence of Church Slavonic or East Slavonic, e.g. брат, is not Church Slavonic (though in the sense 'brother' in a monastery it would be) because the elements were always in that order, cf. the related English *brother*, and there is no Church Slavonic form тлега contrasting with Russian теле́га 'cart', which is in fact a Turkic borrowing.

A nice example of a Church Slavonic word which has come down in the world, i.e. has caught the popular fancy, is прохлажда́ться 'to idle one's life away, take it easy', originally calqued from a Greek verb into Old Church Slavonic and meaning 'to repose (in paradise, i.e. somewhere cool)'. Related are прохла́да 'cool', прохла́дный 'cool'. We might add бла́го used as a conjunction meaning 'since, as', or as a noun in, say, бла́го ещё, что... 'the one good thing is that...', and тишь и благода́ть 'it's nice and peaceful'.

3.3.2 ра-, ла- and ро-, ло-

ра́зум 'reason'	—
распя́тие 'crucifixion'	—
разда́ть 'to distribute'	But masculine past tense form ро́здал; a clear preservation of the East Slavonic form under stress (Church Slavonic forms are favoured by East Slavonic *akańje*, i.e. essentially the pronunciation of some unstressed *o*'s as *a*).
ра́вный 'equal'	ро́вный 'flat' — but равни́на 'plain, plateau'.
ра́зный, ра́зница 'different/-ce'	But торго́вля в ро́зницу 'retail trade', a commercial term.
ладья́ 'rook, castle (in chess)'	ло́дка 'boat'

And many others. This is similar to 3.3.1, but applies to the absolute word-initial position, and always involves inversion.[5] The Native Russian pronunciation of [o] in the position immediately before the stress as [a] (*akańje*) may have aided the penetration of some Church Slavonic forms into the language, concealing to varying degrees their native status — this may be the case in, for

---

[5]Note that some instances of ра-, ла- involving inversion are 'correct' and therefore not unambiguously identifiable as Church Slavonic or Native Russian. Here one can only hypothesize, using, say, semantic arguments. So ра́ло 'plough' and ла́нь 'hind' are both correct, and their meaning suggests they are native. For completeness, note that forms in ES where *o* is expected go back to a falling pitch and those where *a* is expected go back to a rising pitch in Common Slavonic.

example, ладья́, where the ending -ья́ might be seen as native (see 3.3.9). Note that this contrast is present in the very common prefix раз- / рас-, роз- / рос-.

3.3.3 жд and ж

жа́жда 'thirst'	—
неве́жда 'ignoramus'	неве́жа 'uncouth person', — someone who does not know how to behave, cf. неве́жливый 'impolite' (in some English dialects people use 'ignorant' in this sense).
тождество́ 'identity' (learnèd)	—
осуждённый 'condemned' (participle)	осужу́ 'I shall condemn'

Nowadays *žd* tends to be pronounced as it is spelt (which happens to make it 'Church Slavonic'), but the historically 'correct' pronunciation, based on an East Slavonicization, is as a voiced щ, i.e. ж'ж' (3.3.4). Think of the once recommended pronunciation of дождь — дожди́.

What is at issue here is what happens to a Common Slavonic **d* under the influence of an immediately following **j*.

3.3.4 щ and ч

This is the voiceless equivalent of 3.3.3, thus the influence of **j* on an immediately preceding **t* (also the sequence **k/*g + *t* followed by a front vowel). The Church Slavonic pronunciation would have been something like *št'* (as, but not palatalized, in Modern Bulgarian, roughly the original geographical area of Old Church Slavonic), but this was East Slavonicized as *šč*, which in CSR now has a more widespread pronunciation as a long, soft *š*.

мо́щи 'relics' (religious)	мочь 'power'; мо́чи нет 'I can't go on';
пеще́ра 'cave' (geographical term)	Печо́ра (river-name), Ки́ево-пече́рская ла́вра 'Kiev Caves Monastery' (local name);
сокраща́ть 'to abbreviate'	укора́чивать 'to shorten'. Note the inversion vs. pleophony feature here, more visible if we take the perfective укороти́ть.

The present active participle belongs here. The East Slavonic forms of the present participle active do not function as participles; they are usually adjectives. Thus:

горя́щий 'burning'	(горе́ть)	горя́чий 'hot', горю́чее 'fuel'
пою́щий 'singing'	(петь)	певу́чий 'melodious'
летя́щий 'flying'	(лете́ть)	лету́чая мышь 'bat'
стоя́щий 'standing'	(стоя́ть)	стоя́чий 'stagnant'
сидя́щий 'sitting'	(сиде́ть)	сидя́чий 'sedentary'

And many others.You might now see why the third person plural of the verb, with its final -т, is so similar to the present active participle. Comparison with other languages, from Lithuanian to Latin, will be similarly enlightening. Do note that occasionally there will be different vowels — this usually has a historical explanation. Note too, from the last two examples given, that in English the more learnèd forms correspond to the Native Russian forms, a nice indication that languages might really just exploit the resources at their disposal.

3.3.5 е and ё

Church Slavonic is the lack of the expected development of stressed e before a hard consonant or silence to o (not to be confused with the e which comes, regularly, from *jat'*, *ĕ*, and does not become [ɔ]):

нéбо 'sky; heaven'	нёбо 'palate' (= 'roof/"sky" of the mouth')
крéстный хóд 'Easter procession'	крёстный отéц 'godfather'
падéж '(grammatical) case'	падёж 'a cattle disease'
житиé 'life of a saint'	житьё 'life, existence'
бытиé 'existence'	житьё-бытьё 'everyday life, existence'

This is often exploited by poets for stylistic effects or to achieve rhymes.

3.3.6 ю- and y-

юный 'youthful'	East Slavonic ун- (related to English *young*, demonstrating that the *j* might in some cases be quite ancient);
юг 'south'	— (related to *augment*, thus the place to which the sun has increased to its maximum height);
сою́з 'union'	брáчные ýзы 'chains of wedlock' (related to *join, junction*, i.e. Latin *iungo*).

Note also Native Russian ýжин 'supper, dinner' (Austrian German *die Jause*), ýтро 'morning' (related to, say, *Austria*, thus 'eastern'), yxá 'fish soup' (related to Latin *ius* 'broth, soup' and English *juice*). Words such as ю́бка 'skirt' and юбилéй 'jubilee' are recent loans, probably from German, and may be seen as 'Pseudo-Slavonic'.

3.3.7 The Third Slavonic Palatalization of Velars

This was encountered in Chapter 2 and relates to a change of к, г, х to ц, з, с. It is often seen as a Church Slavonicism, though this is controversial (think of весь 'all', which is unlikely to be a candidate for a uniquely Church Slavonic origin, and yet seems to exhibit this palatalization, though the details, given the synthetic character of Slavonic and scope for analogical processes, must have had an impact). Thus:

состязáние 'competition'	тягáться с + instr. 'to dispute (legal), contend with';
осязáние 'sense of touch'	посягáть на + acc. 'to encroach on; make an attempt on', присяга 'oath (probably touching/kissing the cross)' (both legal);
стезя 'path' (rather high-style)	ни зги не вúдно 'it's pitch black (= the path can't be seen)' (The root is СТЬГ; the loss of the soft sign in the Native Russian form led to the contraction and adaptation of the consonant group.);
пóльза 'benefit', нельзя 'it's not allowed/possible'	льгóта 'privilege' (legal);
восклицáть 'to exclaim'	накликáть бедý на + acc. 'to bring (= conjure up) disaster on' (root-stress in the perfective).

3.3.8 The treatment of the weak hard *jer* in prefixes

Recall that in Late Common Slavonic there were two vowels *ь and *ъ. These are the *jers*; they were phonetically probably 'super-short vowels' and in all the Slavonic languages either became full vowels (these were the 'strong *jers*') or ceased to be vowels (these were the 'weak *jers*') according to certain rules. Essentially, putting aside words where the *jer* was either the only vowel in the word or occurred next to л or р, where it tended to be 'strong', *jers* were deleted in sequence from the end of a word, the odd-numbered *jers* being 'weak' and the even-numbered *jers* being 'strong'; the count was restarted each time a full vowel intervened. Thus:

> East Slavonic дь$_2$нь$_1$ницамъ$_1$, giving деннúцам 'morning star (dat.pl.)'

The 'soft *jer*' gave е or ё when 'strong', and left softness or (later, depending on various factors) nothing in the immediately preceding consonant when 'weak'; the 'hard *jer*' gave о when 'strong' and hardness (= 'nothing') in the immediately preceding consonant when 'weak'. The *jers* when 'weak' also cause consonantal assimilations as a result of their deletion.

A hard *jer* could occur in prefixes, where it could, of course, be 'weak' or 'strong', but was more often than not 'weak'. However, the preservation of the original spelling in hymn texts and of all the vowels in the musical notes meant that in church singing *jers* which in everyday speech had been lost were sung. Such *jers* were treated as if strong, and even penetrated everyday words; they joined the Russian language as 'Neoslavonicisms'. The prefixes affected include въз-, съ-, and въ-. Thus:

содержа́ть 'to contain/maintain (imperf.)'	сдержа́ть 'to restrain/hold back (perf.)'
восклица́ть 'to exclaim'	—
во́зраст 'age' (see also 3.3.2)	взро́слый 'adult'
собо́р 'congregation; cathedral'	сбор 'gathering; harvest'
собира́ть 'to gather (imperf.)'	собра́ть 'to gather (perf.)'

In the last example, co- in the perfective verb is actually correct; so the co- in the imperfective can be either a Neoslavonicism or due to the influence of the perfective, or due to a combination of both. They arise from съ₁бирати and съ₂бь₁рати respectively. Note the first example, where the imperfective (actually imperfective-only) verb is, as a simple verb with a prefix, unexpected — can you think of any others?[6]

3.3.9 The tense *jers*

These were already examined in 2.1.2.5. Recall that, in the position immediately before *j* in Late Common Slavonic, the *jers* underwent a special development, becoming 'tense' (so the argument goes) and eventually combining with the *j* as *y* (from the hard *jer*) and *i* (from the soft *jer*). Native Russian doesn't seem to have this feature, and the manifestation of the tense *jers* in Russian words is seen as a Neoslavonicism, and is seen particularly in the contrast between the endings -ие and -ье, and in the spelling of, notably, the unstressed ending of the nominative singular masculine of the adjective. Thus:

житие́ 'saint's life' (see 3.3.6)	житьё 'everyday life'
до́брый 'good, kind'	сухо́й 'dry'

Recall the Old Moscow pronunciation of the unstressed ending in the Native Russian form, namely as if it were written добро́й; and note that, under stress, it emerges clearly that сухо́й is a 'hard' adjective.

Do bear in mind that the treatment of a *jer* before *j* as if weak is arguably never precisely that, since the soft sign (there are no cases of hard signs) here is more precisely a separating sign — it does indeed disappear into, sometimes softening, the preceding consonant, but it also has the effect of separating this consonant from the *jot* beginning the next syllable.

3.3.10. e- and o-

In a very few words Native Russian has an absolute word-initial o- which develops from an absolute word-initial *e-. This should not be confused with the

---

[6]Here are a few examples: состоя́ть в + prep. из + gen. 'to consist in/of (compare perf. состоя́ться 'to take place'), обстоя́ть 'to be', as in Как обстои́т де́ло? 'What's the situation?', зави́сеть от + gen. 'to depend on', вы́глядеть + instr. 'to look (sad, etc.)'.

change of *e* to *o* (spelt ё), i.e. ёж 'hedgehog' does not fit in here, since it does not start with *o*. The words most frequently mentioned in this connection are один 'one', óзеро 'lake', óсень 'autumn', олéнь (masc.) 'deer', and ря́бчик (from earlier оря́бь) 'hazel-grouse'. This development is found only in Russian, Ukrainian, and Belarusian, and is of significance here only because of the first of these words, which occurs in many Russian words in the form един- (note that phonetically this now begins with [j], but this was not the case originally): едúный 'single', едúнство 'unity', соединúть, imperf. соединя́ть 'to unite'.

3.3.11 Certain suffixes

Certain suffixes may be considered Church Slavonic. One example might be -тель, e.g. повелúтель 'sovereign, master (very high-style)', утешúтель 'comforter', предáтель 'traitor'. And compare носúтель 'bearer, carrier (say, of a disease)' with the more down-to-earth носúльщик 'porter'.

In addition, note that Church Slavonic is helpful in preserving, creating, or reflecting semantic distinctions:

ладья́ 'boat (poetic); rook (in chess)' (see 3.3.2)	лóдка 'boat'
странá 'country; (and a direct source of new Russian words, e.g. странúца 'page') (see 3.3.1).	сторонá 'side; district'

and that it may be seen as providing high-style equivalents:

да здрáвствует 'long live' (see 3.3.1)	здорóвье
óчи 'eyes' (poetic)	глазá

Note too that there is nothing intrinsically Church Slavonic about óчи, which is the normal word for 'eyes' in most Slavonic languages. It is simply the use which Russian, with its own peculiar глазá, makes of it, consigning it to a higher register and thus by association to the realm of Church Slavonic.[7]

High-style equivalents might include town names, e.g. Ленинг рáд, Владивостóк (see 3.3.1) — from the first it can be seen that Church Slavonicisms were certainly not perceived as religious in the period after the Revolution — even совéт 'council; soviet' and сою́з 'union' are, strictly speaking, Church Slavonicisms. Furthermore, Church Slavonic provides affixes for the learned language and new terms: зло-, благо-, из-, etc., e.g. злоупотребля́ть + instr. 'to abuse', благодарúть + acc. 'to thank', извлéчь 'to extract (e.g. profit)'. Note that the first two verbs are essentially *prefix*ed rather than *preverbed* stems; in other words, they remain imperfective — the second in

---

[7]Doubtless 'Native Russian' and 'Church Slavonic' come to act as cover-all terms for 'lower' and 'higher' registers of Russian, respectively.

particular 'looks' perfective, as if благодаря́ть is expected (but the perfective is, of course, поблагодари́ть). The third verb has what would, strictly speaking, be referred to as a *preverb*, which has a grammatical effect (in addition to the obvious semantic one) and, in this instance, gives a perfective verb, from which an imperfective is derived: извлека́ть — it fits in nicely with Russian grammatical structure — another example is извини́ть, imperf. извиня́ть 'to excuse'. Perhaps imperfective verbs such as принадлежа́ть + dat. 'to belong (to)' (with к + dat. for belonging to a group), вы́глядеть + instr. 'to look (sad, etc.)' are to be seen as prefixed rather than preverbed — Church Slavonic does not have to mean 'irregular' or 'anomalous'.

Many phraseological calques involve Church Slavonic elements, perhaps because they involve metaphor and thus fit in with the general lexical area favoured by Church Slavonicisms. Thus: пита́ть наде́жду 'to cherish the hope' (see 3.3.3) and влачи́ть жа́лкое существова́ние — French *traîner une vie misérable* (see 3.3.1/4/9). But Church Slavonic elements are not obligatory, e.g. слома́ть лёд 'to break the ice (Fr. *briser la glace*)'. In Chapter 4 there will be much expansion on many of the issues raised here.

Thus, Church Slavonicisms are an integral part of Russian, and it might be argued that the process of integration was well in hand by the time of the Second South Slavonic Influence in the fourteenth-fifteenth centuries, an influence which restored an identity, albeit a less 'real' one, to and imposed a reduced range of usage on the language of the Russian Orthodox Church.

Chapter 4: Identifying and Exploring Stems

4.1 Preamble

Here I wander around a number of words and word-families, drawing out topics of particular and general interest. Much of this will be familiar to certain readers (and will already have been hinted at, even rather heavily, in earlier chapters), but the hope is that by placing it in a looser context some attempt will have been made to satisfy one of the needs learners of Russian have, namely the acquisition of tools supporting their general interest in the language and helping them see links and so achieve vocabulary growth relatively painlessly. Needless to say, what follows is limited and selective.

If you're a student, do you really need to learn all the words listed in your coursebook? To this there is no unambiguous answer. Of course, it is desirable to learn all the 'words', but it is more desirable to work out how to use them. This involves a lot of hard work — there's no other way, for any language, and this work will continue indefinitely. Much vocabulary will be learnt by exposure, in real, everyday life — and doing it 'naturally' will make it authentic and reasonably independent of what is prescribed as correct; but you don't have that opportunity all the time, or even a little of the time, and when learning the language 'actively' you often need to ask questions — and it helps if you have some idea what questions to ask. We can help achieve this through a book such as this one, in which we can also mention things the native speaker might not always be aware of.

And how do you learn the words? Different people will have different ways of assimilating vocabulary. Some people copy everything into vocabulary books — for Russian that's a lot of work if you're going to note down the really useful information from the start (that's probably well nigh impossible; I certainly never managed it). Basic essential information includes stresses and enough information to be able to use a word in a sentence. Some people will have photographic memories. That doesn't mean their Russian (or whatever language) will be 'better', or more 'natural'. Most native speakers of languages don't have photographic memories, so it's clearly not a prerequisite for being a good speaker/writer/user of a language.[1] And, anyway, there are such things as dictionaries! What do you need *them* for, if not to use them? There is, though, the reality of doing translation in exams without dictionaries. This is justifiable only from the point of view of the time it would take to use the dictionary to find

---

[1] This doesn't really follow, as there is a difference between the natural *acquisition* of a language and the state we are in when we already possess the skills desirable when *learning* a language.

the 'mot juste': better without dictionaries, using your 'intelligence' to work out strategies. This approach makes a certain amount of sense, so long as you don't imagine you'll produce translations of seriously publishable quality (though some individuals may). One of the real skills here can be to do things as quickly as possible and then walk out of the exam room (not many teachers would encourage that, but it bears thinking about as a real-life skill): if the results are anything near good, you might be a born *interpreter* (not to mention translator) — this idea came to me from a UN interpreter. So relax and just learn what you can. And remember that one of the ways of learning words, or learning to guess their approximate meaning, is through what this book is in part trying to achieve, namely helping you find out a little about Russian words.

So, the general structure of Russian words follows the following pattern:[2]

> (prefix(es)) + ROOT (+ suffix(es)) (+ ending) (+ particle)

No attempt is made here to establish a hierarchy between the components in the above pattern. Everything in brackets is optional, unless we insist on zero-affixes and endings — in other words, they are always there. The ROOT on its own or together with prefix(es) and suffix(es) is the STEM. In other words, the STEM may or may not be identical with the ROOT. In привéт 'greeting' the ROOT is BET. There is no visible suffix, and it can be argued that there is a zero-ending (in that there has to be an ending, in a language like Russian, to convey grammatical relations). In at least one word, to be met later, there may seem to be no root; given that speakers have no trouble interpreting it, it presumably has a zero-, or underlying, or context-driven root.[3]

4.2 A few issues

4.2.1 Identifying roots

Now, сторонá 'side' is related to странá 'country', which occasionally retains meanings close to 'side', e.g. стрáны свéта 'points of the compass' (some Russian dispute this, insisting on стóроны свéта!). In other words, this is an instance of pleophony and a pre-Russian (and probably pre-Slavonic, see below)

---

[2] There are, of course, also compound words, namely words with more than one root, e.g. пар_о_хóд 'steamer, ship', Влад_и_мир 'Vladimir', typically characterized by a 'link vowel', and italic and stump compounds, e.g. гэс (= г_и_дро_э_лектри́ческая с_тáнция, thus feminine, though indeed indeclinable) 'hydroelectric power station', вуз (= в_ы_сшее у_чéбное з_аведéние, neuter expected but actually masculine and declined because well-established) 'higher educational institution', and, as an example of a stump compound, исполкóм (= испол_ни́тельный комитéт) 'executive committee'. You can often see the compound root as a single root.

[3] A root-free example suggested to me for English might be *superette*.

root СТОРН — the final consonant is needed to trigger the pleophony, which occurs between consonants. Can we justify an ultimate origin in *stor-? Well, yes. What about простóр 'space', which seems semantically close enough? Going outside Slavonic there is Latvian stara 'strip (of land, etc.)', Greek stórnūmi 'I spread, strew', and we might go as far as German die Stirn 'forehead', both the last examples with (presumably) an original suffix in n. Thus in Russian we may justify a root СТОРОН/СТРАН.

Note too the word сýтолока 'commotion', with its prefix су- and suffix-cum-ending -a. The prefix is related to с-, со-, even су- in non-standard words: сосéд 'neighbour', сопéрник 'rival', сопéрничать (с + instr.) 'to rival', and occasionally супéрник, etc. — see супрýжество 'wedlock' in 4.2.3. The root is Т/ЛК, historically ТЪЛК, related to modern Russian толк 'sense', e.g. тóлку нет 'it makes no sense', and verbs such as истолковáть, imperf. истолкóвывать 'to interpret, explain' (note that in the derivation of imperfectives from verbs with the suffix -овá- the o remains intact — compare устрóить, imperf. устрáивать 'to arrange'). It's probably related to English 'talk'. Сýтолока may be a Russian dialect word, since the o's surrounding the л are unusual. There are only a few examples of identical vowels going back to a hard or soft sign preceding р or л between consonants in Russian, e.g. сýмеречный 'twilight, dusk (adj.)' (compare сýмерки, gen. сýмерек 'twilight' (where the second -e- is a mobile vowel before a zero ending)), верёвка 'rope, string', and arguably пóлон, short form masculine of пóлный 'full'. The phenomenon of a hard or soft sign being repeated after an р or л is referred to as the 'second pleophony', which leads us to suppose that the first one is much more important. It indeed is, and as was seen in Chapter 3 is one of the features which contrast Native Russian forms with Church Slavonic forms, all of them now, of course, entirely Russian, just as no-one would hesitate to consider Norman-French venison to be English.

Pleophony is by no means as exotic a phenomenon as you might imagine. Going not too far away, we observe that some Scottish people often pronounce words like form in a way which suggests that the spelling might be 'forom'. Some Irish people don't say 'film', but 'filim'. The Irish name Colm is written Calum in Scotland, and in Scottish Gaelic, whenever we have a vowel followed by l or r , and the vowel + consonant sequence precedes a consonant, the vowel tends to be repeated after the l or r — note the pronunciation of the name for Scotland Alba. This inserting of a vowel is a very well-known phenomenon, and even has names, namely anaptyxis or svarabhakti; the actual exact 'repetition' of the same vowel is what we find in Russian, as must be evident from the spelling — the changes in unstressed vowels came later, and didn't affect the spelling. We can easily list a few examples: гóрод 'town', здорóвый 'healthy', гóлос 'voice', солóма 'straw', бéрег 'shore, bank', берёза 'birch-tree', молокó 'milk' (go by the standard spelling — without a stress mark and ё — which is historical and doubtless reflects the original sound-shape). Now, some of these words occur in English too. It doesn't require much imagination to suspect that garden/yard, *burgh* (or *borough*), *birch*, *milk* are related to the Russian words. This relationship becomes more likely when we cite words from lands closer to Russia, e.g. German *Garten, Berg, Milch*, and Lithuanian *gar̃das, ber̃žas*. But in all these words the vowel comes *before* the *r* or *l*! Well, the fact is that this order of components is the original order. Don't, by the way, pay too much attention to the vowels in English and German, because there have been many more changes and are many more variations in vowels over history. But then we ask ourselves: what of words in Russian like Ленингра́д, where the component град must correspond to 'town' — compare Но́вгород 'Newtown'! And what of Да здра́вствует...! 'Long live...!', согла́сен 'agree', безбре́жный 'boundless, "without a bank/edge"', and Мле́чный пу́ть 'Milky Way', млекопита́ющее 'mammal'. Well, the simple version of the answer (recall 3.3.1) is that in Church Slavonic the *r* or *l*, instead of having the vowel repeated after it, changed places with the *r* or *l*, in a process known conventionally as 'metathesis' or, perhaps better, 'inversion' — variations on this are what happens in all the Slavonic languages other than Russian, Ukrainian, and Belarusian; and it is just as difficult to explain — basically, it all has to do with the vowel-like qualities of *r* and *l* — listen to, say, an American pronunciation of *perception*. Note that -еле- from *el between consonants is rare in Russian; instead of the expected -еле- we get -оло- (after hushers we may have -ело-, as in ошеломи́ть 'to astonish', where the Native Russian version of the root, ШЕЛОМ, corresponds to Church Slavonic шлем 'helmet; crash helmet' (and, bearing in mind the First Palatalization, *xelm-, borrowed from Germanic and reflected in English *helmet*). Quite a nice example of this is the verb for 'to grind', namely моло́ть, which has non-past мелю́, ме́лешь, ... ме́лют; in other words we have -оло- between consonants (м and т), but the original -*el*- preserved between *m* and a vowel — note that the *j* which originally followed the *l* in the non-past had been absorbed into the *l*, so that in the non-past the *l* is truly between vowels, thus ruling out pleophony; we can corroborate this by noting that in Lithuanian the infinitive is *mélti*.

Masses of such examples can be found in Russian, with pleophony vs. metathesis/inversion being a very rich source of vocabulary: taking the *turn* root (see 4.3.55), ВРАТ/ВОРОТ, we have переворо́т 'revolution' against обрати́ться, imperf. обраща́ться + к + dat. 'to treat, turn to' (here -*bv*- becomes -*b*-); taking a *control* root (see 4.3.13), ВЛАД/ВОЛОД, we have вла́сть 'power, authority', владе́ть + instr. 'to own, command (e.g. of a language)' as against во́лость 'province' (pre-1918); taking a *keep* root, ХРАН/ХОРОН, we have храни́ть 'to keep, preserve' as against хорони́ть 'to bury (i.e "to preserve in the ground")'; and taking the *enclosure/town* root, leaving го́род 'town' aside, we have огоро́д 'vegetable garden' with an unusual stress, the prefix о-, and the root ГОРОД/ГРАД in the sense 'fence'. So a *town* is a place with a fence or stockade around it, and likewise a garden — note German *der Zaun* 'fence'. There are related verbs, e.g. огороди́ть, imperf. огора́живать 'to enclose' and, in a Church Slavonic form, загради́ть, imperf. загражда́ть 'to block, obstruct'. Note the different ways used to derive the imperfectives and the vowel alternation in огораживать. Lithuanian *gařdas*, with its originally falling (now rising) intonation, supports the Russian stress in город (we expect the stress on the first of the two pleophonic vowels to be a reflection of the emphasis being on the beginning of a syllable with falling intonation) and the mobility of that stress (original rising intonation tends to be reflected in fixed stress).

As we've already seen (3.3.1), not all possible candidates do in fact belong to the club. To drive this home, колокол 'bell' probably arises from **kolkol-*, where the syllable is repeated. This may be an instance of pleophony, though Sanskrit has *kalakalas* 'noise' (but recall that pleophony is nothing special in languages, so we shouldn't be too surprised). It may be related to English *call, hail*. The root may also be a voiceless variant of ГОЛ, which is found in голос 'voice' (Native Russian, thus pleophony; think of согласие 'agreement') and Church Slavonic глагол 'verb' (originally 'word'; there's a Russian dialect form гологолить 'to natter').

Compare the possible linkage of голова 'head' with Latin *calvus* 'bald'. It looks like pleophony, and it is. Lithuanian obliges, as so often, here: *galvà* 'head'. There is reason to link it to Latin *calvus* 'bald' (French *chauve*). Russian has глава 'head, chief; chapter', and you can immediately sense that this form with metathesis has the figurative meanings. Think, too, of the adjectives: головной 'head-' — главный 'head, principal'. A 'title' is заглавие (do you notice a second Church Slavonicism there?), while in a newspaper a headline is заголовок, less 'lofty'. Now, think back to *chief, chapter* — these come from Latin *caput* 'head'. In French and Italian this has been replaced by a word for an earthenware pot — heads tend to be used a lot in the colloquial: *la tête, la testa*. The original Latin word gave French *le chef, le chapitre*. Now, in German 'head' is the related *das Haupt*, which is only used in the sense of 'chief', 'principal': *die Hauptstadt* 'capital city'. At this point I have to say that pleophony has almost become a term of abuse, however at times affectionate, among some Slavists — a dear colleague would often refer to the study of the Russian language as a 'load of old pleophony'. I hope, however, that I've resuscitated it by linking it with other languages, particularly with English. And, wandering off again, if you're Dutch, how do you pronounce *melk* 'milk'?

Before moving on, it is good to come back on something. Note that *Alba* is not the same as in Russian, in that the *al* is not between consonants. The impetus in Common Slavonic, when all this happened, was towards open syllables, namely sequences of *consonant + vowel*; *a* on its own at the beginning of a word wouldn't work, and in Slavonic what happened here was that the vowel and the following *l* or *r* changed places. Exactly what happened, or how this happened, no-one really knows, but perhaps a Slavonic variation on [alaba] was a first step, with the first vowel then lost. Check 3.3.2.

4.2.2 A note on consonantal groups

Related to привéт, mentioned above, is обéт 'promise'. But what has happened to the в? Remember, when *b* and *v* came together, the *v* dropped out. Note óбласть 'region', cf. влáсть 'power, authority', and обúдеть (обижáть) 'to offend', cf. вúдеть 'to see' (in обúдеть seeing 'around someone', thus avoiding their eyes and so offending them; similarly презирáть'"look over" someone', thus 'despise', and note the related words зрúтель 'spectator', зрéлище 'spectacle', обзóр 'survey', зреть 'to see', etc. — this group of words suggests a root З/Р or ЗЬР — see 4.3.33). In more recent compound words -бв-does occur, e.g. обвестú 'to take around, encircle', обвинúть 'to accuse'. Note too the word обинýк in expressions such as говорúть обиняко́м 'to beat about the bush', говорúть без обиняко́в 'to speak plainly, directly', which is likely to be related to the verb обиновáться, perf. обинýться 'to vacillate', most often met as не обинýясь 'without hesitation', and probably being a combination of об- and a derived form of вúть 'to wind'. Many consonant groups were simplified early on, helping create the context for open syllables (see Appendix 2).

4.2.3 A wander around suffixes

Note зóнтик 'umbrella' and its origin in Dutch *zondek*, namely something which provides cover from the sun (*sun + deck*), giving an original analysis into зон and тик. In Russian the component -ик is a suffix, which means there must have been a reinterpretation by Russian of the structure of the word, thus the form зонт 'umbrella; awning'. In native words we find, for example, стóлик 'small table, restaurant table'. Between the suffix -ик and the root (or rest of the stem) there are often other suffixes. Thus худóжник has the suffixes -/н- and -ик-. The first, originally -ьн-, will have changed г to ж through the First Palatalization. This leaves us with худог (a link to худóй 'thin' seems unlikely), which is an odd root in that it is bisyllabic and not interpretable other than as originally bisyllabic. Well, here this is because it is a borrowing — from Germanic. The y could originally be a back nasal, so *handag-* or something (Gothic *handags*), i.e. English *handy*, which is what an artist is. Another example is рабóт/н-ик (here the -от- is historically a suffix, but РАБОТ seems a reasonable, independent root for modern Russian, rather separate from РАБ and its 'slave' sense). The suffix -от(а) can also be seen in, for example, длиннóты 'long, tedious passages' (the normal word for 'length' is длинá, showing that we have -ьн- even in длúнный 'long'; the other type of length, 'longitude', is долготá). Thus there is the word раб 'slave', someone deprived of freedom, related to English 'orphan'. The word рабóта is itself related in the distant past to the antecedent of German *Arbeit* 'work, toil; suffering', the first three letters reflecting the element order in a prehistoric form of Russian. It's also related to Latin *orbus* 'deprived; parentless, childless'. We begin to see the link between 'slaves' рабы́ and 'child' ребёнок, and note the term for 'house *serv*ants/*serfs*', домочáдцы, where чад reflects the word чáдо 'child', related to the English word. Child labour, slave labour. See 4.3.6.

The suffix -/н- is extremely important and productive, by which is meant 'living, actively participating in the formation of new words', e.g. the adjectives дискéтный 'diskette', читáбельный 'readable', смотрúбельный 'watchable' (the last two are rather nice combinations of a Russian stem with a western suffix). Note that л preceding the -н is soft. If we look at ýмный 'clever', we see that the м is hard, and yet the short-form masculine is умён, where the mobile vowel (appearing because there is a zero-ending) softens the м! The actual suffix, then, has to be seen as something like -/н, and the slash here looks like it had the antecedent *ь.

What about пóлный 'full', though, with its short-form masculine пóлон (not пóлен)? The answer here has to be that we either have a different suffix (-ън-) or no suffix at all and the mobile о just separates the two final consonants. Compare подпóльный 'underground', composed of под-, the root ПОЛ (or ПОЛʲ?) 'field', and the suffix and ending. Working through words related to пóлный, we in fact never find the л and н separated, except in the short form masculine, so we do seem to be looking at a root ПОЛН, so far as modern Russian itself is concerned. Slavonic language history suggests an original soft sign for the vowel: *pьln-, something confirmed by Lithuanian pìlnas 'full', with nothing between the l and the n — if there had been something, Lithuanian would have had it.

We might develop this by looking at words with the suffix (actually, suffixes) -ниц(а).[4] Note that wherever there is an л, that л is soft: пéпельница 'ashtray', чернúльница 'inkwell' — compare the words they are derived from: пéпел 'ash', чернúла 'ink', with hard final consonants. So we have the same suffix -ьн-, plus the suffix -иц(а) with its Third Palatalization (a feminine form of -ик, thus рабóтница).

This might be built on by looking at a few other words. First, спосóбность 'ability; capacity' has the suffixes -/н- and -ость, and at least the prefix с/-. The root ПОСОБ- has a sense of 'help, aid', thus посóбие 'handbook, (financial) allocation'. It is *help* in the sense of 'enabling one to do something'. The first syllable, по, is itself presumably a prefix, suggested by such forms as осóбый (and other related forms) 'special', with prefix о-. There is a possible link with свóй 'one's (own)' and свобóда 'freedom' (see 4.3.23).

These suffixes have an even more extensive impact, in the verb pattern exemplified by нéрвничать, non-past нéрвничаю, нéрвничаешь, ... нéрвничают 'be nervous', here a very useful compound productive suffix, which may have pejorative or negative overtones. The suffix these days may be seen as something like -/нича(й)-, since it can be tacked on to complete words, e.g. лакéйничать 'to behave like a flunkey' (лакéй 'lackey, flunkey'). However, from

---

[4]For simplicity's sake a nominative singular ending will often be considered part of a suffix or stem, and the word 'stem' will occasionally be used when 'root' might be more correct.

нéрвный 'nervous' (with -/н- already) we can begin to discern the suffix's composite nature, something we can break down too with скрóмничать 'to be overmodest' — compare скрóмный 'modest', a loanword from Polish ultimately made up of the prefix съ- and the root КРОМ, as in кромá, more often Russian крóмка 'edge', thus 'on the edge, limited, peripheral'; note too крóме + gen., originally a prepositionless prepositional (in early Russian the prepositional was *never* used with a preposition, just as is still the case in Lithuanian and Latvian) 'on the edge of', thus 'apart from, besides', and тьмá кромéшная 'utter/outer darkness' — note the perhaps unexpected hardness of the spatial adjective (compare здéшний 'local', from здéсь 'here').

Now злóба 'malice', with its root З/Л, where the slash indicates a hard sign, as evident from the short form masculine of злой — зол 'evil; angry'. The word is formed with the suffix -ба — the -о- is probably a link-vowel, with the soft sign which would usually start the suffix (think of свáдьба 'wedding') being deleted, thus ЗЪЛ- + о + (ь)ба. Злóба дня 'topic of the day' has its source in the Bible (Matthew 6:34): Довълѣетъ дьневи злоба его 'Sufficient unto the day is the evil thereof'. Note злободнéвный 'topical'. In злодéй we have a compound word, with дей relating to action, doing, e.g. дéйствовать 'to have an effect, act'. In зловóние we have the same, this time with the suffix -ие. The component вон- can be found in вонь 'stench', or обоня́ние 'sense of smell', where the в disappears in the group *bv*. The words for the other senses, of which you might like to work out the families, are зрéние 'sight', осяза́ние 'touch', вкус 'taste', and слух 'hearing'.[5]

The noun шаг 'pace, step' may well be related to the root СЯГ/СЯЗ 'touch', which you've just seen, with the ш- arguably emerging from the influence of -ж- in the diminutive шажóк, supported by the closeness of a soft *s* to a *š*-sound; not to mention that the phonetic realization of *s* varies considerably over languages — that there was variation in the dialects behind English and French is shown clearly by French *pousser* and *huissier*, alongside respectively *push* and *usher* in English.[6] This suggests an diminutive suffix -ьк-, which is odd. It may be more

---

[5]One of them can be noted here: вкус has the prefix въ- and is derived from earlier кусити 'to try, test', borrowed from Germanic and behind English *choose*, borrowed from French. As such it is related to кýшать 'to eat' (presumably with a frequentative or habitual nuance) and, more transparently, то покуси́ться на + acc. 'to lay claim to, make an attempt on'. It is tempting to relate it to куса́ть, perf. укуси́ть 'to bite', and thus кусóк 'piece, bit'. This latter family had a nasal in the root, as indicated by Polish *kąsać*.

[6]We might link *usher* with poetic устá 'lips', which might be reflected in Latin *ostium* 'estuary', like Rome's port of *Ostia*. 'Doorways' (= 'openings, orifices') come in here too. Thus усы́ 'moustache' has a root УС, certainly related to Latin *os* 'mouth' (it also provides *oral* — remember that in Latin *s* becomes *r* between vowels). There could be a slight problem with this, because Polish *węsy*, with the same meaning, suggests a nasal origin. Another example of the *s* - *š* is фáрш 'mince', which probably

an instance of root/stem-final velars undergoing a 'First Palatalization' on analogy with the рука́ — ру́чка pattern: пиджа́к — пиджачо́к 'jacket', бог — божо́к 'god', по́рох — порошо́к 'powder'. We don't actually even need a velar, for instance ко́рень 'root' — корешо́к 'spine of book; small root', бара́н 'ram' — бара́шек 'young ram/lamb; catkin'. This root emerges in осяза́ние '(sense of) touch' (as just seen), to be contrasted with прися́га 'oath' (под прися́гой 'under oath'; and note прися́жный 'sworn; member of a jury'), посяга́ть на + acc. 'to make an attempt on, lay claim to'. The forms with г (and derived ж) are Native Russian — the lexical areas of law, commerce, hunting, and administration are traditionally Native Russian areas, perhaps by tradition conducted orally rather than in writing. The forms with з are Church Slavonic and results of the Third Palatalization.

Карто́фель and its masculine gender might be used to say that nouns in -ель are masculine (though it is a borrowing from German, the actual component -ель encourages us to think of it as native). Actually, it would be more correct to say that nouns with the suffix -тель are masculine. One true exception to this is доброде́тель 'virtue', which is feminine — note too the position of the stress immediately before the suffix (which obtains for the singular — but note учи́тель 'teacher', ending-stressed in the normal plural: учителя́, etc.). An exception from the point of view of stress is де́ятель 'figure, agent'. The noun мете́ль 'snowstorm, blizzard (fem.)' is not an exception, since its suffix is -ель, affixed to a root МЕТ 'sweep, whirl' (мести́, мету́, мете́т 'to sweep, whirl; be a snowstorm (impersonal)'). We might bring in смета́на 'smetana' here; it has a sense of milk which has been concentrated, in that it is a participial form of an old verb съмѣта́ти 'to throw together'. Think too of предме́т 'subject', something which has been 'thrown' (-jected) (МЕТ) close up to (sub-) something (and note междоме́тие 'interjection'). You might think that there is something odd here. Do the verbs мести́ (clearly no jat', given мёл in the past tense) and мета́ть, non-past мечу́, мéчешь, ... мéчут 'throw', with a jat' (history tells us there was a jat' here — a lengthened grade, as shown in лете́ть — лѣта́ть before 1918), belong together? The answer is almost certainly that they are indeed related, though there are possible oddities caused by analogy. For instance, in CSR we have смета́ть 'to tack (together)', which has imperfectives мета́ть and смётывать (note the ё). And note the adjective сметли́вый 'quick-witted', someone good at making connections. For another angle see 4.3.22.

Borrowings from other languages can be tricky: ме́бель 'furniture' is feminine, and the second е, which is not mobile, is initially unexpected— compare French *meuble*, which is masculine and has no vowel between the *b* and the *l*. But does the Russian word come directly from French and have insertion of a vowel? Perhaps it came into Russian through Polish *mebel* from German *das Möbel*? Whatever the case, do we have suffix substitution here? Well, perhaps,

---

comes from German *Farsche*, ultimately from French *farce* 'stuffing, filling', derived from *farcir* 'to fill, stuff' — that Old French special *s*.

since, as we have seen, the suffix -ель does not necessarily force masculine gender and the е there is not mobile. And then bear in mind меблировáть 'to furnish', as in меблирóванные кóмнаты 'furnished rooms'!

Sometimes suffixes disappear. In нúзменность 'lowland' we seem to have the suffixes -енн- (here not an augmentative suffix, as it is in здоровéнный 'burly, strapping') and -ост-. However, this leaves -м- unexplained. In fact the suffix is -мен-, to which the suffix -/н- was added. In early Russian there was низмень 'low place, depression', now низúна (note *that* suffix again), something preserved in сухмéнь 'dry weather (dial.), dry soil' — we discover such things by using reverse dictionaries (e.g. Zaliznjak 1987), which are absolutely invaluable for the study of languages like Russian. More interesting and relevant to the study of the modern language is a consequent expectation that the word for 'low' be нúзий, rather than нúзкий. In other words, the к is a suffix -/к- (ък-). So we begin to understand why the short comparative is нúже, i.e. the к disappears (or came later). You may have noticed this in other adjectives, e.g. дáльше 'further' — далёкий 'far', ýже narrower' — ýзкий 'narrow', вЫше 'higher' — высóкий 'high', шúре 'wider' — широ́кий 'wide', блúже 'nearer' — блúзкий 'near', тóньше 'finer, more slender' — тóнкий 'fine, slender' (note the soft sign). Note too низы́ 'the masses' (i.e. the *low(er)* elements of the population), превы́сить, imperf. превышáть 'to exceed' (and note inversion or metathesis in the prefix; cf. Native Russian пере-), сýзить(ся), imperf. сýживать(ся) 'to get narrow', удалúть imperf. удалять 'to remove, extract, dismiss', расшúрить(ся), imperf. расширять(ся) 'to broaden', приблúзить(ся), imperf. приближáться 'to bring/come closer'. Sometimes the к is much more assimilated, thus утончúть, imperf. утончáть 'to make thinner, refine', облегчúть, imperf. облегчáть 'to facilitate, lighten, relieve', смягчúть, imperf. смягчáть 'to soften, alleviate', related respectively to тóнкий 'fine, thin' (ТЪН(ЪК) — we know the first vowel was a hard sign from the evidence of other Slavonic languages, e.g. Polish *tenki*, where the vowel and preceding hard *t* indicate a hard sign), лёгкий 'easy, light' (ЛЕГ(ЪК)), and мя́гкий (МЯГ(ЪК) — the я indicates an earlier front nasal, as still in Polish *miękki*, with the preceding soft consonant indicating a front or palatal nasal). The г is probably by analogy with that in лёгкий. In this connection we might mention мукá 'flour', which probably has the same origin as мýка 'torment', and is related to мя́гкий 'soft'; thus there are different original nasals in each. The origin can be seen in, say, Lithuanian *mìnkyti* 'to crush, knead', *minkštas* 'soft'. So you soften something up by pummelling it, creating torment! Мя́коть 'flesh, pulp (fem.)', which fits in semantically, is also related to мя́гкий.

As another example of an adjective in -ък-, we might start with the noun я́рость 'fury', which has, as might be expected, the root ЯР. This is ancient, in Proto-Indo-European *$y\bar{e}r$, meaning 'year, spring' (thus related to the English). It probably meant 'warm, hot' to start with. In Russian dialect there is я́рка 'lamb of this spring', and in Russian itself яровáя пшенúца 'spring wheat'. It itself has developed to a meaning 'angry, furious, severe', but with the suffix -/к- it means 'bright': я́ркий, with the suffix -ък-.

Now consider ха́нжество 'sanctimoniousness, hypocrisy', along with similar words, e.g. произво́дство 'production', челове́чество 'humanity', ца́рство 'kingdom, realm', большинство́ 'majority', меньшинство́ 'minority', мно́жество 'a great number, multitude', дово́льство 'contentment; prosperity'. In the last one, note the soft sign, just as with the -ьн suffix, when л precedes. Clearly, the suffix is underlyingly -/ство or -ьство. But what of the forms with -ество? Part of the answer can be found by reference to plural formation in English: *fishes, churches* — but *caps*, etc. In other words, after certain sounds a vowel sound is inserted; so this is not specifically Russian, but a more widespread linguistic feature. The sounds concerned are hushing and hissing sounds, which may seem to need to be kept apart from hushing/hissing sounds beginning the next component of the word.[7] Actually, this doesn't have to happen, and in Polish we find such forms as *mnóstwo*, equivalent to Russian мно́жество — in Polish the 'correct' development went through, with contraction of the awkward consonant group. It has been suggested that the -e- is a Church Slavonic feature; that may well come into it, but it isn't necessary, as we've seen from *churches*, etc. It might be argued, by the way, that Russian tends to treat the *jers* very correctly, which means they would have been expected to disappear when appropriate, as indeed in this suffix when there's no preceding hisser or husher. What is also interesting here is that, given the *fishes* argument, we might not have to posit a soft sign or some vowel beginning the suffix — it would have happened anyway. But the example дово́льство indicates that there *was* one there. Slightly differently, note мно́жество, but мно́го 'much, many', челове́чество but челове́к 'person' (ханжество́ is from ханжа́ 'hypocrite', from a Turkic word meaning 'tramp', so doesn't fit in here). In other words, once again the alternation arising from the First Palatalization; this must have been caused by a front vowel, e.g. and i.e., the antecedent of the soft sign, beginning the suffix.

What of матери́нство 'maternity, motherhood', where we have мать with its extra syllable -ер- (it's an ancient *r*-stem noun, just as is дочь 'daught*er*' and, though there have been changes, брат 'broth*er*' and сестра 'sist*er*'). Here we have the suffixes -ин- (related to the possessive, as in ма́мин 'mum's', та́нин 'Tania's', осли́ный 'ass's') and -/ство (= -ьство) again.

Превосхо́дство 'superiority' has the root ХОД, the suffix -/ств-, and the Church Slavonic prefixes пре- (in Native Russian пере-, another case of pleophony[8]) and вос- (underlyingly в/з or въз). Note the related verb

---

[7]In this connection, compare the past tense of the English verbs *change, itch, fizz, kiss*, and *fish*.

[8]We might consider the following too, bringing in a few more factors of interest: перерыв 'interval' also has the prefix пере- (Native Russian; Church Slavonic пре-), and рыв representing the root Р/В, where the vowel was ъ, lengthened as ы, as also in

превосходи́ть (imperf.) 'to excel in (= + в + prep., or + instr.); surpass (= + acc.)'. What would the perfective be? Well, it is превзойти́. Note the new mobile vowel, *not* corresponding to an original *jer*, and the native form of the prefix — or rather the expected zero in the prefix, given the о in the next syllable, arising before a consonant group. In other words, note that prefixed идти́ 'to go' becomes -йти́, and a vowel is inserted before the *jt* consonant group (remember that *j*, i.e. й, is a consonant). Compare отойти́ 'to depart', разойти́сь 'to separate; go one's separate ways', and разогна́ть 'to scatter, chase in separate directions', among many others. Analogy causes this о to hang on in inappropriate circumstances, e.g. отошла́ 'departed (fem.)' is fine, but we would expect отшёл instead of отошёл 'departed (masc.)'.

In супру́жество 'matrimony; wedlock', on removing the suffix there emerges супру́г 'spouse (masc.; the fem. form is супру́га — no inserted suffix, just -а; but note the colloquial form супру́жница), which is made up of the prefix с/- (= съ-) in the sense of 'together, with', which has either become су- under the influence of words with that prefix, e.g. сутя́га (obs., coll.) 'litigious person' or, more likely, reflects the fact that the prefix could have a final nasal element (thus: *sъn-*), which before a consonant, as here, would have given сѫ-, which would have become су- by the tenth century. Note Polish *sąsiad* but Russian сосе́д 'neighbour', where the nasal vowel didn't develop. The nasal element comes out in, for example, сня́ть 'to take (off)', of which more in 4.3.5.2. Thus the root is ПРУГ. This has a basic sense of something pulled together/tight, which comes out in such words as пружи́на 'spring', упру́гий 'taut'. With a different nasal (perhaps *in* as in French *fin* rather than the *on* as in French *bon* which we might have behind many cases of у, the two reflecting different ablaut grades) we have запря́чь, non-past запрягу́, запряжёшь, ... запрягу́т, past запря́г, запрягла́, impf. запряга́ть 'harness'. Perhaps English *spring*, with *in*, reflects this other combination of vowel and nasal consonant.[9]

---

the derivation of imperfective verbs, e.g. прерва́ть 'to interrupt (= "tear across")', imperf. прерыва́ть. Note that this is definitely the root because the stress is on -а́ть; if the verb suffix was -ыва-, then the stress would be ⁺пре́рывать. The word переку́р is relatively easy to guess, meaning the same as переры́в but with the object of having a smoke, thus КУР — related to a meaning 'smoke, smell', Lithuanian *kùrti* 'to heat'.

[9] At a late stage in Proto-Slavonic there were at least two nasal vowels: ǫ — ę, the former originating in a tautosyllabic (= 'same-syllable') sequence of back vowel (*o/u*-type vowel) and nasal consonant (= *n/m*) and the latter in a tautosyllabic sequence of front vowel (= *e/i*-type vowel) and nasal consonant. In Russian ǫ became *u* (у, sometimes ю) and ę became *a* preceded by a soft consonant (thus я, which spelling rules might change to а, e.g. the а in часть 'part', cf. Polish *część*). The soft consonant might subsequently harden, e.g. ж in жать where, remember, the nasal element re-emerges when the vowel-consonant sequence is heterosyllabic (= 'other-syllable'): жму, жну.

4.2.4   The *jers*

4.2.4.1   The mobile vowels

The *jers* are the historical basis for the mobile vowels of Russian and of the other Slavonic languages. It's worth, however, knowing about a few other phenomena.

First, the numeral один, which loses its й. Thus одного, etc. At an earlier stage there must have been an optional form with a *jer*. Other Slavonic languages show reflexes of a *jer*: Polish *jeden* (a hard sign), Serbo-Croatian *jedan* (a soft or hard sign). Secondly, the adjective достойный 'worthy', which has short form masculine достоин, where достоен might have been expected, cf. спокоен from спокойный 'calm'. Thirdly, заяц 'hare', which, with its other cases based on зайц-, suggests an alternation between zero and *a* (which would be a nasal, historically), and пояс 'belt', where the spelling is retained but the pronunciation is as if the spelling were пойс-. This leaves us, fourthly, with analogical instances of reflexes of hard and soft signs. Recall that the strong hard sign gave o and that the strong soft sign gave e (or ё). Though there are chronological issues here, that both can give *o* suggests that their pronunciation might have been rather similar, such that any difference was transferred to the hard or soft pronunciation of the preceding consonant. This can be contrasted with the development in the dialects preceding Macedonian, where the hard sign gave *o* and the soft sign *e*, and there was no distinction of hard and soft consonants — on the surface just as in Russian, but underneath perhaps rather different.

Now, from 4.2.3 recall that in instances where in Russian there were consonant-final prefixes preceding consonant groups, analogical 'hard signs' were inserted, giving o. Thus отходить, perfective отойти 'to go away', where the second o is an analogical hard sign before the consonant group йт. Think too of рагонять — разогнать — разгоню 'chase off', слиться — сольюсь 'blend', разбирать — разобрать — разберу 'analyse' (try this with other prefixes, e.g., предо-, изо-). And, coming back to отойти, we expect the mobile vowel in отошла, but not in отошёл (in front of a single consonant) — in other words, analogy extends the mobile vowel to the whole of the past tense. As usual, there's much more to this: what of разодеться, and разостлать — расстилать/расстелить. What do these verbs say to us? Well, the first looks surprising, but it's a colloquial form, meaning 'to get dressed up (in all one's finery)'; the unexpected o serves perhaps to differentiate the verb from раздеться 'to get undressed, take off one's coat'. In расстилать/расстелить, perf. разостлать 'to spread out, lay' we have разо- in the perfective before three consonants. Is there a difference between разостлать and, say, расстроить 'to upset', with its three consonants? Well, three differences might come to mind: first, the difference in the three-consonant groups, where the т of стр is often epenthetic, i.e. inserted, e.g. встреча 'meeting'. In the стл of разостлать the *t* is perhaps less natural, and indeed would often be dropped, as in завистливый 'envious' or, slightly similarly, известный 'well-known'. Secondly, keeping the т helps differentiate the verb from разослáть, imperf. рассылáть 'to distribute'. And thirdly, note that vowels arise between the т and the л in the imperfectives; in other words, there is a mobile vowel here, so there is a slighter unity between the three consonants and perhaps an underlying tendency to insert an analogical mobile vowel.

4.2.4.2 The tense *jers* in adjectives

Russian has short and long adjectives, the former predicative-only and becoming more and more restricted. Thus, respectively интерéсен — интерéсный 'interesting'. The short adjective declined just like many nouns and, just like many masculine nouns, originally ended in -ъ or -ь in the singular. The long adjective, if we decline it, seems to have something reminiscent of тот and the third-person pronoun (*jь, *ja, *je, in a friendly Cyrillic version и, я, е) tacked on to it: интерéсн<u>ого</u> 'interesting', здéшн<u>его</u> 'local', и́скренн<u>ему</u> 'sincere'. And that, in fact, is exactly what is found, since the long adjective is made up of the short, nominal (= noun-like) or indefinite (because it tended to have a sense '*an* interesting one') adjective, to which, to start with, the third person pronoun was added as a way of defining or restricting it, say, '*the* interesting one'. Now, the nominative case of this pronoun does not survive in Russian — он 'he', etc. has another origin — it just slotted in to provide a nominative, probably for reasons to do with avoiding confusion and the general phenomenon of replacement, e.g. the emergence in most of Romance of the reflexes of *ille* 'that' as definite article and third-person pronoun. The original nominative singulars were (simplifying the spelling) и, я, е, thus, for дóбрый 'good, kind', добръ<u>и,</u> добра<u>я</u>, добро<u>е</u>, and the genitives, for example, would have been добра<u>его</u>, добрые<u>ѣ</u>, добра<u>его</u> — you can see that contractions and simplifications have taken place over time, but in some forms the situation remains relatively transparent.[10] In case this seems far-fetched, the non-Slavonic but quite closely related Lithuanian has precisely this, with much fewer contractions: thus the word for 'he' *jìs* can be tacked on to *naũjas* 'new', giving us the long adjective *naujàsis*. And this little word is, believe it or not, cognate with Latin *is, ea, id* 'he, she, it' — everyone is familiar with 'i.e.' 'that is', expanded *id est*.

So, to cut a long story short, the ending of the long adjective in the masculine singular nominative would have been -ъjь (for soft adjectives -ьjь), where we can see the hard and soft signs in front of a *j*-sound. What we get in modern Russian is, of course, -ый, -ий — these are Church Slavonic spellings.

---

[10]The **-go* component in pronouns is mysterious, and may be a particle not unrelated to же. The pronunciation of the г as [v] in Russian is almost exclusive to that Slavonic language. The explanation is probably a combination of things: analogy with possessive adjectives in -ов, Church Slavonic influence, and Balto-Finnic contact.

As soon as the stress is final, we have (only the hard adjectives) -óй, e.g. сухóй 'dry', большóй 'big', худóй 'thin'. See 2.5.3.

4.2.5   Calques, or 'loan translations'

As a nice example of a calque, consider the complex form непосрéдственность 'spontaneity'. Here there is the negative prefix не-, the prefix по- in its spatial sense of 'through, along, via', the root СРЕД (also СЕРЕД, since this is an instance of pleophony — note that the Church Slavonic forms have an e which never becomes ё). And the suffixes -/ств-, -ен- (possibly), -/н-, and -ост-! It can be imagined that with a root suggesting 'medium, way', a meaning 'spontaneity' can emerge from action which does go along various ways before emerging — *immediacy* (reflecting the pattern for behind the calque). The adjective непосрéдственный means 'spontaneous, direct', as expected. What of посрéдственный and посрéдственность? Well, these mean 'mediocre, mediocrity', suggesting that something not inspirational, spontaneous, cannot but be 'mediocre' — and note the component *medi-* in the English word. Calquing has been at it again. In this connection note that *medium* has a sense of 'middle', i.e. things done between the start and the end of something. Spontaneity implies you miss those out. So we can make the link to середúна 'middle' and средá 'Wednesday' (the middle day of the week; if you know German, *Mittwoch*).

Why not move on to сосредотóчиться, imperf. сосредотóчиваться на + prep. 'to concentrate on' (can you see the English components in the Russian verb?). Something else that is 'in the middle' is the *heart*. *Heart* is related to *cardiac*; the first three consonants, *c*, *r*, *d*, correspond to Russian с, р, д, because the first, a *k*-sound, was originally a palatal *k*, which would become *s* in Slavonic. And 'heart', etc. are related to средá. You might ask why there is no pleophony in сéрдце; the simple answer is that, in this particular form of the root we did not have *serd-, but *sьrd-.

Now we might start from многообрáзие 'variety, diversity; "multiformity"', which is interesting as a compound, with the Church Slavonic suffix -ие. At an early stage in the history of Russian compounds were a characteristic of the Church language. Note that о after мног- is the link vowel. Can you think of related words?[11] Well, for a start the adjective многообрáзный 'varied'. To this we may add разнообрáзный, разнообрáзие 'varied, variety'. But what of однообрáзный, однообрáзие and единообрáзный, единообрáзие?[12] Well,

---

[11]If you go outside Russian, to English, then the *m* and *n* of this word might make us think of *many*, or German *manch-*. And why not, so long as there could have been a vowel in between them. After all, many surviving consonant groups in Slavonic are secondary. And indeed, in OCS we have мъног-.

[12]These are fine examples of the fact that the -о- in certain compounds is not part of the first component — the и of the first component is not removed.

the former pair, Native Russian, mean 'monotonous, monotony' (presumably *undesirable* uniformity), and the latter pair mean 'uniform, uniformity' (presumably *desirable*). We can easily imagine the latter, Church Slavonic, pair fitting well in with the Soviet period — but this would be to oversimplify: by then many features of Church Slavonic as established in Russian between the tenth and the fifteenth centuries were an integral part of Russian.

As a final example, let's look at воображéние 'imagination' and воображáть/вообразить 'to imagine', from в 'in' plus óбраз 'image; form; shape; way (каким óбразом? "how? in what way?"); icon'. The verb is a calque, with the reflexive pronoun, from German *sich einbilden* 'to imagine': *ein-* = во plus *Bild* = óбраз. Another verb with this meaning is предстáвить себé, imperf. представлять себé 'to imagine', arguably more generally used, e.g. Предстáвьте (себé)! 'Just imagine!', itself a calque from German *sich vorstellen*, e.g. *ich stelle mir vor* 'I imagine': *before*/пред/*vor* + *put*/став/*stell* and a dative reflexive. The Russian prefix пред- is Church Slavonic, to be compared with Native Russian pleophonic пéред 'in front of; (immediately) before', which now functions exclusively as a preposition.

4.2.6 Compounds

A nice and straightforward example of a compound is летоисчислéние 'chronology'. We can identify лет- as one component; the -о-, which we might wish to link to the 'word' лето 'summer; year', is probably actually a link-vowel here, as in парохóд 'steamer, ship' (пар 'steam' + -о- + ход 'motion'). Earlier links are either zero, as in хлеб-соль 'hospitality', or и, as in Владимир. And note that in other early compounds the hard-soft opposition in consonants may be irrelevant: конокрáд 'rustler, horsethief' — but конь 'horse' — thus кон-+-о-+-крад-, the final component from крáсть, крадý, крадёшь, ... крадýт 'steal' (in Russian morphology you will note that the hard-soft opposition is often overruled where *e* and *i*, are concerned, favouring acceptance of ы as a sixth phoneme). What of -ис-? This is the spelling of the prefix из- 'out of, from' (in Russian usually quite high-style, as against more 'Native' вы-): in English we might expect *out*- or, more learnèd, *e(x)*- here. Next comes ЧИСЛ, the root, related to числó 'number, date' — at an early stage the root would have been **čit* followed by a suffix **-sl(o)*, the consonant group then simplifying. That earlier group helps understand why считáть, perf. сосчитáть and счесть (сочтý, сочтёшь, ... сочтýт) mean 'to count' as well as 'to consider', and also links 'counting' and 'reading', i.e. 'telling' (a 'tally') and 'recounting'. We expect the basic verb for 'read' to be честь, something found in Czech, namely *číst*: non-past *čtu, čteš,* ..., *čtou*, past *četl, četla*. Note how the т of the root disappears before -сло. This happens in Czech too, namely *číslo* 'number'; but not in the past tense before *l*, namely *četl* — compare Russian -чёл, e.g. óн прочёл 'he has read...'. This is because there are in fact two separate phenomena here, the sequences **tl, *dl* being simplified to **l* in all the Slavonic languages but the

West ones (subject to a very few exceptions). So we have the verb исчислить 'to enumerate, calculate, compute', the e- of 'enumerate' relating to Latin *e(x)* 'out of', compare из, therefore a calque: *e- + numer-*! The suffix/ending -éние gives us a verbal noun (remember the tense *jer*). Note that this noun is probably relatively recent, since the -сл-group in such derivations can become -шл- (by jotation) in more ancient words, e.g. мы́слить'to think' — мышле́ние 'thinking'. And here it doesn't.[13]

4.2.7 A nod to word-formation in the grammar

4.2.7.1 Alternations in plurals

Note the к - ч alternation in клок - кло́чья 'rag' and су́к — су́чья 'bough' (useful here as a way of differentiating this word from су́ка — су́ки 'bitch', but mind the possessive adjective су́чий, as in су́чья жизнь 'nasty rotten life'). The plural ending was originally a collective. When unstressed, the genitive is -ьев. When stressed, it is -éй, except in кум - кумовья́ - кумовьёв 'godfather'. Thus: бра́тьев 'brothers' (бра́т, бра́тья), пру́тьев (пру́т, пру́тья) 'twigs' — друзе́й (дру́г, друзья́) 'friends', сынове́й (сы́н, сыновья́) 'sons'. But is -éй an ending in these words? Remember, given -ья, which might be rewritten as -ьйа, the genitive plural arguably has a zero ending, namely -ьй, where the soft sign will become a full vowel, thus -ей. This may be seen as another instance of mobile vowels, given the original ending *-ьjь (and note that the first *jer* precedes a jot, which suggests a 'tense *jer*'; so here we have a Native Russian reflex, while the ending -ий, with the same origin, would be Church Slavonic.

4.2.7.2 Collectives and singulatives

Note that клубни́ка '(cultivated) strawberries' may be a collective, like земляни́ка 'wild strawberries', мали́на 'raspberries', горо́х 'peas', карто́фель (masc.) 'potatoes' (more often, and colloquial, карто́шка). The collective may also convey a single item in certain cases (though it *is* odd, or at least less frequent, to refer to *one* small fruit/vegetable). Another example is лук 'onion(s)', which is probably from Germanic, i.e. *der Lauch* 'allium; leek'. Лу́ковица is a way of indicating a single onion. In the case of горо́х and карто́фель this is achieved by a singulative suffix -ина, thus горо́шина, карто́фелина (note the alternation x-ш and that the stress does not move). There is nothing special about singulatives — Celtic languages abound in them, e.g. Breton *gwez* 'trees' — *gwezenn* 'tree'. This makes good sense: for concepts which 'tend' to be non-singular (how often do you talk about a *pea*?) the plural, or a collective, presents the basic form, and the singular is formed from it.

---

[13] There's no 'jotation' in the derived imperfective, namely исчисля́ть, either.

Just for interest, consider óвощ 'vegetable', more often used in its plural form, óвощи 'vegetables'. Originally it may refer to 'growing' and be consequently related to German *wachsen*, English *to wax* ('and to wane'), Lithuanian *áugti* 'to increase' (we may even go as far as Latin *auxilium* 'help'). In other Slavonic languages the meaning may be 'fruit', and Ukrainian óвоч indicates that the Russian word is Church Slavonic.

4.2.7.3   Coming and going and the origins of x

Taking вершúна 'summit', we have the suffix -ин(а) again, with the ш *probably* emerging from x under the influence of the following *i* — the First Palatalization.[14] The x of верх 'top, peak' actually goes back to *s, with a midway stage reflected in Lithuanian *vir̃š* 'above' and the original reflected in Sanskrit *várṣma* 'top part, surface' and in Latin *verruca*, the second *r* originally *s*, giving French *une verrue* 'wart' (i.e. something raised, 'eminent'). This development is an instance of the *ruki*-rule, whereby *s became *x (there are certain qualifications to this, which can be disregarded here) after *r, *u, *k, *i and provided a consonant did not follow the *s. Examples for the last three are: ýхо 'ear' — Lithuanian *ausìs* 'ear' (Latin *auris* reflects the *s becoming *r* between vowels, so *aural* is linked to Russian ýхо); лохмóтья 'rags', arguably from a Common Slavonic form *$lāks$- and if so linkable with English *lacerate*, ultimately from Latin *lacer* 'torn, mangled' and, among others, with Greek *lakís* 'scrap'; тúхий 'calm, quiet' — Lithuanian *teisùs* 'fair', *tiesà* 'truth'. This development is particularly interesting as there is evidence suggesting it even began before the change of Proto-Indo-European palatal *k and *g to *s and *z (important in the conventional picture of the west-east dialectal division of Proto-Indo-European) respectively, so писáть 'to write, paint', related to the ancestor of English *picture*, must have developed the *s from the palatal velar (which is what it was) *after* the *ruki*-rule had ceased to be productive — otherwise we wouldn't have *s*. See 4.3.59.

One place where x is particularly in evidence in Russian is the prepositional plural. The ending here is -ах (-ях), which, with the x coming after *a*, suggests something amiss; however, the modern prepositional plural acquired the *x* by analogy from other declension types, thus *-ьхъ, *-ěхъ, *-ъхъ, the vowels before *x reflecting original *i, *oj, and *u respectively), where the *x* arose according to the rules. Pronouns often behave oddly, in most languages, and the original *s is preserved nicely in the prepositionals нас 'us', вас 'you'.

Recall, by the way, that one of the most important verbs in Russian, идтú 'to go', has a weird past tense шёл,... The older form, шь(д)лъ (reflected in, for example, Polish *szedł*), suggests a First Palatalization, but for this to happen we

---

[14]*Probably* because some people might argue, if the next few lines of the text are read, that an intermediate stage *$š$ between *s and *x was retained and overlapped with the period of jotation and the First Palatalization.

would need *x, from which the *š would come (let's assume that's the scenario). There would have to have been something in front of the original *s to cause the change to *x. Well, this is a verb very often accompanied by a prefix, and one such as *per- 'across' would have fitted the bill (or the antecedents, say, of the prefixes *pri- or *u-). Then we recall ходи́ть 'to go', with initial x! Things begin to make sense. At this point we must ask ourselves about going, walking travelling. After the movement, the rest, perhaps 'sitting', and we realize that the verb 'to go/walk' in Russian is very likely to be related to сиде́ть 'to be "sat down"'. This seems bizarre, but in fact it is not unlikely. In Greek, after all, we have *hodos* 'road, way', with the initial aspiration coming from *s. Perhaps the *x, which arose quite regularly in Slavonic, was then generalized as a way of differentiating 'walking' from 'sitting'. Before you ask, идти́, like English *go — went*, is a suppletive verb, with the non-past иду́, etc. from a different root.[15] The Proto-Indo-Europeans didn't *necessarily* confuse 'walking' and 'sitting'.

4.2.7.4 Position: *be — move — put*

	hang	stand	sit	lie
be	висе́ть	стоя́ть	сиде́ть	лежа́ть
move	пове́ситься	станови́ться/стать	сади́ться/сесть	ложи́ться/лечь
put	ве́шать/пове́сить	(по)ста́вить	сажа́ть/посади́ть	класть/положи́ть

Note how the 'be' verbs are all second conjugation (and have fixed ending-stress in the non-past (and don't lend themselves semantically to having perfectives)) and that three of the 'move' verbs are semi-suppletive (i.e. the pairs aren't morphologically as apparently linked as many pairs), with the perfectives exhibiting nasal affixes (lost in сесть and лечь since they were pre-consonantal, becoming nasal vowels which then denasalized). Three of the 'put' verbs too provide morphologically odd pairs. Note in addition that посади́ть and положи́ть have mobile stress in the non-past. Сади́ться and ложи́ться have it fixed on the ending, while in станови́ться it is mobile. The 'move' perfectives all have the stress fixed on the stem.

Staying with positions, обстоя́тельства 'circumstances' is interesting, in that it is a calque ultimately from Latin *circumstantia*, probably through French *circonstance* or German *der Umstand*, i.e. we can see in Russian a prefix meaning 'around' and a root meaning 'stand', СТОЙ, with suffixes -тел- and -/ств-. And висо́к 'temple (of the head)' has a mobile vowel, thus indicating a root ВИС and suffix -/к-, the slash concealing a hard sign, which becomes о when there's no ending. The root may well be related to висе́ть 'to hang, be in a hanging position', thus perhaps referring to hair hanging from the temples.

---

[15] Though we can never be sure — much of what we propose is to a greater or lesser extent speculation, but speculation which reflects linguistic intuitions.

These verbs are extremely useful in Russian. Consider the following examples:

взве́сить, imperf. взве́шивать 'to weigh up, consider, ponder' (note the 'up' prefix and recall French *peser* 'to weigh' and *penser* 'to think', the latter learnèd, but both coming from a Latin root meaning 'hang' and 'weigh')

заста́вить, imperf. заставля́ть + acc. 'to make (someone do something); to stuff'
оста́вить, imperf. оставля́ть 'to abandon'

осади́ть, imperf. осажда́ть 'to beseige' (note the Church Slavonic form of the imperfective)

отложи́ть, imperf. откла́дывать 'to put off, postpone'
приложи́ть, imperf. прикла́дывать 'to hold to/against; add; apply (force)'
положи́ть, imperf. полага́ть 'to suppose' (note предположи́ть, imperf. предполага́ть 'to (pre)suppose') (mobile stress in these and related verbs)
сложи́ть, imperf. скла́дывать 'to set/put down/together; add'[16]

уста́ть, imperf. устава́ть 'to get tired'
отста́ть, imperf. отстава́ть 'to lag behind, fall behind; be slow (of a watch)' (constructed with от + gen.)
приста́ть, imperf. пристава́ть к + dat. 'to stick to; join; pester'[17]

присе́сть, imperf. приса́живаться 'to take a seat'
присе́сть, imperf. преседа́ть 'to curtsey'
усе́сться, imperf. уса́живаться 'to settle down'[18]

приле́чь (perf.) 'to lie down for a while'
приле́чь, imperf. прилега́ть 'to adjoin' (constructed with к + dat.)

зави́сеть от + gen. (imperf.) 'to depend on'

---

[16] The adjective сло́жный 'complex ("folded together")' reflects the complexity of something 'put together': сложи́ть, imperf. скла́дывать. That verb means 'to add', amongst other things. Addition is сложе́ние; its antonym is вычита́ние 'subtraction'. Note the link to число́ 'number' and the root for 'count' and 'read': вы́честь/вычита́ть 'to subtract', mentioned earlier. And also note that of the two deverbal nouns, one is formed from a perfective and the other from an imperfective.

[17] Note the adjective приста́льный 'intent, fixed (of a look)', as in приста́льно смотре́ть 'to stare', which is derived with the suffix -/н- from приста́лый, the long form of the *l*-participle (later past tense) of приста́ть 'to adhere; join; pester'. The sense is one of having come to stand close up to someone or something.

[18] It's quite interesting to check the 'sit down, seat/plant' set in a dictionary. Do you find many forms with prefixed сади́ться?

отстоя́ть, imperf. отста́ивать 'to defend, withstand, stand up for'
настоя́ть, imperf. наста́ивать на + prep. 'to insist on'
состоя́ть (imperf.) 'to consist in (в + prep.), to consists of (из + gen.)'
состоя́ться (perf.) 'to take place'

принадлежа́ть 'to belong' ('to' = dat., unless an association, when it is к + dat.)
подлежа́ть + dat. 'to be liable/subject to'

We might briefly mention the basic verb meaning 'to put', which tends to have been somewhat marginalized in that sense in the language. This is деть, with the root ДѢ and non-past де́ну, де́нешь, ... де́нут, a perfective with imperfective дева́ть, non-past дева́ю, etc. Best known in the 'dressing' family, e.g. оде́ться 'to get dressed', разде́ться 'to get undressed; take one's coat off', and переоде́ться 'to change one's clothes', it is often used on its own in the sense 'do with', e.g. Куда́ она́ де́ла мои́ кни́жки? 'Where's she put my books?' It may also be used reflexively, as in: Куда́ он де́лся? 'Where's he gone?' Заде́ть, imperf. задева́ть means' to brush against; offend', perfective (!) задева́ть means 'to mislay', perfective задева́ться means 'to disappear', and imperf. издева́ться над + instr. means 'to mock'.

4.2.7.5 Some notes on adjectives

We might draw attention, should it be necessary, to the very comforting fact that the stress is always fixed in long adjectives — it's one of those obvious things that one doesn't notice, and drawing attention to it allows us to realize we should be thankful for small mercies. Of course, the short adjective is quite another matter! Note too that soft adjectives are never end-stressed, and that ending-stressed adjectives whose stem ends in к, г, х, ш, ж will have -о́- — in other words, they are not soft adjectives. Note further the short comparatives of густо́й 'thick' and чи́стый 'clean; pure', namely гу́ще and чи́ще: the development of ст to щ in an original group *stj (the comparative can be formed by a j suffix) is regular.

Note the soft adjective за́дний 'behind, rear', with root ЗАД. Most adjectives in -ний which have a spatial or temporal sense are soft, and soft adjectives are, with the exception of ка́рий 'brown (of eyes)' (which we may come across hard), all in -ний (don't confuse these with the 'possessive' adjectives like медве́жий 'bear's', and тре́тий 'third'). Note еженеде́льный 'weekly', which is hard but temporal; and note си́ний '(dark-)blue', which is soft, but apparently atemporal. Examples: ве́рхний 'upper', зде́шний 'local', та́мошний 'relating to "there"', сего́дняшний 'today's', за́втрашний 'tomorrow's', вчера́шний 'yesterday's', нового́дний 'New Year's'. It is tempting to see the adjective и́скренний 'sincere' having an origin in 'from (= из-) the blood/heart' (кровь 'blood', or се́рдце 'heart' (related to *cardiac*, thus k+r), and so conceivably spatial — more likely there is a link with ко́рень 'root' or край 'edge, country', both of which would admit the spatial interpretation too. Note that its usual adverb is и́скренно (hard!), though и́скренне would probably be the form found in the closing section of some letters.

Now note нестерпи́мый 'unbearable'. Link it first of all with терпе́ть, терплю́, те́рпишь, ... те́рпят 'to bear, endure' (it has a perfective стерпе́ть). It is the form of the present participle passive, with a meaning 'who/which is X-ed'; but this participle is relatively little used in everyday language and on the whole provides straight adjectives. Sometimes the participial origin can be discerned, e.g. люби́ть, люблю́, лю́бишь, ... лю́бят 'love', giving люби́мый 'who/which is loved/liked', 'lovable', whence 'favourite'. Just to help understand, if we used it participially we would have expressions such as люби́мый мной го́род 'a town loved *by* me'. You can see how it develops to 'my favourite town', which you would be more likely to render as мой люби́мый го́род. A very common use of such participles is, particularly negated, to form the Russian equivalents of English adjectives meaning 'X-able', e.g. 'inadmissible, unshakable, indomitable, incomparable, unrepeatable, indispensable', respectively недопусти́мый, непоколеби́мый, неодоли́мый, несравни́мый, неповтори́мый, and необходи́мый.[19] Very often, but not always (thus необходи́мый) these are formed from perfectives, itself unexpected for a 'present' participle. Compare the adjectives производя́щий 'producing' and ужаса́ющий 'terrifying' (among many others), from the present participle active, with the basic meaning 'who X-s (someone/something)'. Several such participles have become normal adjectives, e.g. блестя́щий 'brilliant', выдаю́щийся 'outstanding', бу́дущий 'future' (in the neuter it provides the noun бу́дущее '(the) future')).

Two other originally present active participles are предстоя́щий 'coming' and настоя́щий 'present; real, authentic'. Both are odd in that they are formed from verbs which 'ought' to be perfective: simple verbs with a preverb — but, if this is seen as a pre*fix*, of essentially semantic rather than grammatical import, then we have a way to justify it. And we can see, through examples like зави́сеть от + gen. 'to depend on' and вы́глядеть + instr. 'to look (sad, etc.)' that, while this seems non-native, it is not exclusively Church Slavonic — essentially these are just developments using the resources of the language and which fit in doubtless with the early development of aspect. Note the component щ, which is Church Slavonic, and the prefix пред-, also Church Slavonic and, in Native Russian, пе́ред (but not as a prefix — unless we see the adjective пере́дний as composed of a prefix, suffix, and ending!).[20]

And for past passive participles we might start with поме́шанный 'insane, crazy' and бе́шеный 'rabid, mad', the first from a perfective and having the two н's

---

[19]Note неопису́емый 'indescribable', formed from an obsolete verb describ描 описовать, as against regular опи́сывать.

[20]Though the distinction between a preverb and a prefix is a useful one, in this presentation, for simplicity's sake, the term 'preverb' will be used only when a real need is felt to distinguish between it and a 'prefix'.

of the standard language, the second from an imperfective verb. Thus, помёшанный possibly has a sense of 'disturbed', though we would not normally form a passive participle from the intransitive verb по-мешáть + dat. 'to disturb, hinder'; more likely is it to be from the transitive verb по-мешáть (identical!) 'to mix' (derived from месить 'to knead'[21]), thus someone whose mind has become 'mixed up'. Бёшеный is originally a past passive participle from the verb бѣсити (now вз-бесить 'to enrage, madden'), derived from бес (бѣсъ). If we accept that the *jat'* ѣ in this word has its source in a *j*-diphthong, then there may be a link to боя́ться 'to be afraid' and, going outside Slavonic, to Lithuanian *baisùs* 'awful, repulsive' and *bajùs* 'frightful', and to Latin *foedus* 'vile'. Thus, a group *ds* would have simplified to *s*.

This brings us to... adjectives and food. In солёный 'salty' it is most interesting to note the short form сóлон! The root word, for 'salt', is common to many familiar languages, and, perhaps confusingly, related to слáдкий 'sweet' (note pleophonic сóлод 'malt', солóдка 'liquorice'[22]) — it is interesting that 'sweet' is Church Slavonic. Through слáдкий, in fact, we can see some justification for сóлон, i.e. -оло- and -ла-. Given that солёный is a culinary term and that this sort of structure is found in few such terms, we might straightforwardly relate it to the verb по-солить (fixed stress) 'to salt (something)', as a past passive participle with a single н and formation from an imperfective, cf. копчёный 'smoked', from за-коптить 'to smoke, cure in smoke', related кóпоть 'soot (fem.)', revealing a hard sign between the *p* and the *t*. Is it possible that the long form and the short had slightly different origins, сóлон arguably reflecting a stem *soln-? After all, in Serbo-Croat there is *slan* 'salty', with the metathesis which we would expect to find in a South Slavonic language; this is confirmed by Polish *słony*, with its expected metathesis, and by Ukrainian with its long form солóний. Further investigation into Russian reveals сóлóный, e.g. Dal' IV 1909: 382., so it looks like there indeed are two different forms.

4.2.7.6 Stress and alternations in verbs

In the non-past there is only one type of movement, namely from the ending in the first person singular to the stem in all the other forms (the first person will be stressed if the infinitive is stressed immediately before the -ть ending[23]). Thus:

---

[21]Месить is ancient and can be seen in a form which might, though it is problematic, suit Common Slavonic in Lithuanian *maišýti* 'to mix'. Note too Latin *misceo* 'I mix' (and the English verb too), and German *mischen*. Modern Russian мешáть 'to mix' has arisen from it, perhaps at first as a frequentative. Мешáть 'to hinder' is related, and arises from a root МѢХ, which we still see in помéха 'obstacle'.

[22]I'm told that one finds 'salt liquorice' in Scandinavia.

[23]There are only two exceptions to this, and in one of them all but the third-person forms are questionable. The two verbs may well be related. They are: по-колебáться,

служи́ть, служу́, слу́жишь, ...слу́жат 'serve', трепета́ть, трепещу́, трепе́щешь, ... трепе́щут 'tremble'. First, this is particularly productive in second-conjugation verbs — there may be hesitation, e.g. in грузи́ть 'to load', where the stress may remain on the ending: грузи́шь. Recall that it does not happen in verbs of physical position: сиде́ть, сижу́, сиди́шь, ... сидя́т 'sit, be sitting/seated' — лежа́ть, лежу́, лежи́шь, ... лежа́т 'lie, be lying' — стоя́ть, стою́, стои́шь, ... стоя́т 'stand, be standing/stood' — висе́ть, вишу́, виси́шь, ... вися́т 'hang, be hanging', or in many verbs in -жа́ть / -ча́ть / -ша́ть / -ща́ть / -оя́ть (verbs which particularly denote sounds, or absence of sound, as in молча́ть 'to be silent' — but держа́ть, держу́, де́ржишь, ... де́ржат 'hold'), or, very often, in verbs derived from nominals (though the derivation can be problematic): погоди́ть, погожу́, погоди́шь, ... погодя́т 'wait (a little)' (note год 'year') — говори́ть, говорю́, говори́шь, ... говоря́т 'speak' (го́вор 'dialect') — звони́ть, звоню́, звони́шь, ... звоня́т 'ring' (зво́н 'sound of bells; ring') — объясни́ть, объясню́, объясни́шь, ... объясня́т 'explain' (я́сный 'clear'). Remember too that the stress will never be on the ending if the stress is not on the vowel before the -ть of the infinitive, thus ви́деть, ви́жу, ви́дишь, ... ви́дят 'see' — слы́шать, слы́шу, слы́шишь, ... слы́шат 'hear'. Secondly, all first-conjugation verbs which have different consonants in the non-past and the infinitive, but which have the stress on the vowel immediately before the -ть of the infinitive, will have mobile stress too, as in трепета́ть 'to tremble' above. Thus: писа́ть, пишу́, пи́шешь, ... пи́шут 'write'— дрема́ть, дремлю́, дре́млешь, ... дре́млют 'doze'. Otherwise, the stress is fixed, e.g. бры́згать, бры́зжу, бры́зжешь, ... бры́зжут 'to splash (someone with something, e.g. она́ бры́зжет водо́й на бра́та)'.

4.3 Examples

4.3.1 *Ache, be ill* — БОЛ (**bol*-)

Here we start with the zero-suffix and zero-ending feminine noun боль 'pain' and derived nominal forms like больно́й 'sick, ill; painful', боле́знь 'illness (fem.)', and from this noun боле́зненный 'sickly; morbid', from which we then go on to боле́зненность 'sickliness; morbidity (fem.)'. The etymology is not clear, but there is English *baleful* and we have Old High German *balo* 'evil; ruin' as possible cognates. We have the same root for большо́й 'big', namely БОЛ, as shown in Latin *dēbilis* 'weak', Sanskrit *bálam* 'strength', but there may not be a link. Particularly interesting is the verb, or verbs, боле́ть, with its/their participation in both conjugations. As a first-conjugation verb, non-past боле́ю, боле́ешь, ... боле́ют, it has the sense of 'be ill' and as such fits ill with the

---

коле́блюсь, коле́блешься,... коле́блются 'sway; hesitate', and, here the first and second persons are not really used, колыха́ться, колы́шусь, колы́шется,... колы́шутся (semelfactive, 'once', perfective колыхну́ться) 'to sway'.

argument for this being a component of such verbs as сидéть, спáть (i.e. 'be seated, be asleep'); it fits better with verbs derived from adjectives, e.g. белéть, non-past белéю, etc. 'be white'. Perfectives, though you would not wish to pair them with болéть, can be readily formed, e.g. заболéть 'to fall ill'; an imperfective with a habitual nuance can be formed from this, namely заболевáть, non-past заболевáю, etc. As a second-conjugation verb it has only third-person forms in the non-past, namely болит and болят, and here there may be the sense of 'to cause/make pain', as shown by белить, non-past белю, бéлишь, ... бéлят (the mobile-stress pattern seems to be more frequent in this verb), perf. побелить 'to make white': у меня болят нóги 'my feet hurt'. So we may have a slightly different semantic scene here — perhaps a reorganizing of the meanings and structures.

4.3.2   *Argue* — (СЪ)ПОР (*(sъ)por-*)

Оспóрить, non-past оспóрю, оспóришь, ... оспóрят, imperf. оспáривать, non-past оспáриваю, оспáриваешь, ... оспáривают 'to dispute (tr.)' is derived from спóрить, non-past спóрю, etc. 'to argue (intr.)' (perf. поспóрить, often with the nuance 'to have *an* argument'), where the root ПОР is itself related to пер- as in перéть, non-past пру, прёшь, ... прут, past пёр, пёрла, etc. 'move, make one's way; drag; appear; steal (perf. с-)'. Thus also сопéрник 'rival'. The prefix съ- is reflected as Native Russian с- and, usually, Church Slavonic со-. Perhaps English *to spurn* is related, like Latin *spernō* 'I push away', i.e. the idea of making one's way through things, and from there to rivals and arguments.

Соревновáться is similar, with the root Р/В, usually encountered as the noun рьвьнь or adjective рьвьнъ (in the modern language ревнивый 'jealous'), reflected in Latin *rivinus* 'rival' (and note the *riv-* of *rival*!). There's probably no link to ревéнь 'rhubarb' (masc., gen. ревéня), which seems to go back to Persian via Turkic; but one can imagine the acidity of rhubarb fitting in nicely.

4.3.3   *Ask* — ПРОС (*pros-*)

The basic place to start is просить, non-past прошу, прóсишь, ... прóсят 'ask, request', perfective попросить, reflected in many Indo-European languages, e.g. Latin *posco* 'I request' (from *porcsco*) and German *fragen* 'to ask'. A perfective спросить derived its own imperfective спрáшивать — note the suffixation and vowel lengthening (*and* the jotation), with the nuance 'ask, enquire'. We will these days often hear спросить вопрóс 'to ask a question', but strictly speaking we use задáть вопрóс, imperf. задавáть вопрóс (see 4.3.24). The root can, needless to say, be seen in вопрóс, a zero-suffix noun related to a now obsolete verb вопросить, imperf. вопрошáть, derived via jotation and concomitant stress movement. And there is the adjective вопросительный 'interrogative'.

4.3.4 *Awaken*, or *being awake* and *observing* — БЪД — БУД— БЛЮД (*bъd-, *bud-, *bl'ud-)

We are likely to come first to this word family through something like будильник 'alarm clock'. Setting aside the familiar suffixes, we come to будить, non-past бужу́, бу́дишь, ... бу́дят 'to wake (someone)', with its perfectives разбуди́ть 'to awake' and пробуди́ть 'to arouse, stir up'. Related is возбуди́ть, non-past возбужу́, возбуди́шь, ... возбудя́т (note the stress), imperfective возбужда́ть, non-past возбужда́ю, etc. 'to excite; stir up (against)'. But there is also an adjective бди́тельный 'vigilant', which ultimately leads to obsolescent бдеть, non-past бдишь (no 1 sg.) 'keep watch'. By comparing бд and буд it becomes clear that there must be a root БЪД alongside БУД, but there seems to be no evidence of БЫД. БУД can be corroborated from Lithuanian *baūsti* 'to spur on, encourage'. Now, if we have ablaut in the *w*-diphthong, there should be a possibility of *ew*, which on monophthongization (or however the processes involved actually occurred) could give *ju*, causing jotation. And this is what is evident in наблюда́ть 'to observe, watch over' and соблюда́ть 'to observe (a rule)'. These are derived imperfectives related to an obsolescent simple form блюсти́, non-past блюду́, блюдёшь, ... блюду́т, past блюл- 'watch over; abide by'. Not to be confused with perfective заблуди́ться 'to lose one's way' (mobile stress), with its hard *l* (and original nasal vowel in the root) and its imperfective (though they are hardly pairable) заблужда́ться 'to err, be led astray'.

Coming back to буди́ть, what of бу́дни 'weekdays; workdays; boring existence'. Workdays are presumably days when you are awake, vigilant! The singular is бу́день, and there is are adjectives бу́дний, бу́дничный, and бу́днишний, the first used with де́нь in the meaning 'weekday' and the last two meaning 'weekday' and 'dull'. So we have БУД with the sufix -ьн- and a soft ending reflecting the temporal sense and -шн- component (but not the -чн- component). We can't however, go so far as to include the root of the future tense of бы́ть 'to be' here; this has another root — see 4.3.5.

4.3.5 *Be* — БЫ, БУД — ЕС (*by-, *bǫd- — *es-/*sǫ-)

Need one say that his verb is extremely widely represented in the Indo-European languages and presents a suppletive character, i.e. it has bits of different origins? Note the nasal suffix (or infix) in the future, бу́ду, etc., something noted also in ля́гу 'I shall lie down', ся́ду 'I shall sit down'. The long *u* of БЫ is there, of course, in бы́ть, бы́л, бы́вший, and reflected in Lithuanian *bū́ti* 'to be' and Sanskrit *bhūtíṣ* 'being, good condition'. It is there too in Latin *fūturus* 'future; which will be' and *fui* 'I have been', and in Greek *fuomai* 'I become, grow'. A causative is attested in Sanskrit: *bhávati* 'is, happens, becomes'. Something close to this appears in Slavonic too: Polish *bawić się* 'to play', Russian уба́вить 'to decrease', разба́вить 'to dilute', заба́вить 'to amuse', доба́вить and приба́вить 'to add', thus respectively and very approximately 'being away, being spread, being covered, being supplemented, brought to', all non-past -ба́влю, ба́вишь, ... ба́вят, imperfective through jotation to -бавля́ть, non-past -бавля́ю, etc.

Есть is what essentially remains of the present tense of быть, and is precisely what we find in numerous other Indo-European languages: *est, is, ist*, and so on. Residually we also have the third-person plural, суть (also functioning as a noun, 'essence', itself from the verb 'to be' via Latin); the у is historically a back nasal, retained in Polish *są*, and there too in French *sont*, among many others. Though есть can still be used as a copula, i.e. 'is, are', even 'am' for identification purposes, it is perhaps more usefully characterized for Russian with the meaning 'there is, there are', as in the 'to have' construction, where it is, on the whole, expressed unless something other than possession is being emphasized, e.g. the character of what you have rather than that you have it. Also, as a copula its negative form is не, i.e. the verb 'to be' is not expressed, whereas in the sense 'there is, there are' its negative form is нет, constructed with the genitive case. The situation is different for finite forms other than the present.

4.3.6 *Begin, end* — ЧЬН — КОН (*čьn-, *kon-)

One of the first Russian nouns we come across is коне́ц 'end'; the word for beginning, нача́ло, tends to come later, and it is surprising how much trouble some learners have with it. Perhaps because they mistake it for a past-tense form — and why not? As a neuter noun, the beginning is what has begun, though the verb would be началось (if non-reflexive, на́чало). The basic verbs are нача́ть, non-past начну́, начнёшь, ... начну́т, imperf. начина́ть, non-past начина́ю, etc. 'begin' and ко́нчить, non-past ко́нчу, ко́нчишь, ... ко́нчат, imperf. конча́ть, non-past конча́ю, etc. 'end', both transitive and rendered intransitive by reflexivization. The transitives take direct objects and imperfective infinitives — we might, given that the perfective aspect is often associated with beginnings and endings, expect the perfective infinitive, but, given the presence of the actual lexical verbs for 'beginning' and 'ending', it seems quite natural to go for the less constrained aspect, the imperfective. But there may be more to it. Take, for instance, English, where we might say 'I finished *reading*'— the use of the -*ing* form somehow underscores this and brings in the realization that what we are beginning or ending is a process, and for that the imperfective is appropriate. This goes too for the use of the imperfective infinitive also after verbs of continuing and getting into and out of habits. Now, in нача́ть we note the presence of a prefix and of a nasal consonant appearing in the non-past. This happens too in the derived imperfective, with -а́- and what may be lengthening of a front *jer* between ч and н. So the root looks like being ЧЬН. The post-root a in нача́ть could, then, be a front nasal, arising immediately a consonant and denasalizing to [a], spelt as я except when the spelling requires a, as here. We also find the transitive and intransitive verb зача́ть, imperf. зачина́ть 'to conceive', and related forms such as зача́тие 'conception' and зача́ток 'embryo';

beginning', зачáточный 'rudimentary', confirming на- as a prefix. This, and the nasal, are also confirmed by Polish *począć*, non-past *pocznę*, ... 'begin' — and we could add historical evidence. Looking back at the root, we might expect that the *č* arises by the First Palatalization, given its location before a primary front vowel, so we might assume an earlier form **kin-*.

If we look at конéц, we might suppose that -ец reflects the suffix -ьц-, as also found in отéц 'father', пáлец 'finger'. The е drops, which reinforces this supposition. Moreover, the *c* might be assumed to arise by Third Palatalization, such that an earlier form is **-ik-*. This leaves the way open for the ancestor of кóнчить to arise by the First Palatalization, with кончáть derived from it, or arising by analogy, or arising directly from, simplifying things, **konikěti* — otherwise we would have had концать, by the Third Palatalization. Now, if конéц does include a suffix, as seems likely, there is a root КОН — and, of course, that looks rather like ЧЬН before the palatalization of **k*. So *les extrêmes se touchent*! Beginnings and endings are derived from ablaut forms of the same root. Can this be confirmed? Taking конéц, we assume a base noun кон or конь. The latter is quite tempting, as there is an adverb исконú 'from time immemorial; from the *beginning*', which suggests **iz* 'out of' plus the genitive of an *i*-stem noun (i.e. not конь 'horse', which is a *jo*-stem).[24] Whatever the case may be, and many authorities in fact go for кон, the root does here seem to be confirmed.[25] What of 'begin'? Well, there is the somewhat obsolete word чáдо 'child' and derived домочáдец 'house servant', which look like they arise from **kindo*, and that looks as if the stem could be at least cognate with German *das Kind* 'child' (not to mention the English word), and children are beginnings. At this point we also feel tempted by a link with *kin* 'sort; family, *genus*', and the semantic circle is complete — and *genus* is likely to be cognate.

Expanding slightly on кóнчить, we note relatively straightforward derivational patterns: прикóнчить, imperf. прикáнчивать, non-past прикáнчиваю, etc. 'use up; finish off' and окóнчить, imperf. окáнчивать 'to graduate'. Related forms like окончáтельный 'final', окончáние 'end' suggest a verb окончáть — which can be found elsewhere, e.g. in Ukrainian, and which is imperfective, presumably by opposition to окóнчить. Recall that кóнчить and кончáть make for a slightly odd aspectual pair — the latter may have started off as an iterative. In this connection we note the isolated perfective скончáться 'to pass away', where the absence of opposition allows specialization as perfective.

---

[24]Note also испокóн and úспоконь 'from time immemorial', and the adjective искóнный 'original, primordial'. One might also note the word кон meaning 'target' or 'kitty' in games.

[25]Bear in mind that many of the forms arose before the opposition of hard and soft consonants acquired real significance, and so we often need to refer only to the basic, hard consonant. This is something which arguably remained relevant even when the opposition had arisen: a soft *m* remained an *m*, at least in Russian.

The more we look at Russian verbs, the more we become aware of the secondary nature of aspect as often presented in textbooks.

Rather than saying more about verbs of beginning and ending, try to explore the roots for yourself and see if you can find any more roots. Can you build anything on верх 'top' — after all, things do come to a head.[26]

4.3.7 *Blow* — ВѢЙ — ДУЙ (ДѪ) (*vě(j)-, *dъm-/*dǫ-)

In развева́ться, non-past развева́ется, развева́ются (third persons only) 'flutter, blow about', we have a formation on the basis of ве́ять, non-past ве́ю, ве́ешь. There is a perfective разве́ять(ся), non-past разве́ю-, разве́ешь-, ... разве́ют- 'disperse, scatter', but this does not really go with развева́ться — think about the meaning! Things don't easily flutter perfectively. The imperfective of разве́яться is разве́иваться 'to be scattered, dispelled'. None the less, do note the formations: развева́ться with the imperfectivizing suffix -ва́-, and разве́иваться with the imperfectivizing suffix -ив(а)-, with the stress on the syllable nucleus immediately preceding the suffix. Similarly conjugated verbs include ла́ять 'to bark', та́ять 'to melt', наде́яться 'to hope', смея́ться 'to laugh' (fixed ending stress: non-past смею́сь, смеёшься, ... смею́тся), and се́ять 'to sew'. Compare second-conjugation боя́ться, non-past бою́сь, бои́шься, ... боя́тся 'fear' and стоя́ть 'stand'— the only two such verbs in the language. Note similar derivational procedures with се́ять, namely рассе́ять(ся), imperf. рассе́ивать(ся) 'to disperse, scatter', and the useful adjective (from a past passive participle) рассе́янный 'absent-minded, scatterbrained'. None of these verbs has the -ва́- suffix found in развева́ться. Thus та́ять has its normal perfective partner раста́ять, but note отта́ять 'to thaw, defrost', imperfective отта́ивать (note the suffix and stress). And derivatives with a sense of 'hope' are based on the Native Russian form of the noun наде́жда, namely надёжа, namely обнадёжить, imperf. обнадёживать 'to calm someone down by giving them hope'. Развева́ться, moreover, does *not* follow the usual conjugational pattern for -ева-/-ова-, but the pattern одева́ть(ся) (одева́ю(сь), одева́ешь(ся), ... одева́ют(ся)) 'dress; get dressed'.

Another 'blow' verb is дуть, non-past ду́ю, ду́ешь, ... ду́ют. Note its non-past, following the same pattern. Here, however, there is an interesting complication. We might imagine that 'blowing' has something to do with 'smoke', which in Russian is дым. The vowel у may reflect an earlier back nasal vowel. In Russian there is a participial form наду́тый 'inflated; haughty', which also exists in a form надме́нный 'arrogant'. In this latter form there is a suggestion of a root ДЪМ, in Common Slavonic *dъm-, with a short *u, to which дым, with the reflex of a long *ū, neatly corresponds. So надме́нный reflects what we might expect, namely the survival of the nasal consonant before a vowel. As may be supposed, дуть has gone over to another non-past pattern.

---

[26]Try соверши́ть and заверши́ть.

Russian дым, by the way, is historically identical with English *fume*. And note the verb дымить(ся), non-past дымлю-, дымишь-, ... дымят- 'smoke (intr.)', the conjugation pattern reflecting a sense of 'to make smoke'.

4.3.8 *Burn* — ЖАР — ГОР — ЖЬГ (*žar-, *gor-, *žьg- or *žeg-)

Обжа́рить, non-past обжа́рю, обжа́ришь, ... обжа́рят 'fry all over', imperf. обжа́ривать, non-past обжа́риваю, etc. is linked through the simple verb жа́рить 'to fry' to жар 'heat' with a zero-suffix and жара́ 'hot weather', in turn linked through ablaut to горе́ть, non-past горю́, гори́шь, ... горя́т 'burn (intr.)'. Жар would have started with *gēr- (the line, or *macron*, over the vowel indicates length), where the g would have become ж and the ē first ě then, given the First Palatalization and its being in the position after a hushing consonant, a. The root is related to Latin *formus* 'hot' and words such as English *thermal*, coming from Greek. Note the unusual derivational pattern of горе́ть, for example, загоре́ть 'to become tanned', imperf. загора́ть, загора́ю, etc., which suggests an ancient iterative with verbal suffix *a, as in several other 'pairs' encountered, something possibly supported here by the Old Church Slavonic present participle active ГОРѦ, ГОРѦШИ, suggesting an athematic form. Lithuanian too, as well as having the verb *garéti*, pres. *gariù*, *gãri* 'burn' (corresponding exactly to горе́ть) has the noun *gãras* 'steam' and the adjective *kárštas* 'hot'. In this connection we can mention греть, non-past гре́ю, гре́ешь, ... гре́ют 'warm (tr.)'; there must have been a vowel between the g and r, as a link imposes itself from the related stem-forms. This root is behind грех 'sin', something leading to the flames of hell.

Within the area of 'burn' we have to think of the transitive verb, namely жечь, non-past жгу, жжёшь, ... жгут, perf. сжечь. Given that сжечь derives a secondary imperfective, сжига́ть, we can propose a root ЖЬГ, with the soft *jer* as usual lengthening to *i* in the derived imperfective. In fact, we needn't go so far as to the secondary imperfective, since the past tense of жечь is based on жёг, жгла, etc. Of course, there might be an vowel here inserted into a non-syllabic root, but that is unlikely: roots are syllabic, at least at this stage in the development of Slavonic.

More to the point, it seems as if жечь is not related to горе́ть and жа́рить. Also, given that the evidence of most Slavonic languages suggests ЖЕГ rather than ЖЬГ, e.g. Old Church Slavonic ЖЕШИ, non-past ЖЕГѪ, etc. (though some manuscripts have the root with a soft *jer*), Serbo-Croat *žeći*, non-past *žežem*, etc., but Polish *żec*, non-past *żgę*, etc., there might be a link with Lithuanian *dègti*, non-past *degù*, *degì*, *dēga*, etc. The development of *ž has not been explained; it could be analogy with the other 'burn' verbs, it could be assimilation of an initial *d to the following *g, and it could be the interaction of a prefix ending in *z with the following *g.

Why not mention here тёплый 'warm', which is related to топи́ть, non-past топлю́, то́пишь, ... то́пят 'stoke; heat (tr.)'. This suggests roots ТЕП and ТОП, with the latter also found in the adjective in, for example, Serbo-Croat *topao* — this may be later, by analogy with the verb. Slavonic evidence from Old Church Slavonic suggests there was no *jer* before the *l* suffix, thus ТОПЛЪ. If there was not and we have **teplъ*, then the *jer* may be an analogical insertion, such that in Russian the short form masculine is тёпел. In Latin we find *Tepula aqua*, the name for a water main in Rome, not to mention Latin *tepidus* 'warm' (not to mention *tepid*), so that, once more, the word is less exotic that we might have thought!

4.3.9 *Calm down* — (ПО)КОЙ (ЧИЙ) — МИР (**(po)koj-*, **mir-*)

In успокóить, non-past успокóю, успокóишь, ... успокоя́т 'to calm; deaden', imperf. успокáивать, non-past успокáиваю, etc. the derivation is straightforward. In Russian we can get down to покóй 'peace' (Остáвь меня в покóе! 'Leave me alone/in peace!'), but in Czech there is *kojit* 'to calm'. So the *po-* started off as a prefix. The plural, покóи, means '(inner) premises, room' (basically a place for peace and quiet). Now, the root КОЙ can be found in an alternative form, namely почи́ть, non-past почи́ю, почи́ешь, ... почи́ют, imperf. почивáть, non-past почивáю, etc., as in почивáть на лáврах 'to rest on one's laurels'. This allows us to speculate on a pre-First-Palatalization form **ki*, and, ultimately, bearing in mind 'peace and *quiet*', we can link it with the antecedent of English *quiet*! (In Proto-Indo-European there was also a labial velar, *k^w*, and in Slavonic this merged with *k*, while the palatal *k* became *s*.)

Coming to another word for 'peace', note that the word мир has two basic meanings — it's a homograph or homophone (if that confuses you, just use 'homonym'): 'world' — 'peace'. Up until 1918 it was written two ways, namely миръ and мiръ, the former meaning 'peace', as in Tolstoy's *Война и миръ War and Peace*. There is the slogan Ми́ру мир 'Peace to the world'. Note related adjectives: мировóй 'world', as in мировáя войнá 'world war', and ми́рный 'peace(ful)'; but obsolete мировóй судья́ 'justice of the peace'.

4.3.10 *Change* — МѢН (**měn-*)

This root is possibly linked to an original meaning to do with 'think, opinion, mind', as if we've never been so sure of our own minds — perhaps we can see something useful in измени́ть 'to betray', where there could be a sense of someone 'coming away from/out of their idea' (see 4.3.39). Possibly the basic verb here is мени́ть, not found in Russian in that form, but existing in other Slavonic languages, e.g. Czech *měnit* 'to change', and arguably in Baltic Lithuanian *mainýti* with the meaning 'to have an opinion'. But the basic verb extant in Russian seems to be меня́ть, non-past меня́ю, etc., perf. поменя́ть (also reflexive). However, there are verbs where prefixed меня́ть is *imperfective*: изменя́ть(ся) 'to change', переменя́ть(ся) 'to change', заменя́ть 'to replace', сменя́ть 'to exchange', with resp. perfectives измени́ть(ся), перемени́ть(ся), заменить, сменить. This suggests either that менить really is basic but lost, and that менять has been secondarily created by removing the prefix from, say, изменять, or that менять was originally derived from менить (which it subsequently replaced), perhaps with an iterative or frequentative nuance.[27] This would then fit in with such pairs as разменивать / разменять, обменивать / обменять, подменивать / подменять, which could be seen as more recent, formed when менять had become established (and arguably replaced менить). Note too that many nouns in this family have a hard *n*: мена, размен, обмен, замена, смена. So, the safest word for 'change' in general is probably изменить(ся). Don't confuse the noun derived from it, изменение, with измена 'treachery, betrayal (of = dat.)', from the other изменить. There is also the word мена, possibly revealing the basic root МЕН, which you will meet in the saying Мена не грабёж 'Exchange is no robbery'. Note too перемена 'change, alteration; interval, break' and смена 'shift (at work)'. The verb заменить 'to replace' is constructed with the accusative and instrumental: Он заменил стул табуреткой 'He replaced the chair with a stool' (the same goes for заместить, imperf. замещать, which is very common in this meaning). The related noun is замена 'substitution, replacement'. Note that in general, if you change something for something else, the construction is + acc. + на + acc.: Я меняю/обмениваю квартиру на дачу 'I'm (ex)changing my flat for a dacha', Она разменяла пять фунтов на рубли 'She changed five pounds to roubles'. The related noun is размен (not размена!). The verb обмениваться 'to exchange' is constructed with the instrumental: Они обменялись мнениями 'They exhanged/had an exchange of opinions'. The related noun, also constructed with the instrumental, is обмен — again, note the gender and form.[28] The last verb in the list needs explanation, since the perfective is actually подменить, and it has two imperfectives, подменивать and подменять. Clearly, this verb wants to have its cake and eat it. This last example means 'to substitute', in a slightly surreptitious, underhand sense (note the prefix, под 'under', and English *sub-* (concealed in *surreptitious* and *suspect,* but not in *subordinate*) and *under-*; also French *rire* 'to laugh', *sourire* 'to smile' (= *sous* + *rire*). In Russian we substitute something (accusative) with something (instrumental): Он подменил англо-русский словарь русско-английским словарём 'He substituted an RE dictionary for an ER one' (note the reversed order). The related noun is подмен *or* подмена, for once.

---

[27]See Appendix 3.

[28]The usual word for 'exchange' in regard to money is обмен, i.e. обмен валюты (is обмен always followed by a genitive?). Размен, as the prefix indicates, suggests the exchange of something larger into something smaller, e.g., разменять трёхкомнатную квартиру на две однокомнатные 'to exchange a three-room apartment for two one-room ones'. So the earlier example Она разменяла пять фунтов на рубли conveys the message that there were more roubles received for, say, a single five-pound note.

In all this connection note the Russian word лицемéр 'hypocrite', where we would expect лицемѣнъ 'face-changer', but where there has been a change in the second component — note what may be a calque from Slavonic in Lithuanian: *veidmainỹs* 'face-changer'.

4.3.11   Clean — ЧИСТ — ЦѢД (*čis(t)-, *cěd-)

In чи́стить there is a root ЧИСТ. We can imagine that the ч is related to an original *k* through the First Palatalization, something seen in the likely related Lithuanian *skáistas* 'bright', *skaidrùs* 'clear'. There is a likelihood (conceivable if we bear in mind Lithuanian *skaidrùs*, without the *t*) that the word is related to цеди́ть, non-past цежу́, цéдишь, ... цéдят 'strain, filter', i.e. 'clean, purify', thus the link. This latter form may be more closely linked to Lithuanian (the Lithuanian *i*-diphthong indicates a Second Palatalization, which fits in with the root ЦѢД), so that the difference between the two Russian forms is one of the particular vowels in the root. Also, if the link is correct, then the -т- of чи́стый may well be a suffix, but a very ancient one. Can you work out why?[29]

4.3.12   *Continue, long, short* — ДОЛГ (ДЪЛГ) — ДЬЛ — КОРОТ, КРАТ (*dъlg-, *dьl- — *kort-)

Дóлгий is a straightforward hard adjective with spelling adjustment as required by the stem-final velar. The masculine short form, дóлог, is in line with expectations, being an inserted, rather than historical, vowel, as also in пóлный — пóлон 'full'. It is not an instance of pleophony. The actual vowel of the root in Common Slavonic was probably a back *jer*, though a wider range of evidence suggests hesitation, perhaps ablaut, here. Thus Lithuanian *ìlgas* and Sanskrit *dīrghás* 'long', but Greek *dolikhós* 'long' and Latin *indulgeō* 'I dwell on'. First Palatalization is reflected in the derived verb продóлжить, non-past продóлжу, продóлжишь, ... продóлжат, imperf. продолжáть, non-past продолжáю, etc. 'continue (tr.)'. The imperfective is almost certainly derived from the perfective, with redundant jotation or by analogy. In Dal' I 1903:1144 you'll find должи́ть and должáть, both roughly 'to last, be drawn out'. It's entirely possible that there is some connection between this root and долг 'debt, duty', although it tends to be be assumed it's an ancient word related to Gothic *dulgs* 'debt'. The repayment of debt is something one tends to wait a long time for, so why not? Note the verbs одолжи́ть, imperf. одолжáть 'to lend ("to" = dat.); to borrow ("from" = y + gen.)', both fixed-stress, and obsolete за-должáть 'to owe ("to" = dat.); to borrow ("from" = y + gen.)'.

---

[29]Because the root-final *d* would have come up against the suffix *t*; the consonant group would have become *tt* by voice assimilation and the first *t* dissimilated in manner of articulation to the voiceless fricative *s, as in вести́ 'to lead' (non-past веду́, etc.) and плести́ 'to wind, braid' (non-past плету́, etc.).

The other common adjective for 'long' is дли́нный, a straightforward hard adjective, this time with a masculine short form, дли́нен, which reflects a historical mobile vowel, the soft *jer*, as in the suffix -ьн-. Thus there is a root ДЛИН; however, this root corresponds to the noun длина́ 'length', itself derived by the suffix -ин-, so that the root is more likely to be ДЛ. We really need a vowel (why?) and, though the *l* might be interpretable as such, comparative and historical evidence removes this need: we find, in the Old Rus' language, д(ь)ля 'length'. So there is a root ДЬЛ, where the *jer* never manifests itself as a full vowel, unless we take into account the almost certain link with до́лгий — the *g* may well be an ancient suffix. Note too that the *jer* is front, fitting in nicely with the evidence of variation (there is lots of evidence for front vowels retracting before *l*). In Modern Russian we find дли́ться, non-past дли́тся, perf. продли́ться 'last' (only the third person is used). Nominal forms are derived, as expected, e.g. дли́тельный 'protracted'.

Turning to 'short', we find коро́ткий and кра́ткий, both hard adjectives with the suffix -ък- providing the short forms ко́роток, кра́ток. The forms reflect respectively pleophony and metathesis, the meanings fitting in well with 'concrete' for Native Russian and 'abstract' for Church Slavonic. Thus: 'short' as against 'brief'. This is reinforced by derivatives: укороти́ть, non-past укорочу́, укороти́шь, ... укоротя́т, imperf. укора́чивать, non-past укора́чиваю, etc. 'shorten (e.g. trousers)' (note the Native Russian jotation too and also the lengthening of the vowel before the imperfective suffix), корота́ть, non-past корота́ю, etc., perf. скорота́ть 'to while away (e.g. time)', both as against сократи́ть, non-past сокращу́, сократи́шь, ... сократя́т, imperf. сокраща́ть, on-past сокраща́ю, etc. 'to abbreviate, abridge' (note the Church Slavonic jotation and vocalization of the weak *jer* in the prefix). Note too how, for once, this fits in nicely with English, where one would not 'abbreviate one's trousers'. It is interesting to see that there is a non-prefixed form in the shape of корота́ть, doubtless ancient and perhaps iterative, and we might hypothesize коротить, perhaps factitive. Compare what was said above for 'long'. As for origins, we doubtless have the same root in German *kurz* 'short', appearing in French, for example, as *court*. The Latin sense, in its adjective *curtus*, of 'shortened, chopped off', surfaces in English *curtail* and, closer to Slavonic, Lithuanian *kartùs* 'bitter', i.e. a taste cut short (we also find it in, for example, *kartù sù* 'together with', which might indicate proximity, 'shortness'). In case the idea of 'cut' does not convince, there is probably an ablaut connection with черта́ 'line, limit', linked to Sanskrit *kṛtā* 'split, ravine', and the related черти́ть, non-past черчу́, че́ртишь, ... че́ртят, perf. начерти́ть 'draw (up)' and derived forms to do with drawing and draughtsmanship.

4.3.13 *Control* — ВОЛОД — ВЛАД — ПРАВ — МОГ (МОЧ, МОЩ) (**vold-*, **prav-*, **mog-*)

Вла́ствовать, non-past вла́ствую, etc. 'rule, hold sway (with над + instr.)' and управля́ть, non-past управля́ю, etc. 'manage (+ instr.)' lead us into this area. The first has the Church Slavonic root ВЛАД, which we find, pleophonically, in Воло́дя, во́лость 'province (obs.)'. The suffix **t*, tacked onto the original **vold-*, led to a regular change of **dt* to **tt* to **st*, thus вла́сть 'power, authority'. We can discern interference of the suffix -ьств- in the formation of the verb. The root is nicely reflected in Lithuanian *valdýti* 'to rule, master'.

Управля́ть is linked with пра́вый 'right'. It has no perfective these days, though there is a reflexive pair, упра́виться — управля́ться с + instr. 'to finish something off, to deal with something'. We see a link in Latin *probus* 'upright, worthy' and, possibly, words referring to 'front'. So there is a root ПРАВ. There may be a link to a form such as Old English *fram* 'strong, bold'. The root may be expanded, giving such forms as пра́вда 'truth', where the suffix must be -ьд-, given пра́ведный 'righteous' and справедли́вый 'fair, just', with the *jer* becoming a full vowel before the *jer* of the additional suffix. Note too оправда́ть, non-past оправда́ю, etc., imperf. опра́вдывать, non-past опра́вдываю, etc., 'justify', the genesis of the perfective quite difficult to explain: simply the tacking-on of a widespread new non-past pattern, namely -а́ю, etc. onto the stem правд, perhaps supported by the fact that this derivation is onto a stem (hence more recent) and not a root, or, less likely, some influence of да́ть 'to give' (without its non-past), and then, without any doubt, a unusual imperfectivization strategy?

Finally, the form мочь, both a feminine noun 'power' and an infinitive (restricted to language books) 'to be able'. This goes back to **mog-*, which is cognate with *might* 'power'. In Gothic there is *mahts*. Ultimately there may be links with Lithuanian *mė́gti* 'to like' ('liking', 'loving' are empowering phenomena) and even Greek *mēxanḗ* 'tool', thus *mechanical*. The non-past is rather odd: могу́, мо́жешь, ... мо́гут — one doesn't expect the mobile stress. But modals do behave oddly. The perfective, смочь, probably bears the semelfactive nuance of the prefix с-. In other words, a rather special perfective — the more we think about aspect, the less, or at least the clearer and more restricted, its role. The root manifests itself also in a Church Slavonic form, e.g. мо́щный 'powerful', мо́щи 'saint's relics'. And one can imagine the rationale for помо́чь 'to help'.

4.3.14 *Cover, hide* — КРЫ, КРО (**kry-/*krъ-*)

In задви́жка 'catch, fastening', застёжка 'fastener, clasp', and засо́в 'bolt, bar' there is the prefix за- in its sense of covering/closing something, particularly on a surface, thus запо́лнить can mean 'to fill in a form' (i.e. a sheet of paper is a surface) or a table-top. It may also, like напо́лнить, mean 'to fill a volume', e.g.

ззрйтели запо́лнили зал 'the spectators filled the hall'. One might argue that the spectators don't go up to the ceiling, so perhaps it's really a case of 'filling all over the place', as in пол был заста́влен сту́льями 'the floor was covered with chairs'. Note накрыва́ть for setting a table — perhaps a sense of depth or height or better of simply putting things *onto* the surface rather than *over* it.

In the first word we have the root ДВИГ 'move' with the now familiar suffix -/ка (= -ька), the soft sign causing the First Palatalization consonant change. In the second there is exactly the same, this time with the root СТЕГ, related to German *stechen* 'to prick, sting, stick'. In Russian there is the verb стега́ть, perf. стегну́ть or отстега́ть 'to whip, lash' and the verb стега́ть, perf. вы́стегать 'to quilt'. Probably not linked, with a different root-vowel, is СТЬГ, related to German *der Steg* 'path (obs.)' or *der Steig/die Steige* '[mountain] path'), and present in Russian in стёжка 'path' (it also means 'quilting'!) and in the non-diminutive form зга, encountered only in ни зги не ви́дно 'it's pitch black' (i.e. 'one can't even see the path') — the non-diminutive and Church Slavonic form, стезя́, was encountered in Chapter 3 under the Third Palatalization (3.3.7). The latter probably appears most in the verb дости́гнуть, imperf. достига́ть 'to reach, achieve (+ gen.)', with a lengthened root vowel, probably linked to the imperfective structure, with the perfective derived from it. Whatever the relationship between all these forms, there do seem to be various ancient vocalic grades here. Particularly common are the verbs застегну́ть(ся), imperf. застёгивать(ся) 'to fasten, button up', отстегну́ть(ся), imperf. отстёгивать(ся) 'to unbutton, undo'. Worth noting is that nouns with the suffix -/ка have stress *fixed* before the suffix; compare рука́ — ру́чка hand, arm — handle, pen', нога́ — но́жка 'foot, leg — little foot; furniture leg'. The source nouns may have mobile stress or, as in кни́га — кни́жка 'book', fixed stress. The reason for the fixed stress in the diminutive is complex, but may well be connected with the loss of the soft sign of the suffix being compensated for by an increased salience of the immediately preceding vowel (redundant if the stress is already there, as in кни́га; but think of голо́дный 'hungry', short-form masculine го́лоден, or noun го́лод).

Here it might be appropriate to mention the word family concerning 'cover', namely based around the verb крыть 'to cover, conceal' (particularly common reflexively, i.e. кры́ться 'to be covered, concealed, lurk'. We find a related form in Baltic, Celtic, and Germanic languages, not to mention Greek *krúptō* 'I hide' (think of, for example, *cryptography*, or *cryptic*). Given a non-past кро́ю, кро́ешь, ... кро́ют we can suggest a root КРЫ or КРОЙ, ultimately *krū* and *krъj*, where the long vowel variant broke up into *uw* (= *ъw*) before a vowel but was retained before a consonant, thus giving related forms like кров and кро́вля 'roof', as against крыша 'id.', кры́шка 'lid, cover'. If we remove a cover, cover with a cover, and bring down a cover we get the common, indeed indispensable verbs откры́ть 'to open', закры́ть 'to close', скры́ть 'to hide' (and many others), with the imperfectives derived from them with the suffix -ва́-: открыва́ть, закрыва́ть, and скрыва́ть.

4.3.15 *Cut* — РѢЗ (*rěz-*)

Coming to the subject of 'cutting', the basic verb in Russian is péзать with non-past péжу, péжешь, ... péжут. Here the root is РЕЗ, and we note the e doesn't become ё, suggesting an original *jat'*, something confirmed by Ukrainian pізати. The root manifests itself in the zero-suffix form of the adverb наотрéз 'flatly', as in наотрéз отказáться 'to refuse flatly' and the noun резьбá 'carving', with the suffix -ьба, also found in судьбá 'fate', свáдьба 'wedding', молотьбá 'threshing', related respectively to the more basic forms суд 'judgement, trial', сват 'matchmaker' (note the assimilation in voice reflected in the spelling; but contrast with the last example), and молóть 'to grind'.[30] What is the perfective of this verb? Well, we come across срéзать, нарéзать, зарéзать, to mention but three — look them up, and seek out others. The perfectives on the whole reflect different types of cutting, so are only arguably actual perfectives within a pair — and clearly it is odd that each one be paired with péзать. On top of that, these perfectives have their own derived imperfectives. As imperfective we might quite reasonably expect the suffix -ыв(а)-, e.g. зарéзывать (if you can find that in a dictionary!), and indeed we do encounter forms on that pattern, but we also have отрезáть, etc., i.e. the suffix -á-, yielding a non-past -резáю, -резáешь, ... -резáют. Can you think of any other verbs which behave like this?[31] Staying with this verb, we might mention the town of Рязáнь, which might be related to the nearby *Erzja* Mordvin Uralic people, or to the past passive participle of péзать, thus рѣзанъ, a personal name meaning, as suggested by Vasmer, 'cut (from the womb)', the vowel change reflecting *jakańje* (the *a*-pronunciation of e in the first pre-tonic after soft consonants).

We might also mention the verb рубить, non-past рублю, рубишь, ... рубят 'to fell; hack, chop; mince'. We find the root РУБ (the vowel goes back to a back nasal, reflected in Polish *rąb* 'hem, edge'), which suggests, correctly, links with рубáшка 'shirt', рубáнок '(woodworking) plane', рубéж 'boundary' (за рубежóм 'abroad', на рубежé двух столéтий 'at the turn of two centuries'), зарубéжный 'foreign (lit. "over the edge")', рубéц 'hem; scar', the relatively transparent compound мясорýбка 'mincing-machine' with the linking vowel -о- and suffix -ъка, and almost certainly рубль 'rouble (originally 'bit of a *grivna* ("ten-copeck piece; pound; gold or silver medal around the neck")')'. Here again there are problems with perfectives: порубить comes very close, but also has the familiar по- related sense of 'to do a bit of X'. And, if we have отрубить 'to hack

---

[30]While on the subject of this verb, note хлеб 'bread', with a link easier to see if it is translated as 'loaf', since they are the same word (the Russian word is a borrowing from Germanic). In Gothic there is *hlaifs*, which shows us the e is ѣ (setting aside some special cases, ѣ comes, as here, from *aj* and *oj*, as well as from a long *e*), and so doesn't become ё.

[31]We might mention сыпать 'to spread, strew', двигать 'to move', бéгать 'to run'. Look them up, with prefixes.

off', what is the imperfective? We would, again quite reasonably, expect отру́бливать or отрубля́ть, when it is actually отруба́ть, non-past отруба́ю, отруба́ешь, ... отруба́ют. So note two things here: first, that 'cut' seems to be an activity verb which does not lend itself in any straightforward manner to functioning within an aspect pair; and secondly, that this is one of a number of verbs with an unexpected feature, namely the suffix -á- without softening, in derived imperfectives. These derived imperfectives may well reflect ancient 'iteratives' or 'frequentatives', e.g. the now disappeared руба́ть, sometimes still extant in their underived form, e.g. ступа́ть 'to step', броса́ть 'to throw' and paired with forms in -ить.[32] Note, too, the specialized past passive participle ру́бленый 'minced' (a culinary term; from an imperfective in modern Russian terms, and with a single н, as etymologically correct in this participle — the second н is the familiar adjectival suffix, which came to characterize the long form of the participle in course of the nineteenth century).

And we might mention стричь, non-past стригу́, стрижёшь, ... стригу́т, past стриг, стри́гла, etc. 'cut, clip' (the perfective is остри́чь). Taking into account the non-past, thus стригу́, etc., the root emerges as СТРИГ, with the usual development of г, or к, before т, and before a front vowel. When specifying haircutting, we often use подстри́чь(ся), reflexive in the sense 'to get one's hair cut', and the imperfective is подстрига́ть(ся), the derivation bringing out the root-final consonant and adding the imperfectivizing suffix -á-.

Another verb to mention is коси́ть, non-past кошу́, ко́сишь, ... ко́сят 'mow; cut', which is related to коса́ 'scythe'. We might link "looking sideways' with a long curved knife like a scythe, so, unsurprisingly, we find косо́й 'slanting, squinting/cross-eyed, sidelong (glance)', и́скоса 'aslant, sideways', ко́со 'aslant' (смотре́ть ко́со 'to look askance, scowl'), вкривь и вкось 'all over the place; indiscriminately'. And one other verb you might explore is вы́-сечь 'to cut to pieces' (see 4.3.22).

4.3.16 *Decide* — РѢШ — ВАЗ (*rěš-, *vęz-)

In реши́ть, non-past решу́, реши́шь, ... реша́т, imperf. реша́ть, non-past реша́ю, etc. 'to decide, resolve; discuss' we can assume a root РѢШ, the ш probably traceable to *s* given related forms like Latvian *rist* 'to tie' and, better for the *jat', ràisît* 'to tear' (*š* in the Russian form is most simply seen as reflecting a First Palatalization of an *x* which arose from *s* via the *ruki*-rule — but it could have got stuck there). In other words, there is a sense of 'disentangling' something in order to 'resolve' it. And note how once more there is an odd aspect pair here: no prefixation, two verbs with an equal number of syllables, First Palatalization or partial *ruki*-rule in the perfective and analogy or jotation in the imperfective (and possible stress indicating derivation there too) — not to mention the problems to do with the actual meaning of the verb, i.e. we tend to

---

[32]See Appendix 3.

'decide' perfectively, so an imperfective would mean 'discuss' or 'try to decide', with a habitual or iterative nuance. The fact that this verb has to a great extent become remote from its 'untying' sense is perhaps indicated by Ukrainian, where 'to decide' is вирішити, imperf. вирішувати, with the prefix reinforcing the sense of getting out of something. Similar pairs we've met (e.g. 4.3.15) include ступить, imperf. ступать 'to step' and бросить, imperf. бросать 'to throw' — if решить/решать is indeed on a similar pattern, the argument for consonantal analogy and 'imperfective' (at the early stage probably iterative or frequentative) derivation becomes more persuasive.

In this connection think of one verb family which is semantically linked. The simple verb вязать, non-past вяжу, вяжешь, ... вяжут 'to tie; knit' (also its reflexive вязаться 'to tie in with; work out well') creates many very useful verbs, e.g. завязать, imperf. завязывать 'to tie up, knot; start (friendship, etc.)', связать, imperf. связывать 'to connect', and related forms, e.g. вязь 'ornamental ligatured script', вязка 'tying; knitting; bundle', связь 'link', завязка 'lace; start', развязка 'untying; dénouement; "roundabout, junction"' (think of French *nouer* 'to tie'), вязкий 'viscous', and we might perhaps come full circle, back to вязать, with вязнуть 'to sink into, get stuck in, tied up in (imperf.)'. And one example we should not forget is обязан- 'obliged', where a *bv* consonant group has been simplified, which calques *ob-* + *ligat-* (*ligature*, Latin *ligo* 'I tie', French *lier* 'to link, connect').

At this point we think of the word узел 'knot'. Could that be linked? The answer is that it almost certainly is; moreover, the я - у pattern begins to suggest nasal vowels, something confirmed by earlier texts and related words in other Slavonic languages. And when something is linked, there must be a constriction, a narrowing, thus узкий 'narrow'. A nice example, mentioned in 3.3.6, is брачные узы 'the bonds of wedlock' (a Church Slavonic version of this is reflected in союз 'union'). The sense of 'knots' might be reflected in Lithuanian *ãžuolas* 'oak-tree', something which does not transfer to Russian, where, however, there is the вяз 'elm-tree'.

An English synonym not so far mentioned is 'join'. This verb, which goes back to Latin *jungō* 'I join', is very likely linked: it has the nasal consonant which could have led to a nasal vowel, and the *g* very likely was a palatal velar, giving Slavonic *z*. Don't think of юг 'south', which goes with Latin *augeō* 'I increase, "augment"', i.e. where the sun has increased its height.

4.3.17 *Destroy* — РУХ (*rux-*, the vowel coming from a *w*-dipthong)

The most common word here is разрушать, разрушаю, разрушаешь, ... разрушают, with perfective разрушить, разрушу, разрушишь, ... разрушат. Related is нарушать, perf. нарушить 'to break (silence), infringe (a law)', with the same non-past pattern. Note the stress patterns. We also have the deverbal, formed from the perfectives, nouns разрушение, нарушение — note the stress. Related is the biaspectual verb рушиться 'to collapse, be destroyed', and the perfective-only verb рýхнуть, рýхну, рýхнешь, ... рýхнут, past рýхнул (the -ну- is retained) with the same meaning. There is a basic meaning of 'movement', as in the Ukrainian political movement/party Рух 'The Movement' (also 'traffic'!).

4.3.18 *Die, be born* — МЬР, МЕР, МОР — РОД (*mьr-, *mer-, *mor- — *rod-)

The standard word for 'die' is умерéть, non-past умрý, умрёшь, ... умрýт, imperf. умирáть, non-past умирáю, etc. That we find it also with other prefixes, e.g. померéть 'to die', a rather demotic form, and замирáть 'to fade away', indicates that the basic form is мерéть, something found in other Slavonic languages, e.g. Old Church Slavonic МЬРѢТИ, non-past МЬРѪ, МЬРЕШИ, ... МЬРѪТЪ, Czech *mřít*. The data from the two Slavonic languages just mentioned in addition indicates that we do indeed have pleophony in -мерéть. So there is Common Slavonic *merti* 'to die' alongside non-past *mьrǫ* 'I die', reflected in the modern verb. This is worth establishing, because the imperfective, which we might glibly state to be derived via root-vowel lengthening and the suffix -á-, is in fact true only if we see it as derived from the non-past stem *mьr-. (This also goes for verbs exhibiting similar patterns, e.g. заперéть, non-past запрý, etc., imperf. запирáть, on-past запирáю, 'lock' — but contrast собрáть, non-past соберý, etc., imperf. собирáть 'collect'.) The additional ablaut form with *o is reflected in nominals, e.g. óбморок 'faint', dialectal умóра 'exhaustion' (and a colloquial predicative 'it's killing, really funny'), and in the Church Slavonic form in мрáчный 'dark; dismal' (with *ь also in сýмерки 'twilight, dusk' and смеркáться 'to grow dark). And we find *o in морúть, non-past морю́, морúшь, ... моря́т, perf. with the prefixes вы́-/по-/у- 'exterminate, wear out', thus a factitive or causative. If we move outside Slavonic, then Lithuanian *mirti* 'to die' and *mirtìs* 'death' are clearly related, the *i* of the root echoing Slavonic *ь. Latin *morior* 'I die' does likewise. Which cannot but lead to *mortal*. We then wonder about German *der Schmerz* 'pain', and indeed it too is linked. It is but a short step from this to Russian and смерть 'death'. Here we have *sъmьrtь and assume the prefix *sъ- 'with, co-'. But on what basis? In fact, it is more likely to be the formant *su- meaning 'good' that is seen in здорóвый 'healthy' (*sъdorv-). This formant, by the way, may well be linked to свой 'one's own'; after all, 'one's own' is most often 'good'. When someone dies a 'good', natural death, that person умирáет своéй смéртью.

Another example of this formant is probably счáстье 'happiness, good fortune', from Common Slavonic *sъčęstьje, where the root is ЧАСТ, as found in чáсть 'part' — a part, as in French *la part*, is a share, one's lot (think of дóля 'lot, share', an ablaut of делúть 'to divide', as well as ýчасть 'lot, fate') — the root is linked by ablaut, with the First Palatalization as consequence, of КѪС (*kǫs-). This is the root of кусáть 'to bite' and reflected in кусóк 'piece, bit', something bitten off (like French *le morceau* and English *morsel*), nicely confirmed by Lithuanian *kąsti* 'to bite' (the *ą* indicates an original nasal, now long oral) and *kandù* 'I bite'. So счастье refers to one's 'good lot'.

As for birth, родиться, non-past рожусь, родишься, ... родятся 'be born (biasp.)' is based on род '*genus*, sort'. It is probably not a case of initial metathesis, although persuasive arguments may be made for a link to Latin *orior* 'I rise', *arduus* 'high' (the *Ardennes*), Greek *órmenos* 'shoot, stem', and thus to расти 'to grow' and its extensive family, e.g. рост, возраст, взрослый. In Lithuanian we have the definitely related *rasmė* 'harvest', amongst others. Old Church Slavonic has the ablaut form РЄДЪ 'food, nourishment'. This brings us to урожай 'harvest, the ж arising by jotation, as reinforced by Polish *rodzaj* 'sort, kind'. Church Slavonic forms appear in, for instance, Рождество 'Christmas (= "Nativity")', эпоха Возрождения 'Renaissance'.

4.3.19 *Equal* — РАВЬН, РОВЬН (*orv-*)

Пара 'pair' is a straightforward loanword from German *Paar* via Polish, ultimately from Latin *par* 'equal'. Note *par* in English *compare* and its Slavonic equivalent in Russian сравнить, imperf. сравнивать, where the prefix с- is historically the same *com-* of *compare* (Latin *cum* 'with', in verbs *co-*, *com-*, *con-* — the *k*-sound of Latin goes back to a palatal *k'*, which in Slavonic became *s*) and the root is Church Slavonic РАВ, the root very early supplemented by the suffix -/н- (= -ьн-), thus равный 'equal' (compare Native Russian ровный 'level, flat').

4.3.20 *Excitement* and *anxiety* — ВЪЛ(Н) (*vъln-* (= *vuln-/*viln-*)

Волноваться 'to get excited/anxious' is one of the familiar -ов(а)- verbs, part of an extremely productive conjugational pattern. Remember that -ов- was originally a diphthong *ow*, and that before a vowel this became *ov* and before a consonant *u*. At first glance we seem to have -у- before a vowel in -ую, etc., but remember the functions of я, е, ё, ю, namely as indicating the softness of an immediately preceding consonant, and the presence of a *j*-consonant when absolute word-initial, after a hard or soft sign, and after a vowel: я ['ja] 'I', съем ['sjɛm] 'I'll eat', солью ['sɔlʲjɷ] 'salt (instr.sg.)', моя [mʌ'ja] 'my/mine (nom.sg.fem.)', and волнуюсь [vʌ'lnujɷsʲ] 'I become excited/anxious'. The meaning of the verb suggests the meaning of the immediate root ВОЛН 'wave (at sea)'. Comparison with other Slavonic languages refines this to В/ЛН or ВЪЛН, but this is irrelevant to Russian. More relevant is that -н- is a suffix, allowing us the semantic link to вал 'a big wave', German *wallen* 'to boil, seethe, churn (of the sea)', English 'to *well* up', and Lithuanian *vélti* 'to roll' — think too of *revolutions* — do they really mean 'change', or is it something cyclic going on?

The perfective, взволноваться, provides an example of the Native Russian form of the 'up' prefix. In Church Slavonic forms there is воз- (though, if the *jer* were strong, воз- would be correct in Native Russian).

4.3.21 *Fear* — (У)ЖАС — БОЙ — (О)ПАС (**žas-*, **boj*, **pas-*)

In the verb ужасáть(ся), non-past ужасáю(сь), ужасáешь(ся), ...
ужасáют(ся), perf. ужаснýть(ся), non-past ужаснý(сь), ужаснёшь(ся), ...
ужаснýт(ся) 'to terrify/be terrified' there is a root УЖАС (unusual, probably with
the prefix **u-*) and the suffixes -a- and -ну- before the ending and reflexive
particle as appropriate. Note how roots are sometimes identical with actual
words, thus here the noun ýжас with a zero-suffix. And if we add the suffix -ьн
and an adjectival ending to the noun, we have ужáсный 'awful, terrible'. The
origin is obscure, though it is attested widely in Slavonic and may occur without
the prefix. There is no evidence of a front nasal or of a *jat'* after the *ž*; it is
suggested that there may be some relation to гасúть 'to extinguish, put out', an
idea possibly strengthened by Lithuanian *gèsti* 'to extinguish' and its front vowel
(though that isn't necessarily very helpful); we might expect some link to гад
'reptile; repulsive person', гáдкий 'vile', but there seems to be no evidence.
　The suffix of the perfective of this verb would have originally had a sense of a
single, or sudden, action — it would be what is conventionally known as a
semelfactive verb. In many verbs this is now either a marker of or simply
coincides with perfectivity, but the suffix remains productive in the sense of 'one
action', e.g. спекулúровать 'to speculate' and the informal спекульнýть 'to
make one speculation'. This meaning is so important that the suffix is never lost.
Compare a verb like сóхнуть 'to become dry', imperfective, where ну is lost in
past-related forms, e.g. бельё сóхло 'the linen was drying' (note the wonders of
a language, in that one would not use сóхнуть of a river, thus рекá высыхáла
'the river was drying up'), высохший 'dried-up; shrivelled' (a perfective past
participle active, but the suffix here doesn't have the 'one action' sense). Verbs
like сóхнуть are basically imperfective, with a sense of 'gradual process', never
have the stress on ну, practically always lose it in the past-related forms, and are
restricted — it is not a productive formation in modern Russian. Compare
дóхнуть 'to die (of animals)' with дохнýть 'to blow; emit a single breath', and
пáхнуть 'to smell of (+ instr.)' with пахнýть to puff, blow (once)'. In connection
with сóхнуть do note осушáть, perf. осушúть 'to dry (tr.)' (concrete and
figurative) and сушúть 'to dry out/up (tr.)', and see 4.3.40. Here there is the
relation х — ш, given the adjective сухóй 'dry' and root СУХ. The suffix -и- of
the verb can, as already noted, have a sense of 'to make something something'.
Thus: чернúть, белúть, etc. 'to make black, white'. Compare (по)чернéть,
non-past чернéет, (по)белéть, non-past белéет 'be/become/turn black, white'.
Given the prefix о(б)- in осушúть (thus: 'to dry all over/around'), we
subsequently have a straightforward imperfective derivation: осушáть.
　Continuing our digression, a further example is румяниться, non-past
румянюсь, румянишься, ... румянятся 'to redden, glow; blush', where there
is a derivation from the adjective румяный, namely румянить 'to make red' and
the reflexive 'to become red'. Within the adjective there is a suffix -мѣн- (the
vowel change may be analogical, although we can imagine it coming from a

dialect where the *jat'* was pronounced somewhat like [a]). The root is РУД, linked to рудá 'ore' and рдеть 'to be red' and ржáвéть 'to be rusty', ржáвый 'rusty', ржá(вчина) 'rust' — the examples without a vowel go back to *rъd-. In this connection consider also рýсый 'light brown; ruddy'.

In солúть and перчúть too there is the sense, as in румя́нить, of 'making something something', thus 'making something salty/peppery'. In перчúть we go back to the word for 'pepper', пьпьръ, with a suffix пьпьрьць. Now here there are two identical syllables next to each other — a perfect opportunity for haplology, the removal of one of them. Thus: пьрьць. The development of the soft signs is not straightforward, but there was a tendency in Russian for them to become full vowels when adjacent to (especially before) р or л, and the suffix would behave as in other words, thus пéрец — пéрца, like пáлец — пáльца 'finger'. What of the ч? Well, there is something similar in лицó — лúчный. If the ц arose late, then perhaps we actually have the ч arising from к, thus: пьпьрькъ. By the way, the presentation of these in Cyrillic is misleading, and achronological, but it can be easier to see the words this way. Something to bear in mind is that the word probably comes from Latin *piper* (from Greek *peperi*), so there may be a friendlier explanation for the е in пер-. Loanwords behave in special ways, and do not follow the straight and narrow path of 'truly native' words.

Coming back to 'fearing', the most common verb is certainly боя́ться, non-past бою́сь, боúшься, ... боя́тся + gen. 'be afraid (of)'. This verb is found throughout Slavonic and is linked to, for example, Lithuanian *bijóti* 'to be afraid'. We may imagine that the root, immediately before a consonant, would generate *ě̆, and indeed it probably does, giving бéс 'devil', related to Latin *foedus* 'vile' and giving semantic encouragement to the link of ýжас with гáдкий. Боя́ться, as already noted, is one of only two second-conjugation verbs in -оя́ть and belongs among the verbs originally in *-ěti, where the *jat'* became *a after hushings and *j (see 2.4 fn). It does not have a straightforward aspectual relationship: побоя́ться probably comes close, and from it we derive побáиваться 'to be chairy of'. The derived noun is боя́знь (fem.), one of very few with the suffix -знь, e.g. неприя́знь 'enmity', болéзнь 'illness', and жúзнь 'life', all derived from verbs.

There is also the verb опасáться, non-past опасáюсь, опасáешься, ... опасáются + gen. 'to be afraid (of)'. This looks like a compound root, with a prefix *o(b)- and root ПАС, encountered in the sense 'tend' (see 4.3.43) and so having an implication of being on one's guard. Note the derived noun опасéние, with no immediately identifiable direct source (and certainly no jotation) and, perhaps most familiarly, опáсный 'dangerous' and its antonym безопáсный 'safe'.

Finally, we might mention страх 'terror, dread', with its derived adjective стрáшный and verb устрашúть(ся), non-past устрашý(сь), устрашúшь(ся), ... устрашáт(ся), imperf. устрашáть(ся), non-past устрашáю(сь), etc. 'to terrify (take fright)'. This is attested throughout Slavonic and likely linked to Lithuanian *strègti* 'to set, go cold/numb' and German *strecken* 'to stretch' (and thus the English verb too). Note the vowel variation here, just as, possibly, with ýжас. There is no evidence for a reduced vowel within the group str, though we may find forms without s outside Slavonic. The x could be affective, but it is entirely possible that the ancient sequence *gs became *ks, where the *s became *x, possibly via the ruki-rule. Note, finally, that we have a use of the prefix y- here; given that in a few words this is a negating prefix, e.g. урóд 'monster', урóдливый 'ugly' (quite the opposite in the otherwise identical Ukrainian вродлúвий), cognate with English un-, we are tempted to wonder whether we might not have it here, with an intensifying role. There is, however, no evidence for its being anything other than the prefix *u-, which itself may have an intensifying role, e.g. in убúть, imperf. убивáть 'to kill', derived from бúть.

4.3.22   Flow — ЛЬЙ — ТЕК, ТОК (*lьj- — *tek-/*tok-)

The basic verb here is лить 'to pour' (transitive and intransitive; we may use the reflexive form as the intransitive too: Льёт как из ведрá 'It's tippling down', Водá лилáсь в подвáл 'Water was pouring into the cellar'). The prefix с- together with reflexivization gives a sense of coming together, 'converging'. Thus слúться, with the imperfective derived by the suffix -вá-, giving сливáться 'to blend, converge, flow together'. What is intriguing is the non-past of the perfective, with the inserted о. Is this a fleeting vowel? The answer is 'yes', partly because this prefix is actually съ-, and partly because its appearance is triggered by the prefix being followed by two consonants. This claim seems bizarre, given the spelling сольюсь, but remember that the vowels я, е, ё, ю actually represent two sounds when they occur at the beginning of a word, after a vowel, and after a hard sign or a soft sign. So, taking liberties once again with Russian spelling rules, we actually have сольйусь, and the two consonants in question are a soft л and й. Given that the soft sign here would originally have been a vowel, the two adjacent soft/hard signs would have developed by the one on the right disappearing (at least as a full vowel) and the immediately preceding one becoming a 'full vowel', thus сольюсь. This leaves us with the question of the root, and the answer is ЛЬЙ, with the soft sign either remaining as a marker of the softness of the л or becoming е, as in the imperative: Лей! (from *lьjь — note the two adjacent soft signs, the one on the right disappearing and the immediately preceding one becoming е, just as we expect, given Russian's 'resistance' to 'tense jers'). Why, though, do we have и in сливáться? The answer is quite familiar, given earlier instances, with one novel feature: most likely there is a structure съ + льй + ва + ти (+ ся). Since й and в, two consonants, come together, one is deleted, in this instance the first one. And, as happens in imperfective derivation, the root vowel is lengthened. Given that a soft sign is historically a short i-sound, then we expect a long i-sound; the prehistoric Slavonic long i-sound gave и. So there we are.

As mentioned earlier, this is another rich and important family: наливáть/налúть 'to pour (of a drink for someone: + acc. + dat.)', заливáть/залúть 'to flood, spill over (+ acc. + instr.), quench/extinguish (with water!), begin to pour (perf. only) (also reflexive)', подливáть/подлúть 'to add to', e.g. the saying подлúть мáсла в огóнь 'to add fuel to the flames' (with a partitive genitive). Note, by the way, the non-past perfective with its inserted *o*: я подолью́. See 4.2.4.1. Without wishing to lower the tone, one might also have залúть, imperf. заливáть alone, e.g., он нáчал заливáть, perhaps ellipsis of the expression залúть / заливáть глазá 'to get really drunk'.

And do remember that the same morphological pattern is shared by бить 'to beat', вить 'to wind', пить 'to drink', and шить 'to sew' (there are differences of detail). And it is useful to bear in mind verbs such as мыть 'to wash' and брить 'to shave' when considering this pattern.

Tempting as it must be, there does not seem to be a clear link between пить 'to drink and петь 'to sing', though поúть 'to give to drink', with the clear suggestion of a *j*-diphthong (**oj*) giving the *jat'* of петь and links such as Latin *pōtus* 'drunk' and *bibō* 'I drink' (from **pibō*) and Old Prussian *poieiti* 'let him/her drink' are interesting. Whatever the case may be, singing and drinking *do* go together! The root for петь would seem to be ПОЙ with a pre-consonantal variant ПѢ (we might collapse the two if they were seen as respectively pre-vocalic and pre-consonantal, as in Late Common Slavonic), and for пить ПЬЙ.

Now take истóчник 'source, origin'. Once again the prefix ис-, concealing the more transparent из- 'out of'. Note too, for example, искýсство 'art', исконú 'from time immemorial', исслéдовать 'to research, study' — издевáться над + instr. 'to mock', изъя́ть 'to withdraw, remove' (изымý, изы́мешь ... изы́мут, imperf. изымáть, изымáю,...), and obsolete избóрник 'anthology'. And there is the familiar compound suffix -ник, made up of -/н- (= -ьн-) and -ик. The root seems to be ТОЧ, but, as already known, a consonant like ч is likely to be secondary. In Russian it will conceal original к or т. The meaning 'source' suggests 'coming from' — compare also происхождéние 'source, origin' and the verb происходúть/произойтú. Since истóчник can be used for a 'spring', i.e. water, then течь, текý, течёшь, ..., текýт 'flow' might come to mind — think too of the double-prefixed проистéчь, imperf. проистекáть из + gen. 'to spring from, result from', e.g. Из этого проистекáет, что... 'The consequence is that...' Thus we have a root ТОК, as in тóк 'current', where the vowel *o* reflects an ancient alternation with *e* (thus also ТЕК) — don't confuse this with the *o* in the masculine past tense of the verb, тёк (fem. теклá), which is more recent, is an underlying *e*, and is preceded by a soft consonant. By the way, ТОК is probably not related to тóчка 'point, dot' and the related ткнуть, ткну, ткнёшь, ... ткнут and ты́кать, ты́чу, ты́чешь,... ты́чут[33] 'to jab'. Here the vowels reflect an ancient reduced grade *u* and lengthened reduced grade *ū*, giving respectively ъ (which could lead to nothing, as in ткнуть, and о, as in тóчка) and ы (as in ты́кать) — as already noted in дожидáться 'to wait', we can also have reduced grades *i* and *ī*, giving respectively ь and и. It is interesting too to

---

[33]Not to be confused with ты́кать, ты́каю, ты́каешь,... 'to address as "ty"'.

see how the derivation of imperfectives through the suffix -á- (without preceding softening or jotation) may go hand-in-hand with length in the root vowel. A less visible example is летéть 'to fly (punctual)' and the related verb летáть, in which the -е- of the latter conceals a historical *jat'*, i.e. the reflex of a long *e, while that in the latter is *e, as in полёт 'flight', etc.: летѣть — лѣтáть until 1918.

It can be useful to look at similar verbs and see if they suggest comparable patterns. Thus сечь 'to cut to pieces (imperf.); flog (вы́-, perf.)' has non-past секу́, сечёшь, секу́т, past сёк, секла́. And we have секи́ра 'hatchet' and сечéние 'cutting; section' (кéсарево сечéние 'Caesarean'); with a prefix we can create, for instance, the very useful пересéчься 'to intersect', and its more common derived imperfective пересекáться. From the perfective вы́сечь we can derive a secondary imperfective высекáть, in which case the meaning is 'to cut out, sculpt', note вы́сечка 'carving, hewing'. But there is no form with о (сок 'juice' is somewhat mysterious, but may be related to words for 'pitch' or 'juice' in other languages, and to со̱сáть 'to suck', in which case the final -к of сок would be a suffix added to a root *so). What about печь 'to bake'? Well, here there is non-past пеку́, ..., past пёк, пекла́. So there's a root ПЕК; could there be a related root ПОК? Well, the word пéчень 'liver' is likely to be related to ПЕК; and the word пóчка 'kidney', derived from a now disappeared пока (dial. опока 'clay') could well be too, in which case there will indeed be ПОК. Note too the word пóчка 'bud'; but the root here is likely to be П/Т (= ПЪТ), which is related to Lithuanian *pùsti* 'to swell' (*putù* 'I swell') (buds swell before opening!). There is also the quite unrelated word пóчва 'soil': this word is a variation on подóшва 'sole', from подъшьва; the strictly correct modern form is подóшва; пóчва, which happens to mean 'sole' in West Slavonic languages, is a consequence of д and ш colliding, becoming тш (the voiced *d* becomes voiceless *t* in front of the voiceless *š*), and so ч.

Things can be brought back round to течь by referring to a related verb, мочь 'to be able', where we have г instead of к: non-past могу́, мóжешь, ..., мóгут, past мог, могла́. Well, we can assume the infinitive of течь goes back to *tekti (Ukrainian actually has текти́ in Ukrainian, but for another, more recent, reason: analogy with other infinitives; the *ti, incidentally, is a simplified version of what there was in Proto-Slavonic); so мочь might well go back to *mogti; the voiced *g* becomes *k* in front of the voiceless *t*; the group *kt in front of an front vowel becomes ч in Russian.[34]

Could we still be in the world of 'baking' with печáль? After all, sadness can 'burn', be painful. And that may well be the case here. The suffix appears in the form -áль, really the realization of -ѣль after a hushing consonant or *j*. Ask

---

[34]In this verb we can seem similarity with English *might*, German *die Macht* 'power' — being able is associated with power, with 'potency', something more transparent where мочь appears in its original nominal shape; мóчи нет 'I can't manage any more/haven't the strength', refleected nicely in Spanish *no puedo más*.

yourself why there are lots of second-conjugation verbs in -ать (including two in -ять), e.g. слышать 'to hear', стоять 'to be stood/standing'. They reflect what happened to conjugation-two verbs in -еть (the -е- was a *jat'* after *jot* and *k*, *g*, *x* which had, of course undergone the First Palatalization, e.g. such verbs as сидеть 'to be sat', видеть 'to see' (see 2.4 fn).

By the way, note a related meaning of печь in the structure печься о + prep. 'to take care of, look after' — note беспечный 'careless, carefree', опекун 'guardian, trustee'. Thus, 'care' goes with 'pain' and 'heat' and 'baking'.

4.3.23   *Free* — ВОЛ — СВОБОД (**vol-*, **svo(bod)-*)

In повелитель 'sovereign (rhet.)', used for Golding's *Lord of the Flies* Повелитель мух, we have a familiar structure. The perfective verb повелеть 'to command' is pairable with повелевать 'to command (+ instr.) (obs.); to enjoin (+ dat. + inf.)'; the verb велеть 'to command (neg. = "to forbid"' (+ dat. + inf. or + чтобы + past), non-past велю, велишь, велят, is biaspectual and related to воля 'freedom, will' (presumably someone who is free can give commands — control freakery has a long history), itself derived from a basic form visible in произвол 'arbitrariness; arbitrary rule'. Again, note the *e/o* alternation: ВЕЛ — ВОЛ.

The word воля is the typical, and very resonant, word for 'freedom' in Puškin. But we might be more familiar with свобода 'freedom' and the related adjective свободный 'free' and a verb such as освободить, imperf. освобождать 'to free'. In Serbo-Croat we have *svoboda* or *sloboda* 'freedom' (note the adjective *slobodan*, used as a name too), in Slovak *sloboda* 'id.', so, if we assume the form starting in *sv-* to be original, there might have been a labial dissimilation (*svob-* becoming *slob-*). In Polish we find *swoboda* and *świeboda*. The latter might suggest a *jat'* and emergence from **xv-*. But it can't, can it?[35] Might we justify **svob-* on semantic grounds? If we cast our mind around the vocabulary of Russian for words which look the same and have a possible semantic relationship, then свой 'one's (own) (etc.)' might seem likely. 'Freedom' is closely connected with a sense of self. So that is likely, and we might even consider a word such as особа 'person' and собственный 'one's own'. So far so good, but isn't there a quite different word in Russian too, namely слобода 'settlement'? Well, it does denote a settlement of free peasants, and we might want to see some link with the root СЕЛ 'settle', as in посёлок 'settlement'; but this is unlikely, though the resonance of the *-sl-* cannot be denied, prompting a casual link.

---

[35]No, because that change does not occur in the antecedent of Polish (so far as we are aware, and disregarding borrowing), as is clear from *kwiat* 'flower', *gwiazda* 'star'. And where would the **x* have come from, anyway?

4.3.24   *Give, know, stand* — ДА — ЗНА — СТА(Н) (**da-*, **zna-*, **stan-*)

These are the three roots in Russian with the suffix -ва- after a, where the -ва- is lost in the non-past and the present participle active: достаёт, достаю́щий, but доставая (imperfective gerund) 'take, get, obtain'. The three roots are ДА, ЗНА, and СТА(Н), as illustrated (for the last two) in узна́ть, non-past узна́ю, etc., imperf. узнава́ть, non-past узнаю́, etc. 'find out, recognize' and прода́ть, non-past прода́м, прода́шь, прода́ст, продади́м, продади́те, продаду́т, продава́ть, non-past продаю́, etc. 'sell'. It is difficult to give an explanation which covers all three. However, in the case of ДА there was also a verb дая́ти, probably iterative, at an earlier stage. This verb had non-past forms in даю, даеши, etc., and it is possible that this provided the modern imperfective forms. However, this leaves the end stress unexplained. Possibly the stress -ава́ть comes into it, and the need to differentiate between, say, узнава́ть and узна́ть in the non-past, namely узнаю́, узнаёшь — узна́ю, узна́ешь respectively. Basically, however, there is a uniform treatment of the imperfectives, with three different treatments of the perfectives: доста́ну, доста́нешь — узна́ю, узна́ешь — разда́м, разда́шь. Useful verbs include, for the 'stand' root: заста́ть, imperf. застава́ть 'to find someone somewhere/doing something': Я заста́л её на рабо́те, Ма́ша заста́ла сы́на спя́щим; приста́ть, imperf. пристава́ть 'to attach oneself to/tag along with (a group)' (к + dat.) and 'to pester someone (= к + dat.)', among other meanings; and отста́ть, imperf. отстава́ть от + gen. 'to lag behind; to be slow (of a watch)' (see 4.2.7.4); for the 'know' root: позна́ть, imperf. познава́ть 'to get to know, become acquainted with', созна́ть, imperf. сознава́ть 'to realize, be aware of' (refl. + в + prep. 'to confess (to)'), and призна́ть, imperf. признава́ть 'to recognize, acknowledge, deem' (refl. + в + prep. 'to confess, own up to'); and for the 'give' root: разда́ть, imperf. раздава́ть 'to distribute', изда́ть, imperf. издава́ть 'to publish; emit; utter', and вы́дать, imperf. выдава́ть 'to issue; betray; pass off as (+ за + acc.)'.

The last group cannot be left without mentioning the verb созда́ть, imperf. создава́ть 'to create', which follows this pattern too but has a strange prefix, namely соз-. Now, assuming the prefix in fact to be со- and the base verb to be дать, -з- is left over. Could зд then be the root, with the verb analogically transferring into the 'give' family? If we consult a dictionary we come up with, in addition to the unhelpful созда́ние 'creation' and созда́тель 'creator', the intriguing and lofty сози́да́ние, сози́да́тель (with the same respective meanings), and сози́да́тельный 'creative'. Given the patience to try lots of other prefixes (substitution is an excellent strategy in word-formation), we can come up with назида́ние 'edification' and назида́тельный 'edifying, instructive'; and if we look up the sequence зд with and without an intervening vowel (е and о, because those are the orthographic reflexes of strong *jers*) as absolute word-initial sequences, we encounter зда́ние 'building, *edifice*' (did you ever think what an odd Russian word this was?), зо́дчий 'architect', зо́дчество 'architecture', and зо́дческий 'architectural'. So we have З/Д, — but what *jer* do we have between the consonants? The historical evidence suggests the front *jer*, the soft sign, as indicated by созида́тельный, etc., with its lengthened front *jer*; there is, too, the actual verb созида́ть, which has an optional obsolete non-past созижду, etc. And, for instance, Serbo-Croat *zid* 'wall'. But what of зо́дчий, etc, with their o? Well, these forms are Church Slavonic, and the reduced palatalization of Church Slavonic could have played a role; and the form could be artificial and borrowed. If you're desperate, then you might even see it simply as an o inserted before two consonants, just as in разобра́ть 'to analyse', etc. Or there may be a reflection of ablaut or some sort of analogical development.

Note that ЗНА is much more familiar than we might imagine. It is, in fact, the same root as English *know*, and the essential link is given away by the *gn* we get in *gnosticism*, *recognize*, *know*, German *kennen*, etc. The Slavonic *z* is historically a Proto-Indo-European palatal *g.

And СТА(Н) is itself, as might be expected, linked to *stand*. The contentious area here might be the *n* and whether it is to be linked to the *n* found in verbs in -нуть and thus a member of that class of Slavonic verbs (see 2.4 fn). On balance it might be simpler to see it as a nasal infix (or suffix, given it is added to the root), such as is found in many verbs in many Indo-European languages — in Russian we have only to think of лечь — ля́гу 'lie down', сесть — ся́ду 'sit down', and быть — бу́ду 'be' (there is another, namely -брести́ 'find', as in изобрести́ 'to invent' and приобрести́ 'to acquire', where the non-past was -бра́щж before the verb was regularized on the плести́ — плету́ 'braid, plait' pattern.

And now for the real verb 'to know', fossilized nicely in the expression Бог весть! 'God knows!' Can весть be a verb form, or is it the noun весть 'item of news'? Well, nowadays either the latter or just a set phrase which we don't attempt to interpret. But there is есть '(there) is/are' (and, slightly altered, ест 'eats' and даст 'will give'), and indeed it does turn out that this is the third-person singular of the now-disappeared verb вѣдѣти 'to know'. Given the root ВѢД, this is an instance of ст from *tt from *dt, e.g. вести́ — веду́ 'lead'. The first-person singular вѣдѣ survives in the particle ведь 'after all, y'know'. Though the actual verb has disappeared,[36] the root is still very much present in Russian: языкове́дение 'linguistics', востокове́д 'orientalist', и́споведь 'confession (fem.)', *Моско́вские ве́домости The Moscow News*, све́дение 'piece of information' (compare сведе́ние, from the ВЕД root, 'reduction, settling'), све́дущий в + prep. 'knowledgeable about, well-versed in', дове́даться, non-past дове́даюсь, etc. (perf.) 'find out by asking', заве́домо 'wittingly, knowingly, known to be (+ adj.)', and probably заве́довать, non-past заве́дую, etc. (imperf.) + instr. 'be in charge of, manage' (заве́дующий +

---

[36]Though obsolete in the sense знать, a form ве́дать, non-past ве́даю, etc. is still used in the negative, mainly in set phrases, e.g. не ве́дает стра́ха 'knows no fear', and is fully used in the meaning 'to manage', as in он здесь ве́дает все́ми дела́ми 'he's in charge of all business here'.

instr. 'manager of, in charge of'). And we might mention зловещий 'sinister; ominous', with as second component the root ВѢД 'know', but in the form revealed in the noun весть 'he/she knows; item of news'; jotation of the group ст gave щ.[37]

Finally, it would not do to omit to mention свидетель 'witness'. Anyone coming across this word thinks of it as referring to someone who *sees*, or shares the seeing of, something. Actually, this is a case of 'popular etymology'. The word was съвѣдѣтель, because a 'witness' is someone who shares the *knowledge* of something, as indicated by *wit*. After all, English has a special word for a witness who sees, namely an *eyewitness*, as indeed does Russian: очевидец. (This should not prevent us from bearing in mind that at a very early stage 'seeing' and 'knowing' were probably related, something in fact suggested in the similarity of the Russian roots ВѢД and ВИД.)

4.3.25 *Happen* — ЛУЧ — ЛѪЧ (**luk-* — **lǫk-*)

We are most familiar with случиться, non-past случится, imperf. случаться, non-past случается 'happen'. That the component с- is the prefix съ- can be demonstrated by substitution, thus получить, imperf. получать 'to happen, улучить, imperf. улучать 'to seize, find (an opportunity)'. And we may come across the verb without a prefix, as in the expression Коли Бог лучит 'If God allows'. So there is a sense of 'give, grant, allow' in the simple verb. Something which happens is something which is somehow granted, allowed. Historical evidence indicates that there was no back nasal in the root, and there is a likelihood that the Lithuanian verb *láukti* 'to wait, expect' is cognate, both semantically and through the *w*-diphthong, which would give Slavonic **u*.

There are, however, verbs such as отлучить, non-past отлучу, отлучишь, ... отлучат, imperf. отлучать, non-past отлучаю + от + gen. 'separate (from), excommunicate', the reflexive meaning 'to be absent from' — note the noun отлучка 'absence'. Taking another prefix, we have разлучить, imperf. разлучать + acc. + с + instr. 'to separate X from Y', and reflexively + instr. 'to separate from', plus the noun разлука 'separation'. Even more, we have случить(ся), imperf. случать(ся) 'to couple, link (mate)'. So what is going on? Are these the same root? Well, the historical evidence indicates a back nasal, which can be linked with Lithuanian *lankýti* 'to visit'. This verb is linked to an adjective *lankùs* 'curved' and verb *leñkti* 'to bend', which we may bring back to Russian лук 'bow' (the weapon). We must suppose, and it is by no means out of the question, that, when we pay a visit, we make some sort of détour. If we look into dialect, we can find a verb such as ляцать 'to tense, bend' (this is very close

---

[37]Do not associate this adjective with вещь 'thing', a Church Slavonic word arising from Common Slavonic **vektь* — in Native Russian we would expect **вечь*. There may be a link with Latin *vōx* 'voice', something supported by the fact that речь 'speech' may mean 'thing' in other Slavonic languages.

to Lithuanian *leñkti*, plus a Third Palatalization; see Vasmer II:84), and a dog with a concave back may be referred to as a ляка. In Ukrainian лякáтися means 'to be frightened', and we can begin to see connections. Coming back to more concrete things, а лукá is a 'bend' in a river and a лукомóрье a 'creek', and we cannot but see some connection with лукáвый cunning'.

None the less, if asked to think of a Russian word for 'bend', those surveyed just now would not come to mind. In fact, you might first think of words of the 'turn' family, in which case take a look at 4.3.55. We would be amazed, but on mature reflection probably not (and, one might hope, certainly not after reading this book), just how much in our linguistic expression these days is ultimately based on, and doubtless still plugs seriously into, basic concepts of the simplest states and activities within space and time.

So, we might be inclined to think of поклони́ться, non-past поклоню́сь, покло́нишься, ... покло́нятся 'bow', with its intriguing imperfective кла́няться, non-past кла́няюсь, etc., with its -я- suffix and its expected (but not really without a prefix) root-vowel lengthening, but unexpected stress and absence of a prefix. All predicated on a basic verb клони́ть, non-past клоню́, кло́нишь, ... кло́нят 'bend, incline (tr.); drive at, insinuate (intr.; к + dat.)', which may be reflexive, with the senses 'bow; be approaching'. What we notice is that it has no perfective, and yet there is поклони́ться, which is paired with кла́няться. We must imagine that some reorientation has taken place here — it is always crucial to bear in mind that the descriptions we get of languages are based on many factors in addition to linguistic ones, particularly when a language is being codified and then given prestige through standardization. And there is an imperfective поклоня́ться + dat. 'to worship' — note there is no change in the root о. Quite possibly there is something expressive about the а of кла́няться, reinforced by its being placed under the stress. The root о of поклоня́ться *could* be an а, but it's never stressed, so all we have is the о of the etymological root. The root is probably cognate with Lithuanian *klãnas* 'puddle', essentially a depression, and with a long vowel we have *klõnis* 'low spot in a field' (*o* and *a* are basically reversed in Russian and Lithuanian). We might imagine links with Lithuanian *kálnas* 'mountain', Latin *collis* 'hill', Greek *klı̄nō* 'I lean over', thus *incline*. There are many other verbs in the family, e.g. наклони́ться, imperf. наклоня́ться 'to stoop', накло́нность 'inclination', отклони́ться, imperf. отклоня́ться 'to diverge', склон 'slope', скло́нен 'inclined'. Not, however, слон 'elephant', though there is the very useful (not related to сло́н) verb прислони́ться, imperf. прислоня́ться + к + dat. 'to lean (against)'. Here the *s* is problematic. Both seem related, so could one of them somehow reflect a Proto-Indo-European palatal **k*?

And as a last example, we might be familiar with нагну́ться, non-past нагну́сь, нагнёшься, ... нагну́тся, imperf. нагиба́ться, нагиба́юсь, etc., 'bend down, stoop'. From this we imagine imperfective and intransitive гну́ть, which means 'to bend; cringe; insinuate' — note the similarity to клони́ться. The derived imperfective indicates a root Г/Б — which *jer* comes between? It has to be the back *jer* (rather its antecedent), otherwise there would have been a First Palatalization here. So: ГЪБ. The lengthened root vowel in the derived imperfective was *$*y$, which eventually became *i* after the velar. The consonant group *$*bn$ simplified to *n*. The verb developed a perfective согнýть, with a semantically appropriate prefix: 'down'. The root has a sense of 'bend, fold'. In Modern Russian we find also гúбнуть 'to perish (imperf.)', doubtless related to a disappeared iterative гибáть. The retention of *bn* suggests a less remote development. Modern Russian also has погибáть 'to perish', and the shared perfective is погúбнуть. We find a somewhat similar form in Latvian, namely *gūbuoties* 'to bend down' (remember the long *$*ū$ gives *$*y$). There is no semantic problem in associating 'bending low' with 'perishing'. An ablaut form gives the transitive form губúть, non-past гублю́, гýбишь, ... гýбят, perf. погубúть 'to destroy', which in most other Slavonic languages means 'to lose'. Recall that there is no nasal here, so the root should not be confused with that of губá 'lip', which does have an original back nasal: *$*gǫba$, Polish *gęba*.

4.3.26 *Healthy* — ЦѢЛ — (СЪ)ДОРОВ (*$*cěl-$ — *$*(sъ)dorv-$)

Coming in at a tangent, for лекáрство 'medicine' we can refer to English *leech*. The root is ЛЕК, and can be seen in лечúть 'to treat', with the к was palatalized to ч. The word family is almost certainly ultimately from Germanic: Gothic had *lēkeis* 'doctor' and in Swedish, for example, we still have *läkare* 'doctor'. With an agent suffix we have лéкарь 'doctor', the standard word in several Slavonic languages — the stress indicates it may be from a form of Polish *lekarz*. Note that the e does not become ё, indicating that it was originally *$*ě$, something immediately clear from Ukrainian лікáр, with its i, a vowel which in that particular position (an open syllable) is more than likely to have come from *$*ě$ in that language.

Целéбный 'healing, medicinal' is related ultimately to цéлый, the same word as English 'hale, healthy'. The form we need can be found in Old Prussian *kailīstiskan* 'health', where *kail-* reflects the source needed for цел- (ЦѢЛ) — a *j*-diphthong which by becoming *$*ě$ would create the conditions for the Second Palatalization. From цел-, with the suffix -ьба, there is a form цельба; if to this we add the adjectival suffix -ьн-, giving цѣльбьн-, we have the basis for a quite regular derivation of целебн-.[38]

---

[38] The two other velars affected by the Second Palatalization are reflected in друзья́ 'friends', plural of друг — there has been suffix substitution here, but the original consonantal alternation of the old nominative plural, дру́зи, has been retained, and in седóй 'grey (of hair)', where there is a root СЕД (with an e which never becomes ё, thus originally *$*ě$, in Cyrillic ѣ). Along with the more general word for 'grey', сéрый, which has a similar origin, седóй may be related to *hoary*. That it seems cognate with *hoary* and that we have *š* in West Slavonic (the WSl reflex of *$*x$ under the Second Palatalization), e.g., Polish *szady*, indicate that this must be a case of the Second

Now for another word to do with 'health'. In дре́вний 'old, ancient' there is a Church Slavonic metathetic form, древ-, derived with the adjectival suffix and soft endings, to fit a sense of time (adjectives with a sense of place and time are very often soft, ending in -ний, e.g., ле́тний 'summer', зде́шний 'local'. The root, ДРЕВ (with *jat'* in Church Slavonic), is, as we might expect, related to pleophonic ДЕРЕВ. Celtic is quite nice here: in Breton *derv* means 'oak-trees'. The same root with a different vowel reveals a link to здоро́вый, здоро́вье 'healthy, health', thus a suggestion of strength. We might wonder about the prefix з-. Well, a hard sign has dropped here, bringing the original consonant, $*s$, up against the $*d$ and causing its voicing to z; since it is reflected in the spelling, it must be ancient. But $*su$- is normally linked to meanings of co-, 'with'. But not this time, as we already saw with смерть (see 4.3.18). This is an ancient formant, meaning 'well', and found in *swastika*, originally a token of 'well-being' ($*su$ + $*asti$ 'be, is' in Sanskrit; incidentally, an *āstika* in Sanskrit is 'he who believes in the existence of something', thus a 'theist', while a *nāstika* is 'he who does not believe in the existence of something', thus an 'atheist'). Though it is not the same formant, we have identical voicing in здесь 'here': from сь 'this' + де '"place"' + сь 'this', a big like 'this place 'ere'. And compare где 'where', from къ 'what' + де '"place"'. It makes sense, and we can confirm such things from Celtic, e.g. Breton *pe* 'what' + *lec'h* 'place' giving *pelec'h* 'where'.

And what of Russian вра́ч 'doctor'? In Bulgarian and Serbo-Croat the meaning is resp. 'magician' and 'fortune-teller', which suggests a link to врать, non-past вру, врёшь, ... врут 'to lie, fib', itself related to ворча́ть, non-past ворчу́, ворчи́шь, ... ворча́т 'to mutter, grumble'.

4.3.27   Include — КЛЮЧ (*$kl'uč$, *$kl'uk$-)

These verbs are fine examples of calques, Slavonic elements focussing on the zero-suffix and zero-ending noun ключ 'key' being used render Latin *claudō* 'I shut', found widely in Indo-European and ultimately cognate with the Slavonic root itself. In Latin we also find *clāvis* 'key' (giving Russian кла́виш(а) 'piano/typewrieter key (masc. and fem.)' via Polish) and *clāvus* 'nail' (French *clé* and *clou* respectively), and in Lithuanian *kliùti* 'to hook (on)' and *kliáuti* 'to bend'

Palatalization. If it were the First (remember that *jat'* developed in two stages), the original *jat'* would have become *a* and we would have ша-. Thus, in Common Slavonic we would have had something like *$xojd$-.

As another example of an adjective in -ебный we might take вражде́бный 'hostile', with the suffix on the Church Slavonic root ВРАГ. We find the Native Russian equivalent, ворог-, in обворожи́ть, imperf. обвора́живать 'to bewitch'. Враг 'enemy' also means 'devil', which helps understand its relationship to the verb. The adjective is formed on the noun вражда́, which has to be враг plus a suffix -ьда, the soft sign changing the г to ж through the First Palatalization — in other words, this word is Church Slavonic through metathesis, not through жд, which has a quite other source here.

— all these examples, and historical and comparative evidence within Slavonic, e.g. Polish *klucz*, makes it clear there was no back nasal here. This brings us to Russian клюка́ 'walking-stick; crook, staff'. Within all this we think of how we close something, e.g. a door, by using a hook. Whether all this is linked with the other meaning of ключ, namely 'spring, source', is uncertain, but it seems likely, given water-divining sticks and the idea of a source being something we 'tap' (in German *erschließen*, where *schließ* is cognate). Thus in Russian we have such verbs as включи́ть 'to include, turn on', вы́ключить 'to turn off, remove', исключи́ть 'to exclude', заключи́ть 'to conclude, shut', подключи́ть 'to attach, connect' (refl. 'to settle down; to tap into, say, a debate (к + dat.)', and many other variations, all regular second-conjugation verbs and with imperfectives in -ключа́ть, non-past -ключа́ю, etc. You can find ключи́ть in Dal' II 1905:308.

4.3.28 *Jump* — ПРЫГ (ПРѦГ, ПРѦГ) — СКАК, СКОК, СКОЧ (*pryg- (*prǫg-, *pręg-) — *skak-, *skok-, *skoč-)

The verb пры́гать, non-past пры́гаю, etc. retains its stress and is essentially a root ПРЫГ expanded by the suffix *a and also by the semelfactive suffix, thus пры́гнуть, non-past пры́гну, пры́гнешь, ... пры́гнут. These might be seen now as an aspectual 'pair'. We might expect derivatives, e.g. 'to jump over', to offer perfective перепры́гнуть with imperfective перепрыга́ть, but the imperfective is in fact перепры́гивать. The same goes for other derived pairs. Another verb structured like пры́гать is толка́ть, non-past толка́ю, etc., semelfactive толкну́ть, non-past толкну́, толкнёшь, ... толкну́т 'to push'. Derivatives here are similar, e.g. оттолкну́ть, imperf. отта́лкивать 'to push away; antagonize; repel'. There are other verbs apparently with this sort of pattern, e.g. дви́гать and дви́нуть 'to move', but here the derived imperfectives are in -двига́ть and the non-past is or can be on the писа́ть model, i.e. дви́жу, дви́жешь, ... дви́жут, whereas пры́гать and толка́ть never exhibit that pattern. Perhaps there is a significant difference here. There are ablaut and nasal insertion links here with roots manifested in such words as упру́гий 'taut, resilient', пружи́на 'spring' (the verb and noun *spring* is itself related), запря́чь non-past запрягу́, запряжёшь, ... запрягу́т, imperf. запряга́ть, non-past запряга́ю 'harness (= "tighten")'.

Another common verb for 'to jump' is скака́ть, which does conjugate on the писа́ть pattern: скачу́, ска́чешь, ... ска́чут. It more commonly, when underived, means 'to gallop'. Here there is a root enlarged by *a and *i (see below), hence the First Palatalization. Other examples include -лага́ть and -ложи́ть 'to put', ката́ть and кати́ть 'to roll', ступа́ть and ступи́ть 'to step' — and we might argue for inclusion here of the вида́ть — ви́деть, слыха́ть — слы́шать pattern. On the whole we do not have imperfectivization through the suffix -ыв(а)- here. However, as stated above, СКАК does have it, e.g. соскочи́ть, non-past соскочу́, соско́чишь, ... соско́чат, imperf. соска́кивать, non-past соска́киваю, etc. 'jump off/down'. Perhaps a factor to bear in mind is the lesser frequency of the semelfactive — of course, times change and whatever went on in the past fades into the etymological fog, and nothing prevents any semantically appropriate verb exploiting that suffix now.

4.3.29   *Learn, habit* — УК (УЧ), ВЫК (*uk- (*uč-), *vyk-)

In the noun учи́тельская 'teachers' room' the root is УЧ and the closest links are to учи́ть, учу́, у́чишь, ... у́чат 'teach' and учи́тель 'teacher'. There are two suffixes (three if we include -и-) and the adjectival ending indicates ellipsis of ко́мната 'room' (think, though it's really quite trivial, of the meanings of столо́вая, and how the word has become liberated from the 'room' sense). We can assume the ч comes from к, something confirmed by the related нау́ка 'science'. Now, у arises either from a diphthong ending in *w, or from a nasal like that in French *bon*. A diphthong in *u* (a *w*-diphthong) may be expected to be in alternation with the vowel *u*, short and long. Well, 'to learn/study' (учи́ться, etc.) means 'to become accustomed to learning', and there is at least the verb привыка́ть, perf. привы́кнуть к + dat. 'to get used to', and related nouns like привы́чка 'habit', обы́чай (б в > б) 'custom' (обыкнове́нный 'ordinary', обы́чный 'usual'), not to mention the fact that приучи́ться, imperf. приучи́ваться к + dat. actually does mean 'to get used to'; or indeed antonyms such as отвыка́ть, отучи́ться. So there's the connection, with the *v* arising as a prosthetic consonant when the long *u* was at the beginning of the word — creating an open syllable (subsequently a prefix could be added).

4.3.30   *Listen, hear* — СЛЫХ (СЛУШ)— СЛУХ (СЛУШ) (*slyš-, *slyx-, *sluš-, *slux-)

Вы́слушать, non-past вы́слушаю, etc., imperf. выслу́шивать, non-past выслу́шиваю, etc. 'to hear out; auscult' is a regular derivation from the source verb слу́шать, non-past слу́шаю, etc. 'listen (to)', which we can link with слух 'hearing; ear (fig.)', слы́шать, non-past слы́шу, слы́шишь, ... слы́шат 'hear', and arguably even слы́ть, non-past слыву́, слывёшь, ... слыву́т + instr' 'have a reputation as ...',   сло́во 'word', and сла́ва 'glory'. We can relatively immediately perceive the sense of sound and fame. There are many derivatives of слу́шать, particularly useful ones including подслу́шать, imperf. подслу́шивать 'to eavesdrop' (of course, we must argue here: the perfective would be more appropriately translated as 'to overhear', i.e. a limited eavesdropping action), and прислу́шаться, imperf. прислу́шиваться к + dat. 'to listen (carefully) to, heed; get used to a particular sound'. A perfective corresponding to слу́шать might be послу́шать in the senses 'to listen for a little' and 'to obey' (also reflexive, constructed with the genitive, though we encounter it with the accusative, e.g. я слу́шаюсь жену́ 'I obey my wife'). In the sense 'to attend a lecture', its perfective might be прослу́шать, and in the sense 'to hear a case, a pronouncement', one might have заслу́шать.The form found in Belarusian and Ukrainian is respectively слу́хаць and слу́хати. Polish has the equivalent of both, *słuchać* meaning both 'to listen (to)' and 'to obey'. This verb is cognate with Lithuanian *klausýti* 'to listen to; obey' ('to listen to' is also refl. *klausýtis*, + gen.; 'to obey', related but with an ablauted form, is also *paklùsti* — 'to hear' is *girdéti*). Note the *w*-diphthong, nicely parallelling у.

Слы́шать, as we've seen, is second-conjugation. Given that there is a nuance of onomatopœia here, we can imagine an origin in **slyxĕti*, the *jat'* causing the First Palatalization and changing to *a* after a husher, just like молча́ть 'to be silent', визжа́ть 'to squeal', etc. The perfective is услы́шать, particularly used in the infinitive and non-past, otherwise tending to require a sense of 'catch sound, "hearing" of' — in other words, just as with 'sight': ви́деть — уви́деть (see 4.3.33). We very often come across слыха́ть, doubtless originally iterative, with equivalent usage to вида́ть.

So, everything is perfectly clear. Or is it? Why, for instance, is слу́шать first-conjugation? We are told that it arises from **sluxĕti*. But this would give a second-conjugation verb. Now, this makes sense, as the *Look, see* family (4.3.33) has смотре́ть as rough equivalent to слу́шать, and смотре́ть is second-conjugation. Perhaps слу́шать has moved into the First Conjugation or started off as first-conjugation (was it iterative?) and acquired ш by analogy with слы́шать. At least this helps us understand why so many people confuse the non-past of слу́шать and слы́шать.

Here we might briefly mention several other connected things. First, the verb слыть, слыву́, слывёшь, ... слыву́т + instr. 'to have a reputation as...'which had an earlier non-past слову́, etc. and in Old Church Slavonic was СЛОⰖТИ, СЛОВⰀ, etc. In Latvian one has *klūt*, 3ps. *kluva* 'become well-known'. There has been a reshaping of the verb here. Going further back, i.e. referring to other languages, one finds Greek *kleō* 'I praise' and Latin *inclutus* 'famous'. In Breton *klevout* means 'to hear'. So there was a Proto-Indo-European palatal **k'*. This also fits in with сло́во 'word' and сла́ва 'glory', the sense of 'fame' being readily attestable in other languages and сло́во being an instance of ablaut (short **o* as against the long vowel of сла́ва). You will have noted the *e* in the examples from Greek and Breton; in the position before **w*, which this is, **e* regularly became **o*, cf. *new* — но́вый.

4.3.31 *Live* — ЖИВ (**živ-*)

In жиле́ц 'lodger' there is a suffix -/ц- (= -ьц-), the ц arising from к. The ultimate root has to be ЖИВ, with the *v* disappearing before a consonant: живу́ — жи ть, жил. This looks like the First Palatalization, and we find the sort of form required in Lithuanian *gývas* 'living, alive', which together with жив- is related to English *quick* (as in 'judge between the quick and the dead'). Another linked word is probably жир 'fat', with a suffix -р-; in other words, you have been fed.

The adjective жило́й 'living, residential, inhabited' here provided the stem жил (also to be seen it in жилпло́щадь 'floorspace, accommodation', from жила́я пло́щадь). Why 'stem'? Well, because the л is a suffix which also provided the past tense and was initially some sort of 'resultative participle'. There still are quite a few 'long forms' of past tenses, e.g. уме́лый 'skilful' — уме́л 'knew how to' (уме́ть), уста́лый 'tired' — уста́л 'tired' (уста́ть), сме́лый 'daring, brave' — смел 'dared' (сметь), про́шлый 'last' (but one/now)' — прошёл/прошла́ 'passed' (пройти́), etc., блёклый — блёк 'faded' (блёкнуть), all usually from intransitive verbs.

As another example we might take спе́шка 'hurry', which reflects a root СПЕХ (another е which never becomes ё, i.e. another *jat'*, *ě*, something confirmed from Lithuanian *spéti* 'to manage to', where *ė* reflects an earlier long *e*, which is partly what *jat'* is). This might suggest a link with спеть 'to ripen' (спе́лый 'ripe') and, of course, успе́ть 'to manage to, to succeed in, to have time to' — we mature over time; and from this we can make the jump to спеши́ть 'to hurry'. Remember that х in front of -/к(а) (= -ьк(а)) becomes ш — the First Palatalization again. Also see 4.3.42.

Coming back to the past tense, we see that Russian precisely does have 'I done': я сде́лал(а). Earlier in the history of Russian, and still clearly reflected in various ways in other Slavonic languages, the *l*-participle was accompanied by an auxiliary verb in the form of the verb 'to be'. Various tenses of this verb could be used, but most commonly we had the present tense, providing the 'perfect tense', namely 'I have done', etc. But the verb быть in Russian hardly has a present tense. In other words, it has lost it. The indications are that it was first lost in phrases of the type 'Ivan is a teacher'; given this, it was omitted in the third person forms of the perfect tense, rendering the expression of the subject or subject pronoun crucial, something which extended to the other persons ('I, you, we, you'). This partly explains why the subject pronouns tend to be expressed in Russian, although the endings of all but the third-person singular of the non-past make it quite clear who or what the subject is. And, for the past, we no longer talk of first-person, etc., forms since everything is based on the gender of the subject in the singular, whatever the person, and in the plural gender has been lost, so we have just one form, which, with its ending -и and softening of the л, is not identical with the short adjective ('we are tired' is мы уста́ли). Perhaps the verbal character and sense of animacy is conveyed by the retention of -и.

4.3.32   *Load* — ГРѪЗ — ГРАЗ (*grǫz- — *gręz-)

Coming back to 'loading' from another direction in order to note an example of just how complex verbal usage can be, we normally have по-грузи́ть (гружу́, гру́зишь, ... гру́зят) това́ры на + acc. 'to load goods onto ...', and на-грузи́ть or нагружа́ть/нагрузи́ть кора́бль това́рами 'to load a ship with goods'. Погружа́ть/погрузи́ть is most often used in the sense of 'to dip something into something' or, reflexively, 'to sink down into, to plunge into, to become immersed/engrossed in' ('in, into' here = в + acc.). Thus он погрузи́лся в себя́ 'he sank into thought', сестра́ была́ погружена́ в размышле́ния 'my sister was deep in thought'. And this word family is linked to грязь 'dirt', which is known to only a few Slavonic languages. An old verb, грязѣ́ти, гря́знути, meant 'to sink, get stuck', from which we can imagine a link with погрузи́ться 'to sink into, become engrossed in' and the word груз 'load, cargo'. Thus, 'loads, burdens', and getting stuck in mud! In грязь there is a derivation with a -ь (*i) theme, as often happens, while in груз there is a zero-suffix.

Note too that the root vowel in грязь indicates a former front nasal vowel, and the evidence is for a back nasal vowel in the root in груз. At this point we might wish to link гру́стный 'sad', for semantic reasons. However, there is no evidence of a nasal vowel in гру́стный (though this doesn't have to rule a link out), and the indications are instead for a link with гру́да 'heap' and a root such as discerned in Slovenian *skrb me grudi* 'worry burdens/saddens me'.

4.3.33   *Look, see* — (СЪ)МОТ(Р) — ГЛАД — ЗЬР and ЗЪР — ВИД — МѢТ (*(sь)motr-*, *ględ-*, *zьr-* and *zor-*, *vid-*, *mět-*)

As usual we can start with a word other than the obvious one: вы́глядеть, non-past вы́гляжу, вы́глядишь, ... вы́глядят + instr. 'look (sad, etc.), have a (sad, etc.) appearance', e.g. Она́ вы́глядит гру́стной 'She looks sad'. There is nothing particularly interesting about this at first sight. But verbal calques are often slightly anomalous, and вы́глядеть, which is one, is no exception. Basically we would expect a prefixed simple verb to be perfective, but вы́глядеть, as might be expected from its meaning, is imperfective-only. Then, we might have read or been told that the prefix вы- is always stressed in perfective verbs. From вы́глядеть we can see that the rule should be that the prefix вы- is stressed when it is prefixed to a simple verb. And вы́глядеть is a calque of Polish *wyglądać*, itself a calque of German *aussehen*, literally 'out-see', thus *er sieht gut aus* 'he looks good'. Note that we just wrote that the Russian verb was a calque of the Polish verb, not a borrowing from Polish. Russian uses its only extant verb form, гляде́ть, whereas Polish has *glądać* — in other words, Polish gives us another, possibly iterative, form, which would have given выгляда́ть in Russian, but didn't — but below ви́деть and вида́ть 'to see', which *do* occur, will be considered.

By the way, the perfective verb with the expected meaning, i.e. 'to look out, peep out', is вы́глянуть, non-past вы́гляну, вы́глянешь, ... вы́глянут with imperfective выгля́дывать, non-past выгля́дываю, etc. Another example is взгляну́ть, imperfective взгля́дывать на + acc. 'to glance at'. Now, are these regular? Well, yes; we just have to note that when *d* and *n* came together the *d* dropped out; and we can suppose that the perfectives to some extent retain a semelfactive, one-time-only, nuance. Now, leafing through a dictionary we will find пригляде́ть, non-past пригляжу́, пригляди́шь, ... пригля́дят 'choose, find, look out for (for oneself)', with imperfective пригля́дывать, non-past приглядываю, etc. — constructed with за + instr. there is a sense 'look after'. Reflexively, with к + dat., they mean 'to look closely at, get used to, to tire/bore (impersonally, with the person bored in the dative and the things boring as grammatical subject)', the last two with an association with one's eyes getting used to something or bored by something, e.g. Áнна пригляде́лась к темноте́ 'Anna got used to the dark' (only with things one's pupils actually do adjust to, so somehow not to тума́н 'mist'), and Са́ше давно́ пригляде́лся э́тот плака́т на стене́ 'Sasha is long since tired of that poster on the wall' (not with films or things that move). And there is приглянýться + dat., perfective-only and colloquial, referring to someone's appearance taking someone's fancy, e.g. Гварде́ец приглянýлся ей 'She took a fancy to/liked the look of the Guardsman'. So note that гляде́ть with a preverb or prefix does not *have* to become -глянýть when perfective. To illustrate this yet again, here is another example: разгляде́ть 'to make out, discern', a perfective verb. Does it have an imperfective? Well, yes and no. Yes, in that there is a verb разгля́дывать 'to examine closely, scrutinize', so it looks a nice neat pair from the morphological point of view. But on semantic grounds we might quibble, since, as indicated already, the perfective means 'to make out, discern', and the imperfective 'to examine closely, scrutinize' — aren't they really two separate, single-aspect verbs? Perhaps we shouldn't quibble, as we can easily imagine 'making something out' being the end result of 'scrutinizing something', and we can note that разгля́дывать can have the familiar conative (= 'attempting') nuance of imperfectives, thus 'to try to discern'. There is a similar problem with lots of verbs: иска́ть can mean 'to look for' or 'to try to find', with arguable perfectives like поиска́ть 'to have a little look for something' and найти́ 'to find' (more the true perfective of иска́ть, at least if we see 'perfective' as essentially 'resultative').

Note, by the way, that -глянýть has mobile stress, which is quite unusual in such perfectives and that there is a *perfective* verb гля́нуть на + acc. 'to glance at', itself with an unusual stress. As for гляде́ть, remember that it is second-conjugation and that the stress is fixed on the ending: гляжý, гляди́шь,... глядя́т, but, oddly, the imperfective (or present, if you prefer) gerund is гля́дя. Though the connection is difficult to prove, odd stresses in imperfective gerunds often go hand-in-hand with them having turned into something other than gerunds. Thus сто́я, лёжа, си́дя, respectively 'standing, lying, sitting' are now adverbs and have more or less replaced the ending-stressed gerunds proper (think of their equivalents in French, i.e. *debout, couché*, and *assis*); сýдя по + dat. 'judging by' may have its unexpected stress because part of a composite preposition; perhaps this explains гля́дя, namely гля́дя по + dat. 'depending on', though it also has that stress as a gerund (and there is no change in, for example, несмотря́ на + acc. 'in spite of'); and, particularly fascinating, благодаря́ + dat. 'thanks to', which keeps its stress but takes an unexpected case. Why does it take the dative when, if it is indeed the imperfective gerund of благодари́ть, it should be the accusative, since that verb takes the accusative: я поблагодари́л его́ 'I thanked him'. Well, the answer might be that the actual gerund *does* take the accusative: Благодаря́ его́, я улыбну́лся 'Thanking him, I smiled'. The preposition is a specialized usage of the gerund which, if you think about it, doesn't actually mean 'thanking...' and can, in non-standard Russian, actually be negative, i.e. благодаря́ его́ глу́пости 'thanks to his stupidity' (Kornej Čukovskij acknowledged this by warning against it ages ago). There may be some sort of calquing going on here, since the dative is widespread in prepositions with this meaning, and it is possible that earlier usage, where the verb took both the accusative and the dative, has been rationalized in this way.

Remember that second-conjugation verbs in -еть, -ать, and -ять tend to have the stress on the non-past endings, thus сиди́шь 'you are seated', молчи́шь 'you are silent', лежи́шь 'you lie', кричи́шь 'you shout', стои́шь 'you are stood', бои́шься 'you are afraid', though we must note exceptions such as держа́ть, держу́, де́ржишь, ..., де́ржат 'hold' and смотре́ть, смотрю́, смо́тришь, ..., смо́трят 'look, watch'. If the stress comes earlier, it stays there: ви́деть, ви́жу, ви́дишь, ..., ви́дят 'see', and слы́шать, слы́шу, слы́шишь, ..., слы́шат 'hear'.

The root ГЛЯД (from the point of view of the modern language) includes the vowel я which, as often occurs, conceals an earlier nasal vowel, reflected in the Polish example given above, namely *wyglądać*. The root itself may be ultimately linked to the antecedents of German *der Glanz* 'brilliance', *glänzen* 'to gleam, be shiny', so we might assume a semantic journey from 'radiation of light' to 'glancing' to looking (for)' to just plain 'looking'!

The standard verb for 'watch, look (at)' is смотре́ть, non-past смотрю́, смо́тришь, ... смо́трят, perfective usually посмотре́ть, constructed with на + acc. when in the sense 'look at' and with the straight accusative when in the sense 'watch', very like English on the surface, though there are differences of detail: compare я смотрю́ на телеви́зор 'I look at the TV' and я смотрю́ телеви́зор 'I watch TV'. With other perfectives the sense changes significantly, thus осмотре́ть 'to examine, look over', imperfective осма́тривать, non-past осма́триваю, etc., and рассмотре́ть 'to discern; examine', approximate imperfective рассма́тривать 'to regard; scrutinize'. From these examples it is clear that смотр behaves as a root. However, in dialects we find мотре́ть and such a root is used in parts of South Slavonic, e.g. Serbo-Croat *mòtriti* 'to watch' (incidentally, in the church language we may also find jotation *over* the *r*: МОТРНТН, МОЩРНЖ). In Slavonic we always find the final *r*, but if we go outside Slavonic then we may find the root without it, e.g, Lithuanian *matýti* 'to see'. So МОТР turns out to have a suffix **r* too.

Coming to another group, озира́ться, non-past озира́юсь, etc. is imperfective-only, with a root ЗЬР, the secondary lengthening in the imperfective formation changing the antecedent of ь (a short *i*) to that of и (a long *i*) as already encountered. In a sense we assert this by assuming a form озре́ться, or there is simply analogy with forms like зреть, non-past зрю, зришь, ... зрят 'see' and презре́ть, non-past презрю́, etc. 'get a feeling of disdain' (презира́ть 'to despise' might not be felt to be its imperfective). Презре́ть is possibly quite rare, but it is definitely 'there', given derivations like презре́ние 'contempt', презре́нный 'contemptible', and презри́тельный 'contemptuous'. Note how the nuance 'contempt' is given through the concrete meaning of the verb, namely looking over the top of someone, not into their eyes. At this point note подозрева́ть, non-past подозрева́ю, etc. 'suspect' (its perfective might be заподо́зрить + acc. + в + prep., the same construction as for подозрева́ть). It certainly has the same root, given that it is probably a calque of something like *suspect*, lit. 'under-look'.

Is there a link with зреть, зре́ю, зре́ешь,... зре́ют 'ripen'? After all, given derivations here like созре́ть, imperf. созрева́ть 'to ripen', there indeed may well have been a confusion. The two verbs may not be related, in spite of having the same basic infinitive, but, after all, when something ripens, it becomes more visible. In the 'ripening' sense we can note some probable relatedness to English *grain, corn* and Russian зерно́ 'grain'.

Now for 'to see': ви́деть, non-past ви́жу, ви́дишь, ... ви́дят does not have a straightforward perfective, though the situation may be regularizing by analogy (note how we have a very similar situation with у-слы́шать). Уви́деть is a normal perfective mainly in the future and infinitive; not, however, in the past, where it tends to have the nuance 'catch sight of, notice'. The root, ВИД, is linked to *video* and thus Latin *videō* 'I see' and verbs of 'knowing' (see 4.3.24). There is also a form вида́ть, perf. увида́ть, which tends to be seen as colloquial, but may also have a greater frequency when negative and in the past. Though it certainly has a perfective, it should be clear that its form, with -а́ть and no indication of jotation, might indicate an ancient, iterative, form. Finally, mindful of презира́ть and its concrete meaning, we might also recall оби́деть, non-past оби́жу, оби́дишь, ... оби́дят, imperf. обижа́ть, non-past обижа́ю, etc., the imperfective clearly derived by jotation. Historically this is *ob- + *viděti (with the consonant group simplifying to *b*), in other words 'looking around someone' and so not looking straight at them, thus 'offend, insult'. In this negative context we might mention ненави́деть, non-past ненави́жу, etc., near-perf. возненави́деть 'hate'. This is a negated form of a verb нави́деть 'to like seeing, to look (someone) up', found more commonly in, say, Polish and Ukrainian, thus resp. *nawidzieć* and нави́дітися — in Russian we may have не нагляде́ться на + acc. 'not to get to see enough of'. We might think of similar turns of phrase in English and French, e.g. *I can't stand the sight of him* and *je ne peux pas le voir*. Note that ненави́деть is not perfective, something which may reflect its slight oddity (a negative and double prefix). Its meaning 'hating' is basically imperfective, unless we suddenly *conceive* a hatred (thus возненави́деть). And recall that prefixes did not originally automatically trigger perfectivity (since it had not really evolved then in the form it has in Modern Russian), but rather just a semantic limitation on the lexical meaning of the verb.

Finally, and because I was often told to use заме́тить by my first native-speaker teacher when unsure about уви́деть (and for a bit of variety), the root МѢТ. Заме́тить, non-past заме́чу, заме́тишь, ... заме́тят, imperf. замеча́ть, замеча́ю, etc. 'notice' is to do with making a mark and measuring, aiming, doing something well. There is a simple verb ме́тить 'to mark' (originally to make cuts or marks in something, for the purpose of measuring) and a large family of derivatives, including nouns and adjectives, e.g. отме́тка 'note; exam mark', замеча́ние 'remark', ме́ткий 'appropriate', сметли́вый 'quick on the uptake', замеча́тельный 'remarkable'. Note how the imperfective derivation is regular and East Slavonic. Намека́ть, non-past намека́ю, etc. на + acc. or о + prep. 'hint at, refer to' must be related to a dialect word мекать meaning 'to understand'. It could be derived from ме́тить. Its perfective is намекну́ть, non-past намекну́, намекнёшь, ... намекну́т, and there is a zero-suffix noun намёк 'hint'. Does this strengthen the argument for a link with МѢТ? Soft *t* and *k* often get confused, by the way, and that 'confusion' is a feature of Moscow-region dialects.[39]

4.3.34 *Love, like* — ЛЮБ — НОРОВ — НРАВ (*l'ub-*, *norv-*)

Most familiar here is the verb люби́ть, non-past люблю́, лю́бишь, ... лю́бят, conveying a state; its near-perfective, полюби́ть, will have the sense of 'fall in love with'. The origin is an an adjectival form *l'ubъ*, with the root found in Lithuanian *liaupsě* 'song of praise', *liáupsinti* 'to praise', Latin *lubet* / *libet* 'is pleasing', *lubīdō* / *libīdō* '(carnal) desire', and with correspondences also in Germanic and Sanskrit, among other Indo-European languages and groups. Note the closeness to ХОТ, as in по́хоть 'lust (fem.)'. We can derive verbs in the usual way, though two suffixes are exploited: влюби́ться, imperf. влюбля́ться 'to fall in love', недолю́бливать + acc./gen. 'not to be too fond of; to be no love lost between'. And see 4.3.57.

We use нра́виться, non-past нра́влюсь, нра́вишься, ... нра́вятся, perf. понра́виться 'to please' to convey a similar meaning, with the object of the emotion functioning as grammatical subject (in the nominative case) and the source of the emotion in the dative case. In Russian we have reflexes of pleophony and inversion here: но́ров 'custom; obstinacy (both obs.)', норови́ть, non-past норовлю́, норови́шь, ... норовя́т 'aim at, strive to (+ inf.); strive to become (+ в + nom.-acc.pl.)', and нрав 'character, disposition', and нра́виться. We find cognate forms in Lithuanian *nóras* 'desire', *noréti* 'to desire, want', and Sanskrit *nar-* and Greek *anēr* 'man'.

4.3.35 *Move* — ДВИГ(Н) (*dvig-*)

In раздви́нуть, non-past раздви́ну, раздви́нешь, ... раздви́нут, imperf. раздвига́ть, non-past раздвига́ю, раздвига́ешь, ... раздвига́ют 'to move/slide apart, draw (curtains)' there is the loss of the root г in the perfective, because of the consonant group, just as in вы́тянуть. The prefix раз- has the sense of 'apart'. It may be used intransitively, with -ся attached. Note here the stress of

---

[39]Basically, no, because *jat'* would not give ё.

the imperfective, as if there had been a perfective раздвигать, given that the simple form of the verb is двигать. We've had the same situation with some other verbs, e.g. сыпать, non-past сыплю, сыплешь, ... сыплют 'pour, strew' (see *Sleep*), résaть, non-past ре́жу, ре́жешь, ... ре́жут 'cut': рассыпать, imperf. рассыпать, non-past рассыпаю, рассыпаешь, ... рассыпают 'spill, strew, scatter', разре́зать, imperf. разреза́ть, non-past разрезаю, разрезаешь, ... разрезают (imperf.) 'cut (apart), slit'. Note, by the way, that двигать conjugates both as двигаю and дви́жу; and with perfective дви́нуть, originally with a semelfactive sense (unless it started out as one of the imperfectives like тяну́ть), there is the development of an alternative base for preverbed perfectives. It comes from the root ДВИГ, which is probably cognate with English 'twitch'. The root itself may have had a sense of 'forked branch', in which case we can compare it with German *der Zweig* 'branch'. We might even think of English 'switch' (look it up in an English dictionary). You can use lots of preverbs with двигать, partly because it in itself refers to something concrete and spatial. Here are a few examples (the reflexive forms are to a large extent intransitive versions of the non-reflexives):

выдвигать(ся), perf. выдвинуть(ся) 'to move out bring forward, promote; to move forward, get on in the world'
задвигать(ся), perf. задвинуть(ся) 'to push, close, bar, draw (a curtain); to be closed'
надвигать(ся), perf. надвинуть(ся) 'to pull up, approach, draw near'
отодвигать(ся), perf. отодвинуть(ся) 'to move aside, put back'
передвигать(ся), perf. передвинуть(ся) 'to move, shift'
подвигать, perf. 'to move for a while'
подвигать(ся), perf. подвинуть(ся) 'to move (a little), shift'
продвигать(ся), perf. продвинуть(ся) 'to move forward, advance' (продвинутый 'advanced'
сдвигать(ся), perf. сдвинуть(ся) 'to move, shift, budge'

4.3.36 *Pay* — ПЛАТ (**plat-*)

One of the useful pieces of information we might come across is not to confuse заплата 'patch' with зарплата 'wage' (from за́работная пла́та — look up платить with lots of different prefixes). Such an explanation innocently encourages us to miss the fact that платить, non-past плачу́, пла́тишь, ... пла́тят 'pay', with usual perfective заплатить is actually linked with заплата, to a time when a piece of cloth could be a unit of currency, or used in barter. So it is good to see пла́та 'fee' as a zero-suffix word, along with the base of плато́к 'handkerchief'. The immediate temptation is to see Church Slavonic metathesis or inversion here, but evidence from other Slavonic languages discourages this, though we are still not clear what the relationship, if any, there is with полотно́ 'linen; canvas', полоте́нце 'towel', and the like — at this point we might argue that 'cloth' and pay' are quite separate roots, thus releasing the 'cloth' sense to link up with 'linen', but the evidence is lacking, and, for instance, we hardly expect the word for a 'patch' to be Church Slavonic — and we haven't mentioned that the colloquial verb за-платáть, non-past -платáю, etc. means 'to patch' (there's also за-латáть, non-past -áю, etc. 'to patch, mend', though it seems not to be related). The first-person non-past jotation of *t, to *č, tends also to suggest that the verb is not Church Slavonic. There may be a link with Lithuanian platùs 'wide'. And we may have one of those ancient *a — *i verbal relationships again.

Though there is no connection, however much 'paying' and 'weeping' might belong together, we might mention плáкать, non-past плáчу, плáчешь, ... плáчут 'weep', perfectives including заплáкать 'to start weeping', поплáкать 'to weep a little'. For a derived pair we might also mention оплáкать 'to mourn', with its imperfective оплáкивать. There is no evidence of плачúть here, so the development is different. Note the zero-suffix form плáч 'lament', derived from the root ПЛАК — again, not metathesis: the family is related to Latin plangō 'I weep, beat my hand on my breast' and to Lithuanian plàkti 'to whip, beat'. There is a link to such words as French plaie and Spanish llaga 'wound'.

4.3.37 Prepare — ГОТОВ (*gotov-)

In приготóвить, non-past приготóвлю, приготóвишь, ... приготóвят 'to prepare, cook', imperf. приготáвливать, non-past приготáвливаю, etc., or the simple verb готóвить we have a straightforward derivation — note -áвливать (with jotation) rather than -овлять, though we do find подготовлять. Compare these forms with those, just mentioned, with the prefix под-, which have the sense 'to prepare, train'. In Russian we can only go as far as a root готов-, doubtless because this is probably a borrowing from Gothic gataws 'ready' and the verb gataujan, but we might assume a form гот-, given Albanian gat 'ready', where related forms convey 'prepare, boil, knead'.

4.3.38 Pull — ТАГ (ТА(Г)Н)— ТАЗ — ТѦГ (*teg-, *tǫg-)

The aspect pair вы́тянуть — вытя́гивать brings somewhat to mind all those words in the гляде́ть family (see 4.3.33). The missing verb here is тяга́ть 'to pull', also (по)тяга́ться с + instr. 'to be at law with; to have a tug-of-war with'. We note that the first consonant disappears when the two come together. Not so in Polish, where we find ciągnąć 'to pull, draw'. And the Polish reveals that the у in -нуть goes back ultimately to a nasal. So the root is ТЯГ, where the vowel also goes back to a nasal — note how Polish has the same nasal in each syllable, while Russian has -я-у-; there is a difference: can you see it?[40]

---

[40]The difference is that the Common Slavonic *front* nasal leaves in Polish its trace in a palatalization of the preceding consonant, while the *back* nasal does not. In Old Polish these two nasals became very similar (except in their effect on the preceding

There are two imperfectives, namely тяга́ть, which is colloquial, and тяну́ть. This latter may be derived from the former, with a processual, gradual sense (or they may be chronologically relatively equivalent, with the ancestor of тяга́ть having an iterative sense). It is one of the small and unproductive group of intransitive imperfectives in -нуть: со́хнуть 'to dry (out)', мёрзнуть 'to be/get cold', до́хнуть 'to die (of animals; pejoratively of humans)', вя́нуть 'to fade', гло́хнуть 'to become deaf', сле́пнуть 'to become blind', etc. (note that with a prefix they can all become perfective).[41] The root is certainly related to that in English *tension, to extend*, etc. — in fact it is ultimately the root we also find in *syntax*, where we draw components of sentences together into a series of grammatical relations (here with the prefix Greek *sun* = 'with').

In the first paragraph it would have been noted that one of the meanings of тяга́ться was legal; this suggests it is Native Russian. If we can find forms of this root with з instead of г, then this will be confirmed, since the forms with з, as seen in осяза́ние 'sense of touch', cf. прися́га 'oath', are Church Slavonic. And we do indeed find such words, e.g. притяза́ние 'pre*ten*sion' (note the components of the English word too!) and состяза́ние 'competition, "con*ten*tion"' This incidence of a з when Native Russian has г may be parallelled in лицо́ 'face' — о́блик 'aspect, appearance'. Recall that this reflects that almost certainly late Common Slavonic sound change, the so-called Third or Progressive or Baudouin de Courtenay Slavonic Palatalization of Velars, which has a rather restricted presence in Russian; in other words, the dispersion of the Slavonic tribes must have been such when it took place that it did not affect those tribes in the extreme north-east — look at a map and you'll see that the Russians are way out on the periphery. We earlier noted it in князь, from *$k_ь neg$-, earlier *$kuning$-, which is clearly identical to the root of English *king*, Swedish *k(on)ung*, and with the first two vowels perhaps beautifully preserved in Finnish *kuningas*. The original nature of the *g* is indicated by such a word as княги́ня 'princess (prince's wife)' and княжна́ 'princess (prince's daughter)', amongst others.

Coming back to the root in question, we can compare Church Slavonic состяза́ние 'competition' and притяза́ние 'pretension', притяза́тельный 'pretentious' with туго́й 'taut' (i.e. pulled together), reflecting an earlier back nasal vowel and likely ablaut alternation between the two — in Old Russian туга meant 'woe' and we still have, for example, тужи́ть, тужу́, ту́жишь ... ту́жат 'to be sad, despondent'.

---

consonant), but were differentiated in length. Length, or quantity, was eventually replaced by quality, the short nasal giving ę and the long nasal ǫ.

[41]This group tends to be contrasted with the perfectives, originally and still partially semelfactive, in -нуть, e.g., рискну́ть 'to take a risk', though historically they may well be semantically equivalent.

4.3.39 *Remember* — МЬН (*mьn-*)

Following on from 'change' and its possible link to 'remember' (see 4.3.10), note Russian по́мнить, non-past по́мню, по́мнишь, ... по́мнят, perf. вспо́мнить. We note immediately that here there is a prefix installed in the imperfective, again suggesting the complexity and secondary nature of the imperfective-perfective aspectual issue in Russian grammar. And indeed there is an obsolescent verb мнить 'to think, imagine', мни́ться 'to seem'. The мн group suggests a possible mobile vowel between the two. Is there any evidence? Well, we must just work through the prefixes and see what turns up. How about запо́мнить 'to memorize (perf.)'; the imperfective is запомина́ть — the imperfectivizing suffix and, if there had been a soft sign between the *m* and the *n*, then the lengthening of a root **i*. And that is indeed the case. And there are more examples: вспомина́ть 'to remember, recollect' (this can be seen as the imperfective proper of вспо́мнить, indicating the likely original aspect-neutral nature of по́мнить). Also припо́мнить, imperf. припомина́ть 'to recall; remind (+ dat.)', and напо́мнить, напомина́ть 'to remind someone of (+ dat + acc. or + dat. + o + prep.)'. Now, 'to mention' is упомина́ть (imperf.) + acc. or + o + prep. We can imagine 'mention' being rather 'perfective' in essence and even 'semelfactive'; and the perfective is indeed упомяну́ть, non-past упомяну́, упомя́нешь, ... упомя́нут — note the interesting mobile stress here, since many verbs in -нуть have a fixed stress. Now, the я is odd and to give an explanation is difficult, but a likely one leads us in an interesting direction. First, however, a general point, namely that semelfactive verbs quite often do have -ануть as the component: махану́ть 'to wave; jump, rush off', in addition to махну́ть, perfective of маха́ть, non-past машу́, ма́шешь, ... ма́шут (related to an earlier form мая́ти, extant in ма́ятник 'pendulum'), the new formation 're-building' the concrete semelfactive sense. That could play a role here, but it is more likely that this is a case of the suffix -ну- being added to the root. So: упомн-нуть. Now, the root is МЬН, and if a vowel + nasal consonant combination comes before a consonant, that combination provides a nasal vowel. And perhaps this is what happened here: **upomęnǫtь* (from **-po-min-non-*). The interesting direction is: are there any related words in -мя-? Well, one is па́мять 'memory (fem.)' and the derived па́мятник 'memorial, monument', with the rare prefix па́- (another example is па́сынок 'stepson'). In Lithuanian we find, for example, *atmintìs* 'memory'. This leads us to English *mind* and Latin *mens*, gen. *mentis*. Мир те́сен! 'It's a small world!

And while on the subject of the mind, Russian ду́мать, non-past ду́маю, ду́маешь, ... ду́мают 'think' is a borrowing from German, probably Gothic, either the noun *dōms* 'judgement' or the verb *dōmjan* 'to judge' — the long, narrow *o* tends to be reflected in Slavonic as the even narrower *u*. The Germanic source is reflected in English *domesday, doomsday*.

4.3.40 *Rest* — ДЫХ — ДУХ — ДЪХ (*$d\breve{y}x$-, *dux-, *$d\breve{u}x$-)

Starting with the imperfective отдыхáть, non-past отдыхáю, отдыхáешь, ... отдыхáют 'rest', it can be imagined that we might assume a derivation from a verb дыхáть or дыхать (and you'll find them in Dal') — intimations, once again, of an earlier state of affairs in the verb which does not immediately fit with what we are often taught for the modern language. Note that the stress of отдыхáть suggests derivation through the imperfectivizing suffix -á(й)-. The perfective of отдыхáть, with a sense of 'to have a/take a rest', is отдохнýть, non-past отдохнý, отдохнёшь, ... отдохнýт, past отдохнýл-. Now, we've come across a verb дóхнуть, imperfective, with non-past дóхну, etc., past дóх(л)-, meaning 'die (of an animal)', and with perfectives in по- and с- (the latter in particular may be used colloquially of people); and there is the verb дохнýть, perfective, non-past дохнý, etc., past дохнýл- 'take/give a breath'. In these verbs the -o- arises from a hard sign, historically a short *u, and we can readily imagine the lengthening of this root vowel (giving *$\bar{u}$, then *y, in Cyrillic ы) along with the imperfectivizing suffix -á(й)- giving, ultimately отдыхáть. The hard sign would normally have disappeared, and indeed it can, giving зáтхлый 'stuffy' (presumably linked with an unpleasant smell; the d assimilates in voice to the x when the intervening hard sign drops, though we do also find зáдхлый), but it can, as is clear from the examples, also survive, presumably partly to avoid the consonant group — there may be some link here too with тýхнуть 'to rot (imperf.)' and тýша 'carcass', and perhaps to do with stress, as in дóхнуть. We can build up this family by reference to, say, вздохнýть, imperf. вздыхáть 'to sigh' and задохнýться, imperf. задыхáться 'to choke; gasp for breath'. And, of course, what of 'to breathe'? Well, in Russian this is дышáть, non-past дышý, дышишь, ... дыша т, doubtless with a First Palatalization, and the noun душá 'soul', with a jotation and monophthongization of a w-diphthong (*$dawxja$). All this not to forget дух 'spirit', with its zero-suffix. To help here we might mention the ever-useful Lithuanian with its *daũsos* 'air', revealing the diphthong. Most important, however, we can get an overall picture of the family and of the vowel and consonant alternations. And, as we might imagine breathing going with smoke, we can imagine these two families (ДЫ(М)) sharing a more primitive root, extended by *s (later *x by the *ruki*-rule) and *m resp.

For a similar pattern recall сóхнуть 'to dry (intr.; imperf.)', сухóй 'dry', засóхнуть, imperf. засыхáть 'to dry up; wither', сушить 'to dry (tr.) (= "to make dry")' (and note culinary сушёное мясо 'dried meat'), сýша 'dry land' (and зáсуха 'drought'), and Lithuanian *saũsas* 'dry'.

4.3.41   Rich, poor — БОГ(АТ) — БѢД (*bog- — *běd-)

Богáтый 'rich' has as ultimate root БОГ, thus God as the one who allots things and as such is the master, and as 'good'. The suffix indicates one as possessing (the quality of) the root, e.g. рогáтый 'horned' (рóг 'horn'). It is probably an Iranian borrowing, as seems to have been the case with a good number of early religious terms. We note it too, another link with the harvest and growth, in, for example, Polish zboże 'corn', perhaps here a secondary reflection of 'wealth'. The fact of being rich is conveyed verbally by богатéть, non-past богатéю, богатéешь, ... богатéют, perf. разбогатéть 'to be/become rich' (a typical deadjectival intransitive), and the factitive or causative by обогатúть, non-past обогащý, обогатúшь, ... обогатя́т, imperf. обогащáть, non-past обогащáю, etc. — note the Church Slavonic jotations and that the reflexive form may render 'to become rich'. Going back to the simple root, we have a verb such as обожáть, non-past обожáю, etc. 'to adore', formed by jotation or analogy with the simpler божúться, non-past божýсь, божúшься, ... божáтся, perf. побожúться 'swear'. The family can be extended considerably.

As for 'poor', the most familiar adjective is бéдный, formed via the -ьн- suffix from the root БѢД as it appears in the zero-suffix noun бедá 'misfortune, calamity'. An exact equivalent is to be found in Lithuanian bėdà 'need'. In verbs the root leads to a sense of 'conquer, persuade', i.e. 'to cause misfortune by getting one's own way'. So, assuming a basic verb бедúть, we expand to убедúть, non-past убедúшь, ... убедя́т, imperf. убеждáть, non-past убеждáю, etc. 'to convince, persuade' and победúть, imperf. побеждáть 'to conquer, defeat' (and побéда 'victory'). Note the Church Slavonic jotation and the avoidance of the first-person-singular form of the perfectives. Church Slavonic also manifests itself in the participles and deverbal nouns, e.g. убеждённый 'convinced' (in spite of ё) and убеждéние 'conviction', предубеждéние 'prejudice'.

4.3.42   Rush, hurry, throw, abandon — БРОС — СПѢ(Х) — ТОРП — КИД (*bros-, *spě(x)-, *torp-, *kyd-)

Бросáться, non-past бросáюсь, etc., perf. брóситься, non-past брóшусь, брóсишься, ... брóсятся 'to rush' has the meaning 'throw' when non-reflexive. It is one of those verbs unusual in that there is no clear derivational path between the two. We might expect a basic брóсить with a derived imperfective брося́ть, but that is not what is found, suggesting an ancient, pre-aspectual relation. The following examples might help work out what happened (the meanings given are rather summary):

Perfective	Imperfective	Meaning
перебросáть	— — —	throw one after another
набросáть		throw about; throw one after another
забросáть	забрáсывать	fill up, shower with, deluge with (+ instr. + acc.)
набросáть	набрáсывать	sketch, outline; note down (+ acc.)
разбросáть(ся)	разбрáсывать(ся)	throw about, scatter; refl. = overdo things
вбрóсить	вбрáсывать	throw in(to)
забрóсить	забрáсывать	throw, give up, abandon, bring, leave behind
набрóсить(ся)	набрáсывать(ся)	throw on(to); refl. = fall upon, go for, deluge someone with
перебрóсить	перебрáсывать	throw over, transfer
подбрóсить	подбрáсывать	throw up, under, in; add; place surreptitiously
сбрóсить(ся)	сбрáсывать(ся)	throw down/off; discardl refl. = leap off/from
брóсить	бросáть	throw, give up, abandon

A clear picture is relatively difficult to achieve. Where there are prefixed pairs, there is a sense that those with a perfective in брóсить are more concrete (this includes a figurative military sense), while those in бросáть more figurative. We note that the two instances given with a perfective-only in бросáть are iterative. Overall, this possibly suggests that in the basic pair бросáть, now the imperfective, was originally iterative, while брóсить was aspectually neutral but is specialized now, by opposition to бросáть and the decay in Russian of the simple iterative, as perfective.

It is interesting to compare the бросáть family with кидáть, non-past кидáю, etc., and its current perfective кúнуть, non-past кúну, кúнешь, ... кúнут 'to throw' (refl. = 'throw oneself; rush'). Here again prefixed кидáть tends to be figurative, while prefixed кúнуть tends to be concrete — look up прикúдывать(ся), and we even have перекидáть on its own as a perfective with exactly the same meaning as перебросáть. But each family has its peculiarities, such that, for example, скидáть can be both imperfective and perfective in the sense 'throw off (coll.)', both conjugated as -áю, etc., while the actual pair will be скúнуть, imperf. скúдывать. Note the simplification in the consonant group and the original *y after *k, meaning no First Palatalization takes place. The verb may be related to English *shoot* (note how *shoot* has senses in English both of 'throw' and 'rush', e.g. 'to shoot off somewhere'). There are other verbs with the meaning 'throw'.

The same goes for 'rush'. Setting aside, for example, нестись, perf. понестись, with its root НЕС (note that носиться is only used of rumours floating around, ideas being nursed, and how material wears), we can turn to the two most common words, по-спешить, non-past спешу, спешишь, ... спешат, and по-торопиться, non-past тороплюсь, торопишься, ... торопятся. The second, as we might imagine, for once correctly, is an instance of pleophony, the metathetic form not attested and the word seemingly restricted to East Slavonic, even though there may be a link with Greek *trépō* 'I turn' and ideas of 'tropes', e.g. *heliotrope*. By turning about we do things quickly. The first is an ancient derivation, via *-x- (like, using modern forms, грех 'sin' from греть 'to heat' — sins lead to the heat of hell), from СПѢ 'have time to'. It is probably related to Latin *spēs* 'hope, expectation' and can be found in Lithuanian *spéti* 'to manage to, be fast enough to'. We readily see this verb in успеть, non-past успею, успеешь, ... успеют, imperf. успевать, non-past успеваю, etc. Recall that there is, in fact, a verb спеть, non-past спею, etc. in Russian, with the meaning 'ripen', in other words 'to arrive on time'. Note спелый 'ripe', a long form of the *l*-participle. See also 4.3.31. We might compare this with the verb зреть, non-past зрею, etc. 'ripen' — most commonly as созреть, imperf. созревать, and зрелый 'ripe'. We cannot resist thinking of зреть, non-past зрю, зришь, ... зрят 'see', with зрелый as the long form of its *l*-participle, in that ripe fruit might be interpreted as visible. And see 4.3.43.

4.3.43 *Save* — (С)ПАС (*(sъ)pas-*)

In the case of запас 'supply, stock' there is the related verb запасти, imperf. запасать 'to stock', where we may assume a prefix за- (the compound запчасть 'spare part' — запасная часть is fascinating, as the root is disregarded in the compound and has, we must imagine, lost its semantic load). We have seen a redrawing of morpheme boundaries also in зонтик 'umbrella'; and we might ask what exactly English *superette* is, made up as it is of a prefix and a suffix, but nothing else. When verbs of 'taking' are considered, questions will have to be asked about вынуть 'to take out'. Consequently, we can assume a verb пасти, which exists in the meaning 'to graze (transitive); tend, shepherd' (visible in пастух 'shepherd') and пастись 'to graze (intransitive)': non-past пасу(сь), пасёшь(ся), ..., пасут(ся), past пасся, паслась. Now, something which you store up is something you look after, keep, thus 'tend' (could there be a link to 'save'?). Related is Latin *pasco* 'I feed, tend' and, though less clearly, English 'fodder'. If this can be accepted, then there may even be a link with пища 'food' (this is a Church Slavonic form, replacing earlier Russian пича), with a root ПИТ visible in питать 'to feed' (there is also an old form пита 'food, bread', which it is tempting, and probably correct, to relate to *pitta bread*!). A problem here is the shape of the root of пасти; is it ПАС, which the verb forms support, or ПИТ (or ПАТ?), which the link to питать suggests? All we might suggest is that there has been some linkage with the *pattern* (no relation) exhibited by a verb like плести́, non-past плету́, плетёшь, .., плету́т 'to braid, plait', where the original infinitive *pletti (approximately) very early became plesti. However, perhaps we should not constantly strain for perfect explanations!

This shouldn't stop the question being asked regarding a link with спасти́, спасу́, спасёшь,... 'save'. Well, the verbs are indeed linked, спасти́ having the prefix съ-. There's seems little reason why 'saving', 'feeding', and 'saving up, stocking up' (so as to be able to eat) should not be related. See 4.3.21 too.

The root ПЕК and its meanings, one related to 'care, protection', has already been encountered. In this same semantic area we might at least mention also БЕРЕГ — БРЕГ, as in бере́чь, берегу́, бережёшь, ... берегу́т, perf. сбере́чь (and imperf. сберега́ть) 'save' (think of пренебрега́ть + instr. 'to neglect (= "not to take care of")', небре́жный 'carefree, careless'.

4.3.44 Say — (СЪ)КАЗ (*kaz-)

We must start with the word сказа́ть (perf.) 'to say, to tell' (not normally 'to speak'). Note that we can see the -a- before -ть as a suffix and the -ть as the infinitive ending, though historically the -t- is itself a nominal suffix) — see Appendix 3. We may speak of a root СКАЗ because, as well as being a word itself, meaning 'skaz' (a sort of first-person narrative), it can be used as the basis for other words, e.g. расска́з 'story, tale', рассказа́ть, imperf. расска́зывать 'to recount, tell', переска́з 'retelling', досказа́ть 'to finish saying', etc. However, we might ask ourselves about каза́ться 'to seem' (and, if you know Ukrainian, каза́ти 'to say' — also to be found in Russian dialects, and in early Slavonic it may have had a sense of 'explain'), and deduce from that that с- is the prefix с/- (= съ-), as in сде́лать, perfective of де́лать 'to do, make'. This enables us to link сказа́ть with a whole family of words where the meaning 'say' can to varying extents be discerned:

доказа́ть + acc. — доказа́тельство 'to prove; proof, evidence' (i.e. to say something to achieve the end': Мы в конце́ концо́в доказа́ли, что она́ вино́вна в преступле́нии 'We finally proved she was guilty of the crime' (note too the colloquial доказа́ть на кого́ 'to inform on someone')

заказа́ть + acc. — зака́з 'to book, reserve, "order"; order, reservation'

наказа́ть + acc. — наказа́ние 'to punish; punishment' (i.e. to 'say something onto someone', compare приговори́ть 'to condemn'): семья́ наказа́ла их 'the family punished them'

оказа́ть + acc. 'to render (a service), exert (influence)': И́горь оказа́л нам услу́гу 'Igor did us a service/good turn', Их посту́пки оказа́ли большо́е влия́ние на результа́т 'Their steps had a considerable indfluence on the outcome'

оказа́ться + instr. 'to prove to be, turn out to be': Вы́ставка оказа́лась о́чень популя́рной 'The exhibition turned out to be very popular'

отказа́ть — отка́з 'to refuse; refusal' (note the construction): Ма́ша отка́жет нам в по́мощи 'Masha will refuse us help'

отказа́ться 'to refuse': Ма́ша наотре́з отка́жется помо́чь нам 'Masha will flatly refuse to help us'; Она́ отказа́лась наотре́з от предложе́ния 'She flatly rejected the proposal'

показа́ть — пока́з, показа́ние 'to show; demonstration, testimony': Она́ показа́ла ему́ на заво́д 'she pointed out the factory to him' (we might construct it with the dative and accusative, after the pattern of English 'to show')

приказа́ть + dat. — прика́з 'to command, "order"; order' (i.e. to say something close up to someone: Я приказа́л ему́ уйти́ 'I ordered him to leave')

указа́ть — ука́з, указа́ние 'to point out, indicate; decree, indication' (note the construction): он указа́л мне на по́чту 'He pointed out the post office to me'

The imperfective of all these verbs is in -ка́зывать, -ка́зываю, -ка́зываешь, … -ка́зывают. Note, by the way, that derived imperfectives have the stress fixed in all forms and are always conjugated on the 'regular' pattern of чита́ть.

Note how the original sense of 'say' might be conveyed in the use of the dative case or constructions involving cases other than the accusative after these verbs, as well as by their meanings and the semantic links with communication. It's worth tying all this in with the fact that 'indicating, pointing out', 'showing', and 'saying' are linked: we point out with a digit, i.e. a finger, and the root for 'digit' in Latin is also linked to Latin *dico*... 'I *say*', which is historically identical with Greek *edeiksa* 'I have shown'; remember the 'deictic' pronouns are those which point out things, i.e. 'this, that'.

Coming back to the root ВЕТ in приве́т, this is to be found also in сове́т 'council; piece of advice', отве́т 'answer, reply', stems involving two other prefixes. The root itself probably originally had a sense of 'speak' — the ancient council or parliament of the city of Novgorod was called the ве́че. The prefix со- corresponds to English 'co-, 'con-, com-', thus 'speaking with', and от- has a sense of 'back' (among others), thus 'say back' = 'answer, reply'. We note the verb отве́тить 'to answer, reply (perf.)', with a suffix -и and an ending -ть. There is the corresponding imperfective verb, отвеча́ть, with the stress on the -а́- and change of т to ч. By contrasting this with посети́ть - посеща́ть 'to visit', and noting the different alternation here, we reveal a Church Slavonic word. In other words, there are different jotation effects in the two imperfectives — and in the first person singular too: отве́чу — посещу́. Can you think of any other forms of these verbs where this is revealed? And note the stressed -а́- of the imperfectivizing suffix. So привéт may have a sense of saying a few words on meeting someone.

4.3.45 *Send* — СЪЛ (*sъl-)

Now for the 'sending' verbs. First, послáть, non-past пошлю́, пошлёшь, ... пошлю́т, imperfective посылáть, non-past посылáю, etc., is the neutral verb (at least as regards the perfective — see below), to be used unless you have good reason to use another. Присылáть/прислáть, with its prefix при- and sense of 'coming' (it may also have an attenuative, 'diminutive', sense), conveys 'sending' from the point of view of the person to whom something is being sent (by the way, if it is a *person* whom you are sending to someone, use к + dat. to convey 'to', and if you are sending something or someone *from* someone, use от + gen. to convey 'from'). And высылáть/вы́слать emphasizes the origin of the sending. We can imagine there is a verb слать, and indeed there is. It is commonly used to convey the continuous sense of the imperfective, whereas посылáть, which one tends to assume is the general word for 'send', actually has an overtone of 'intermittently', or an iterative sense: Рабóчие завóдов и фáбрик, трýженики полéй шлют пи́сьма и телегрáммы в подéржку э́того решéния 'The labourers in works and factories, the toilers in the fields, send letters and telegrams in support of this decision' — посылáют is impossible here.

We seem to have a root СЛ, but the imperfectives have СЫЛ. We can suppose that the ы has something to do with the derivation of the imperfective, but, given СЛ, how can it come from nothing? We might say that it certainly could, but historical study of the language reveals to us that слать was originally сълати (the infinitive used always to end in -и; now this is restricted to those verbs where the ending is stressed, e.g. идти́). Given that the hard sign most often originated in a short *u*-sound and ы in a long *u*-sound, then we can hypothesize that the imperfective was derived from the perfective by lengthening the vowel of the root. And this will turn out to be the case, since the same thing may be observed (and already in this book has been observed and noted) in many other situations, e.g. the и in дожидáться as against дождáться (thus a root Ж/Д or ЖЬД), and the о versus а in отстрóить — отстрáивать. In the first, one origin of the soft sign is a short *i*-sound, while that of и is a long *i*-sound, while in the second that of о is a short *a*- or *o*-sound, while that of а is a long *a*- or *o*-sound. Thus there indeed is a root СЪЛ.

Note that the с becomes ш throughout the non-past: -шлю́, -шлёшь, -шлю́т. This is just like the с-ш relation illustrated by писáть - пишý, but with an л in between which does not block the relation — sonorants do not seem to be strong barriers to palatalizations, something seen also in цвет 'colour; blossom' and звездá 'star', and, amongst others, in мы́слить - мышлéние, extendable to размы́слить (obs.), imperfective размышля́ть 'to consider, reflect on (+ о +

prep.)'. We expect non-past -мы́шлю, -мы́слишь, and indeed this once was the case; nowadays, however, analogy has given -мы́слю, -мы́слишь.

Actually, there may be something wrong with the analogy with verbs like писа́ть: they are not monosyllabic and have mobile stress in the non-past; слать is stuck with its stress fixed on the ending/suffix, something which, given its superficial similarity to, say, ждать, might lead us to expect слу, слёшь (or шлёшь, ...) слут. Interesting.

4.3.46 *Separate* — ДѢЛ (*dĕl-)

The basic verb here is дели́ть, non-past делю́, де́лишь, ... де́лят, perf. раздели́ть 'to divide (+ acc. + на "into" + acc.) and подели́ть 'to share (+ acc. + с "with" + instr.)'. The same meanings are retained if the verb is made reflexive, except that 'divide' loses its direct object and 'share' expresses its 'direct object' through the instrumental case. The independence of раздели́ть(ся) from дели́ть is demonstrated through its possession of its own imperfective, namely разделя́ть(ся). The family is very extensive, e.g. отдели́ть, imperf. отделя́ть 'to separate (+ acc. + от "from" + gen.), удели́ть, imperf. уделя́ть, as in удели́ть внима́ние + dat. 'to pay attention to', and надели́ть, imperf. наделя́ть 'to provide, endow (+ acc. "with" + instr.)'. A cognate is found in Lithuanian *dailýti* 'to divide', revealing the origin of the *jat'* in a *j*-diphthong — compare the *jat'* in де́лать 'to do' and деть 'to put', from a long *ē̆.

4.3.47 *Sleep*, or *being asleep* — СЪП(Н) (*sъp(n)-)

If we link со́н 'sleep, dream', gen. сна with спать 'to sleep' and hypothesize an actual root СЪП(Н), where the two adjacent consonants would be liable to simplify to one in certain circumstances, we can begin to understand засну́ть, non-past засну́, заснёшь, ... засну́т, imperf. засыпа́ть, non-past засыпа́ю, etc. 'to fall asleep' and просну́ться, imperf. просыпа́ться 'to wake up' (conjugation as засну́ть and засыпа́ть), and even, given that *s* at the beginning of words became *h* in Classical Greek, link СЪП(Н) with Greek *hypnos*, and thus that particular sleep which is *hypnosis*. That seems obvious enough, but is it? How, in fact do we get from засыпа́ть to спать, since засну́ть doesn't actually seem to be an intermediate stage (we normally make the derivation via a prefixed simple verb). There is, too, a verb усну́ть 'to fall asleep', which doesn't have an imperfective, perhaps because it would clash with усыпа́ть, non-past усыпа́ю, etc. 'to strew (with)', imperfective of усы́пать, non-past усы́плю, усы́плешь, ... усы́плют — but note усыпа́льница 'burial-vault'. The intermediate stage we would want is заспа́ть, which we in fact get in the form of the past passive participle, now adjective, за́спанный 'sleepy, "puffed up with sleep"'. What we seem to have is a loss of the intermediate forms, replaced by arguably more expressive original semelfactives. Intermediate forms do, in fact, exist, when we look more carefully: поспа́ть 'to sleep a little' (near-perfective of спать), заспа́ть(ся) 'to smother (oversleep)' (imperf. засыпа́ть(ся)), отоспа́ться 'to have a long sleep; catch up on one's sleep' (imperf. отсыпа́ться), переспа́ть 'to oversleep; spend the night (with)", проспа́ть(ся) 'to oversleep; sleep (a certain length of time), (sleep off)', and разоспа́ться to be fast asleep; oversleep' (the last three all perfective-only). And if you look around these verbs in your dictionary you will discover that the assertion regarding avoiding a 'clash', made a few lines earlier, just doesn't work: засыпа́ть can also be the imperfective of засы́пать to fill something with something by sprinkling'. Languages tolerate a great deal of redundancy and ambiguity. But at least we can see how the 'falling asleep' and 'waking up' pairs arose, and that the н in the -ну- of the perfectives does not have to have anything to do with the *n of the root — perhaps the consonant group simplified in the ancestor of the noun and the *n was lost in ancestor of the basic verb, e.g. *u-sъp-nǫ-ti; unless we prefer the more explicit *u-sъpn-nǫ-ti, with contraction of the two n's.

In this connection we might hypothesize that the root with *p provides the verbs (and deverbals) and that that with *pn, and hence simplification to *n, provides the nominals (and denominals). To this we add the rider that we have such a verb as сни́ться, non-past снюсь, сни́шься, ... сня́тся, perf. присни́ться 'dream, have a dream', with the third-person forms most common and being used in constructions as follows: Вчера́ Ма́ше присни́лся беззабо́тный сон 'Yesterday Maša had a carefree dream' (lit. (approx.) "Yesterday a carefree dream made itself into a dream to Maša")' and Вчера́ Ма́ше присни́лось, что все её волне́ния позади́ 'Yesterday Maša dreamed that all her troubles were behind her'.

And, as if you felt that was that, we might bring in the verb усыпи́ть, non-past усыплю́, усыпи́шь, ... усыпя́т, imperf. усыпля́ть, non-past усыпля́ю, etc. 'put to sleep; lull, undermine, deaden'. The ы is arguably not expected here, so we might have an analogical development (using the pattern of засыпа́ть, etc.), and -и́ть plays a transitivizing or factitive role, one it often has. There is also a deverbal noun, усыпле́ние, and adjective, усыпи́тельный 'soporific', as in усыпи́тельное сре́дство 'sleeping-draught'. The analogy, if that is what happened, may in fact be better described as 'differentiation' or avoidance of ambiguity (which sometimes *does* work), in other words to avoid a clash with the Church Slavonic form, which *is* what we expect, without ы: успе́ние 'death (Успе́ние "Feast of the Assumption")', and its adjective успе́нский — note too the absence of the л in these forms, its loss on morpheme boundaries being a feature of the dialects underlying Old Church Slavonic and of West Slavonic. The relations between all the forms are difficult to define in a precise and satisfactory manner — there is method, but it is rarely if ever absolutely explicable. There is, by the way, a Church Slavonic verb ОУСЪПНТН, which, using the modern alphabet and russifying it as успить, may provide the missing link!

The verb спать is itself slightly odd, at least in its infinitive, which has a one-off correspondence with the non-past, which is regular second conjugation, namely сплю, спишь, ... спят. It would be neater if there was an infinitive спи́ть or спе́ть here (the latter perhaps causing problems of confusion) — this would also then create a parallel structure to бде́ть (see 4.3.4) — backed up by semantics, and note Йгорь спит, Йгорь бдит 'Igor' is asleep, Igor' is awake' in the Russian epic poem, the *Сло́во о полку́ Йгореве The Tale of Igor's Campaign*. Whatever the case may be, this reminds one of semantic factors — certain verbs express a state: сиде́ть, стоя́ть, лежа́ть, бде́ть, and спать. And all these verbs are second conjugation. We do expect спеть — усыпи́ть here to parallel бде́ть — разбуди́ть 'to be awake — to awaken (tr.)' (note the Church Slavonic verb just mentioned). But all the Slavonic languages have the equivalent of спать and second-conjugation non-past, so we begin to wonder whether the спа-forms of this verb in fact reflect an originally different nuance of the verb (a different formant/suffix on the root) which has subsequently merged with the спе́- forms of the non-past. After all, there are some verbs which contain relics of other verbs, e.g. бежа́ть, though there they overlap within the non-past whereas here the two stems (given two) remain distinct. Спать might well be an original iterative, if that is what we see in, say, броса́ть 'to throw' as against бро́сить.

Interesting too here is that the vowel can cause softening of the *s* in, for example, Polish (in Russian this possibly happened too, but has been lost — softening does not as a rule cross labials), thus *śpię, śpisz, ... śpią*. This isn't the same as what happened in слать, where the change throughout is a result of jotation — here Polish has *szlę, szlesz, ... szlą*, which also reflects jotation.

4.3.48   *Slip* — КЪЛЗ (*kъlz-)

We might start with вы́скользнуть, non-past вы́скользну, вы́скользнешь, ... вы́скользнут, imperf. выска́льзывать, imperf. выска́льзывать, выска́льзываешь, ... выска́льзывают 'to slip out', e.g. when something slips out of one's grip. On this basis we expect imperfective скользну́ть, but this only occurs as a semelfactive perfective. There is a verb скользи́ть, non-past скольжу́, скользи́шь, ... скользя́т 'slip, slide' (imperf. intr.), which suggests a root СКОЛЬЗ. But, given Polish *kiełzać (się)* 'to stumble', there are two problems, which suggest КЪЛЗ — the vowel has to be a hard sign, otherwise the *k would have undergone the First Palatalization. Note too that the Polish verb is not second-conjugation (i.e. the Russian *i*-conjugation). Moreover, the expected perfective вы́скользить does not occur, so that a semelfactive (again, perhaps not originally one) has taken over the role of perfective, while the isolated imperfective скользи́ть (expected because we expect вы́скользить) provides the source. As mentioned above, there is a semelfactive скользну́ть, though the most likely way of rendering a real slip and fall would be perf. поскользну́ться (fixed stress). Associated verbs include соскользну́ть, imperf. соска́льзывать с + gen 'to slip off', and проскользи́ть (not проскользну́ть!), imperf. проска́льзывать че́рез + acc. 'to slip through'. With the suffix -/к- (= -ък-) we form an adjective ско́льзкий 'slippery; tricky', and we can form a quite regular deverbative noun скольжёние 'slipping, sliding'. There is, as so often once we start to look closely at Russian simple verbs and the prefixal and suffixal derivational processes involved in aspect, suggestion of a different earlier situation, closer to the one we can generalize *across* languages.

4.3.49   *Slow down* — МЬД(ЬЛ) (**mьdьl-*)

The verb замёдлить, non-past замёдлю, замёдлишь, ... замёдлят, imperf. замедлять, замедляю, замедляешь, ... замедляют 'slow down, slacken; take one's time with (c + instr. or + inf.)', is perfectively regular in derivation. The root may be М/Д (the slash standing for an original front *jer*, though comparative Slavonic evidence suggests a back one), given the form is demonstrated in Czech *mdlý* 'weak'. It may be that the за- preverb originally provided an inchoative ('beginning') perfective sense, given that there is a simple verb мёдлить 'to linger, hesitate; take one's time with/over (c + instr.)'. Perhaps the root is most common in the adverb немёдленно 'immediately', possibly originally a past passive participle.

And what of the *l*? It would seem that a Common Slavonic **mьd-*, attested in Middle Russian (16th-17th centuries мотчание 'delaying') and retained in dialectal forms, e.g. модёть, non-past модёю, etc. 'be weakened, tired', was replaced by **mьd(ьl)-*.

4.3.50   *Smile* — ЛЫБ (**lyb-*)

Улыбка contains the root ЛЫБ. Now, this may also be seen as Л/Б, where the slash conceals a hard sign. Since ы goes back to a long *u* and the hard sign goes back to a short one, we see the link. What does Л/Б give us? Well, лоб 'forehead'. So, smiling has something to do with the forehead? Well, no, since лъбъ originally meant 'skull', so 'smiling' must have something to do with baring one's teeth, as skulls do! The verb must come from лыбать, which doesn't survive; in dialects, however, there is лыбить, with the meaning 'smile' (we still find лыбиться in the demotic and slang registers). Лоб replaces the more widespread Slavonic word чело, which may have something to do with человёк. Чело is probably related to *celestial* and thus French *ciel* 'sky', Latin *caelum* 'sky, heaven', and Lithuanian *kélti* 'to raise, rise' — thus something *high*. It is unlikely that this root manifests itself in the word чёлядь (fem.) 'servants, retainers' and a general sense of 'family, group, kin', which, however, may be a component of человёк 'person'. The век component here might have something to do with Lithuanian *vaĩkas* 'child', rather than the initially tempting век 'century, age'. Much is uncertain!

4.3.51 *Stand out, be different* — ЛИК (*lik-*)

First we might look at perfective отличи́ть + acc. (+ от + gen.) 'to differentiate (one thing from another)'; the stress is fixed on the ending in the non-past. It is made up of the prefix от-, suffix -и-, infinitive ending -ть, and root ЛИЧ (to be further defined in a moment). The verbal stem is thus отличи-. The stem for nouns and adjectives is отлич-, e.g. отли́чный 'excellent; different (= something which stands out")', with the adjectival suffix -ьн-, отли́чие 'difference; distinction', with the nominal suffix -ие. We derive the imperfective from the perfective, thus отлича́ть (the spelling rule requires -a- after ч rather than the expected -я-), with the usual stress (note that the stress does not have to *move* to this position; it can be there in the perfective too). The verb means 'to distinguish/differentiate something from something', with 'from' being conveyed by от + genitive (if we wish to tack on *how* one thing is differentiated from another, the instrumental is used). As a reflexive it means 'to be different from' (again using от + gen. to convey 'from') and 'to be characterized by' ('by' is conveyed by the straight instrumental). Thus: Я отлича́ю стол от сту́ла тем, что у сту́ла есть спи́нка 'I differentiate a table from a chair in that a chair has a back' — Стул отлича́ется от стола́ спи́нкой 'A chair differs from a chair by its back' — Ма́ша отлича́ется хра́бростью 'Maša stands out by her bravery'. Use your dictionary to find words meaning 'different' and 'difference'. Note how the prefix is identical with the preposition, and that here they share a meaning of 'from'. 'From' can also convey 'back', as in 'I came back from somewhere'. This is another meaning of the prefix, as in отдава́ть, отда́ть 'to give back'. Less transparent, but still imaginable, is the meaning 'end', as in отстра́ивать, отстро́ить 'to finish building'.

Related verbs include различа́ть, различи́ть + acc. 'to differ, be different' (with a plural object usually; *not* used to differentiate one thing (or more) from another) and слича́ть, сличи́ть + acc. + с + instr. 'to collate something with something; to check something against something'. The prefix in the second can be aligned with the preposition с in its meaning 'with', in English verbs most often conveyed as 'co-, con-' (occasionally as 'with-', e.g. 'withhold, withstand'; it may also render 'down, (down) off', as in сходи́ть, сойти́, and, in reflexive verbs, of 'coming together', e.g. сходи́ться, сойти́сь.[42] In the first there is no related preposition; the prefix раз- separates or distributes: раскрыва́ть, раскры́ть 'to open (wide)', раздава́ть, разда́ть 'to distribute, give out (to different people)', расходи́ться, разойти́сь 'to disperse, go one's different ways, separate ("from" = с + instr.)'.

Now how about that root? If a root contains a sound like that conveyed by the letter ч, we can be reasonably sure that it wasn't always there and that we might

---

[42]Note схо́дный 'similar', where we can see the idea of things going together. The verb too has a nuance of being likeminded on something, say on agreeing a price (сойти́сь в цене́), and схо́дный also has that sense, namely of a fair price.

find related words in Russian containing other sounds. Given that an adjective like личный means 'personal', we might reasonably assume that it is related to, or derived from, a word with the possible meaning 'person'. Such a word exists, namely лицо́ 'person; character (in a play; often qualified by де́йствующее)'. Of course, this word is more familiar with the meaning 'face'. Thus it looks like ч and ц are somehow related. However, ц is itself relatively recent in the language, so we're not there yet! To get at the source it is useful to pick another word with ч at the end of a root. So: ру́чка, derived from рука́, and lots of related forms, e.g. поруча́ть, поручи́ть 'to entrust something/a task (acc.) to someone (dat.)', or вруча́ть, вручи́ть 'to hand, entrust something (acc.) to someone (dat.)'. Unfortunately, we cannot provide a form of this root with ц from modern Russian; however, reconstructing linguistic history by reference to external evidence (= 'external reconstruction') can help: in Ukrainian the dative and prepositional of рука́ is руці́, and in Bulgarian the plural of the Bulgarian equivalent, ръка́, is ръце́. So, without referring to history, though in an earlier form of the language we had руцѣ in the dative and locative singular and in the nom./voc./acc. dual, we can see that there is a к-ч-ц relationship. Does this work for ЛИЧ? The answer is that it does, since there is evidence in, for example, the word о́блик 'look, appearance' — the meaning is a good indication that this word's root, ЛИК, is also the root underlying ЛИЧ. In лицо́, of course, it's that 'Third Palatalization'.

4.3.52   Take — БЬР — ИМ — ЙМ (*bьr-, *jьm-)

We tend to learn брать, non-past беру́, берёшь, ... беру́т (imperf.) first, with its general 'take' meaning and, through its root БЬР quite readily identifiable with English *bear* and thus 'carrying', as in Latin *fero* 'I carry'. This root can be used, with prefixes and then quite regular derivations of secondary perfectives, to provide such verbs as собра́ть, imperf. собира́ть 'to collect, gather' (reflexively 'to meet, gather; be getting ready to'), убра́ть, imperf. убира́ть 'to tidy (up)', подобра́ть, imperf. подбира́ть 'to pick up; tuck up; select' (note the inserted о in the perfective), and вы́брать, imperf. выбира́ть 'to choose'.

Брать's perfective is взять, indicating that the pair is suppletive. The non-past has the pattern возьму́, возьмёшь, ... возьму́т. This suggests the presence of the prefix в(о)з-. Once the prefix and non-past endings are removed, what we are left with is -ьм-. Note that the м precedes a vowel and that the м is absent from the infinitive, and from the past tense, where instead we find я before a consonant: взяТЬ, взяЛ. Recalling that я often arises from a front nasal vowel (the actual letter is probably the recent form of the letter Ѧ, devised to represent this nasal, which was pronounced — until the early tenth century among the East Slavs — perhaps somewhat as the *in* in French *fin*), which arose from a nasal diphthong, it becomes likely that at the root of that a nasal diphthong is at the root of what we find here. Thus: an approximate infinitive *vuzimtej* and a first person singular non-past *vuzimōm*, respectively giving *vъzęti* and *vъzьmǫ*. In

Proto-Slavonic sequences of an oral vowel plus *m* or *n* was a diphthong, just like *ow* and indeed all sequences of an oral vowel and a sonorant — pleophony and metathesis are just one of the ways of dealing with such sequences: essentially, there is no change other than one of syllable boundary before a vowel, but a change of some sort before a consonant, to create an open syllable — thus for the nasal diphthongs we have a nasal vowel before a consonant. Compare the pronunciation of French *moyen* in *moyen âge* 'Middle Ages' and *moyen français* 'Middle French', the adjective preceding a vowel in the first (and being pronounced as if it were the feminine form *moyenne*) and a consonant in the second — the same phenomenon: try pronouncing a nasal vowel before another vowel! In Lithuanian this verb still exists as the normal verb for 'to take', namely *im̃ti, imù*; it is related to Latin *emo, emere, emi, emptum* 'buy', something we encounter in English 'to redeem'. Noting the forms in Latin with *p*, and English *redemption*, we might speculate that English *empty* (something with everything taken out!), might correspond to the Russian and Lithuanian past passive participles взя́тый, *im̃tas* resp. Whence the *p*? Well, it's a consonant inserted to facilitate the passage from one particular consonant to another. An instance in Russian, referred to elsewhere, is встре́тить 'to meet', with an ancient root РѢТ, expanded to сърѣт, and found in, for example, Serbo-Croatian *sresti* 'to meet'. We may also hear страм 'shame' (demotic, dialectal) for срам; and we have only to think of numerous future and conditional forms in, say, Spanish: *salir — saldré — saldría* 'come out'. This can bring to mind Russian струя́, English *stream*, where comparative evidence also reveals the *t* to be inserted. It is tempting to see the same in кастрю́ля 'pan', assuming French *casserole* comes to mind, but here it is a borrowing, the insertion occurring probably in Czech, as the word wandered across Europe from French.

There is another member of this group in обня́ть(ся), impert. обнима́ть(ся) 'to embrace (one another)'. We might take this opportunity to discuss the -н- lying tantalizingly between the suffix and the root. There is no compelling physiological reason why an *n* should be there; Polish, for instance, doesn't have it: Polish *przyjść* — приня́ть 'to receive', *zjąć*— сня́ть 'to take off'. Russian nouns related to these verbs very often do not have the -н- either: съёмка 'filming, making of a film', прие́м 'reception', прия́тный 'pleasant (i.e. "acceptable")', прие́мник 'radio, receiver', прее́мник 'successor (i.e. someone who replaces someone else)', прие́млемый 'acceptable', восприя́тие 'perception', объём 'volume (i.e., what can be embraced/encompassed by something)', объя́тие 'embrace'. A nice related example is сонм 'gathering' with the prefix with the original nasal (but dialectal сойм 'peasant gathering' and суём, also 'gathering', without it). In Polish there is the *sejm*, the parliament.

This *n* is in fact related to another mystery *n* in Russian, namely the one found when prepositions govern the third person pronoun: у него́ 'in his possession, at his place' as against его́ 'him' and в его́ до́ме 'in his house'. What unites the two phenomena is the position after prepositions/prefixes, and historical linguistic study reveals that three prepositions originally ended in a nasal consonant: *wun, *sun, *kun, resp. в, с, к. At an earlier stage the last two had a final m, *n and *m doubtless neutralizing as *n, and can be related to Latin cum 'with' and Lithuanian kám 'to which (dative of the word for "what")' respectively. The first is actually the same as English in; at an early stage it probably could be either *un or *in. Now, given that the preceding vowel was short, this final nasal consonant would normally disappear, but, as is known, prepositions are linked accentually to the immediately following word, thus от меня 'from me' and зá гóродом 'out of town, in the countryside'. Each has only one stress, as if they were each just one word. So, as in the case of the diphthongs already looked at, before a vowel the n could be preserved. This happened in these prefixed verbs and also in the third person pronoun forms. Why in the latter is slightly mysterious, but it must have been early, since it is preserved in every Slavonic language but Belarusian (where it might be a recent loss), and in Serbo-Croatian we even find the forms without a preceding preposition. Perhaps it helps reduce the suppletive nature of this pronoun, i.e. the fact that the nominative forms, with a historical n (i.e. óн from *onъ 'that yonder'), and the rest come from different words! We might ask why all nouns beginning in a vowel do not prefix n when governed by a preposition; perhaps the answer has to be that this would cause chaos, and certainly obscure the declensions. Worse things do happen in languages, but just ask yourself whether forms like на нýзкой ýлице 'in a narrow street' and на нýлице 'in the street' would be likely to survive;[43] they might be seen as unstable and positionally conditioned, whereas there is some grammatical sense in distinguishing between из егó дóма 'out of his house' and из негó 'out of it' — in the former the preposition governs the noun, which is further defined by the possessive, while in the latter the preposition directly governs the personal pronoun. Of course, when the composition was closer, as in those verbs, then the n could survive, e.g. нанять 'to hire'. And there are indeed instances of the nasal surviving in nouns, e.g. снедь 'food', made up of сън- and the root ѢД 'eat', a dialectal word still fully surviving in, for example, Polish śniadanie 'breakfast'. Where the prefix preceded a consonant we might even have the reflex of a nasal, thus the obsolete Russian сусéд 'neighbour' (for сосéд), as against Polish sąsiad. This sort of archaic survival within ancient compounds can be fascinating, as in the word for 'bear', namely медвѣдь, which literally means 'honey-eat(er)', i.e. мёд + ѢД, the -в- reflecting the u- or w-sound which originally ended the word for honey.

You should be saying: But why have this n after на and all those other prepositions and prefixes, when originally it belonged to only three? Well, the answer seems to be that it spread by analogy, i.e. on the pattern of those three. And indeed, it still hasn't got all the way, since prepositions such as благодаря 'thanks to, because of' and вопреки 'in spite of, in defiance of' do not have it: благодаря емý 'thanks to him'.

---

[43]But how about нан, etc. before a vowel?

Going back to 'take' verbs, приня́ть, non-past приму́, при́мешь, ... при́мут, imperf. принима́ть, non-past принима́ю, etc. 'accept, receive, take' presents the prefix при- with a 'coming, towards where the subject is' sense. Note how the non-past of the perfective does not have -ьм-; perhaps this is a contraction of the vowels of при- and -ьм- (represented in a variable way in the current spelling of прийти́ — приду́ — пришёл 'come'). Now, we have seen that, in some aspectual pairs, the imperfective root may have an -и-, which is a lengthened version of what is in the perfective root. The Ukrainian equivalent of приму́ is прийму́, suggesting there may well have been contraction. And perhaps this spread by analogy, allowing an explanation of сня́ть — сниму́ — сни́мешь 'to take off' — compare this with Polish, where the development is historically regular: *zjąć* — non-past *zejmę, zejmiesz*, ... *zejmą* (the *e* of the prefix is equivalent to the о coming from a hard sign, as in the Russian equivalent съ-). We might add that there could be a link with име́ть 'to have' and its earlier variant имати. 'To have' and 'to take' in Slavonic are certainly related, as we might easily imagine, and conventional treatments of Ukrainian routinely link the imperfective future suffixed form -м- + -у, -еш, etc. to 'to take' rather than to what we might expect, namely 'to have', as happened in the formation of the future of many Romance languages.

This situation underlies many instances in Russian where an н or м appears from nowhere and can be shown to alternate with a я (or an a where the spelling rules so dictate, i.e. after ш, ж, ц, щ, ц). Thus:

жать/жал - жму, жмёшь, ... жмут 'squeeze' *and*
жать/жал - жну, жнёшь, ... жнут 'reap';

нача́ть, на́чал - начну́, начнёшь, ... начну́т 'begin'.

And here are a few examples of 'take' verbs:

(i) Perfective non-past in -иму́, -и́мешь, ... -и́мут:

восприня́ть/воспринима́ть 'to perceive';
отня́ть/отнима́ть 'to take away';
предприня́ть/предпринима́ть 'to undertake';
приня́ть/принима́ть 'to receive, accept, take';
сня́ть/снима́ть 'to take off, to take (a photo), to hire/rent'.

Note how the above verbs retain the -н- in the non-past.

(ii) Perfective non-past in -ьму́, -ьмёшь, ... -ьму́т:

> доня́ть/донима́ть 'to pester, vex';
> заня́ть/занима́ть 'to occupy, to interest';
> наня́ть/нанима́ть 'to hire';
> переня́ть/перенима́ть 'to imitate, acquire (habit), to intercept';
> поня́ть/понима́ть 'to understand';
> уня́ть(ся)/унима́ть(ся) 'to calm down, soothe (tr.)' (reflexive = intr.).

Note how the above verbs lose the -н- in the non-past

(iii) Obsolete non-past; now used only in the past:

> вня́ть/внима́ть 'to hear, heed (+ dat.; imperf. non-past вне́млю, вне́млешь (obs.))'

All the imperfectives are derived by lengthening of the root vowel and stress on the infinitive suffix, as very often happens, and conjugate according to the pattern -а́ю, -а́ешь, ... -а́ют.

And remember the verb вы́нуть, imperf. вынима́ть 'to take out'. It must belong to the family, but has an unexpected perfective infinitive. Its non-past rubs this in further: вы́ну, вы́нешь, ... вы́нут. It is as if this word has no root, as we would surely expect вы́(й)му,... It is likely that here the stress facilitated a contamination of the expected -нять with the semelfactive suffix -ну-, and the non-past pattern followed or came along simultaneously. Note Ukrainian, with little reduction or blurring of unstressed vowels, and the expected form: ви́йняти (and the imperfective pattern illustrates greater regularity, viz. виймáти).

Do work through the above list of members of this family. Some will be easier to tie in to the idea of 'take' than others. Thus: поня́ть 'to understand' can be readily linked to 'to grasp, comprehend' — note the root *prehend-* 'grasp, get a grip of' (note the English itself); French *(com)prendre*; German *begreifen*; but доня́ть 'to pester, exasperate (someone)' seems harder to grasp.

4.3.53 *Thirsty* and *waiting* — ЖАД — ЖЬД (*žęd-, *žьd-)

All the alternating involving з and ж might benefit from a discussion of жа́жда and the related adjective жа́дный 'greedy' (the verb жа́ждать 'to thirst (+ gen. = 'for') is obsolescent in its odd conjugation, namely жа́жду, жа́ждешь,...). Given that in the adjective the suffix -ьн- crops up again, it seems there is an alternation of д with жд: жа́дный — жа́ждать. In Chapters 2 and 3 it was noted that д also alternates with ж, and that while жд was Church Slavonic when it alternated with д, ж in the same circumstances was usually Native Russian (we say 'usually' because in East Slavonic texts Church Slavonic words tended to have ж at first, and жд was a later innovative archaicism!).[44] Note that, when жд does not alterate with д, it is not ChSl, e.g. in ждать 'to wait' (there are no related words with ж alone), something given away in addition by the fact that the vowel и can appear in between: дожидаться, suggesting a root Ж/Д).

As a further example of the consonantal alternation ж/жд we can look at the nouns суд 'court, trial, judgement' and судья 'judge'. The verb судить 'to judge' has a first person singular сужу and a derived (verbal) noun суждение; the related perfective verbs осудить 'to condemn (на + acc. = 'to')', обсудить 'to discuss', рассудить 'to decide between, consider' have exactly the same pattern. Their imperfectives are resp. осуждать, обсуждать, and, in the slightly different sense of 'to reason, discuss, debate', рассуждать; the verbal nouns are осуждение, обсуждение, рассуждение; and the past passive participle осуждённый,... Similar verbs may have problems in forming the first person singular — the form which is Native Russian, while there is no problem with the Church Slavonic forms! Thus убедить 'to persuade' and победить 'to conquer' (убежу and побежу are expected) do not have such a form, possibly because of the risk (however incorrect from the point of view of the standard language) of confusion with убежать 'to run away' and побежать 'to run off'.

We can also come across interesting cross-linguistic parallels regarding these doublets. For instance, recall that Russian has невежда and невежа, both epicene nouns deriving from the root ВѢД 'know', itself related to 'to wit' and 'witness', German *wissen*, etc. and, within Russian, forms such as языковедение 'linguistics' (with языкознание a calque of German *Sprachwissenschaft*), Бог весть! 'God [only] knows!' The first is Church Slavonic and means 'ignoramus', while the second is Native Russian and means 'uncouth, impolite person'. Related to them both, but more similar to the second, is невежливый 'impolite' (and, of course, the opposite); and in many dialects of English 'ignorant' means 'impolite'. We can, needless to say, go on and on with examples, e.g. надежда 'hope' — надёжный 'reliable' — обнадёжить 'to fill (someone) with hope', одежда 'clothes' — одёжка 'togs' (a nice riddle, загадка, is: Сто одёжек, и все без застёжек 'A hundred articles of clothing, and all without a fastener'; the solution, разгадка, is: Капуста 'A cabbage') — note that in these last two examples the е can become ё, which, as we know, is an indication of a Native Russian character. In невежа this doesn't obtain, as the *e* is a *jat'*.

Not relevant here, but simply an interesting digression, is another Russian word, this time a preposition. In talking about 'mediocrity' there was reference to things done 'between' the start and the end. Russian for 'between' is между. This is ChS; a native form is меж, as in the expression меж двух огней 'between two fires (= "between the devil and the deep blue sea", "between a rock and a hard

---

[44]We might expect a Native Russian жажа 'thirst', but it seems not to occur.

place")'. The жд — ж contrast suggests original *dj, and that would suggest a source related to *medium* — in Vulgar Latin a syllabic *i* after a consonant and before a vowel changed into a *jot*, and that *jot* wrought the same havoc in Romance that it wrought in Slavonic — think of French *moyen* and Italian *mezzo*. Going slightly further, why the genitive case in the set expression, as мéжду takes the instrumental these days? Well, perhaps because мéжду is historically the prepositional dual of the noun меж(д)а 'boundary' (the surviving form, межá, still means this), i.e. it meant 'in/on two boundaries', and we can easily imagine that 'within two boundaries/limits *of* X and Y' could acquire the sense 'between X and Y'.

4.3.54 *Try* — СТАР — ПЫТ (*star-, *pyt-)

The verb we most often encounter at an early stage in learning Russian is старáться, non-past старáюсь, etc., perf. постарáться The etymology is unclear, though there may be a link with *strenuous* (see 4.3.58) and with Lithuanian *starìnti* 'to pull hard' (also *stóras* 'strong'). We have predictable derivatives, e.g. старáтельный 'assiduous', старáние 'effort', and with unexpected meanings, e.g. старáтель '(gold) prospector'.

We also have пытáться, non-past пытáюсь, etc., perf. попытáться 'to attempt'. Non-reflexively it now has senses of 'torture, torment (fig. and concr.); try for (e.g. "one's luck")'. All this reflects a semantic constraint away from the arguably more general meaning, still prevalent in several Slavonic languages, of 'ask'. Some care is required in this connection, thus пы́тка 'torture', as against попы́тка 'attempt'. Derived forms are numerous, e.g. пытли́вый 'inquisitive, searching', испытáть, imperf. испы́тывать 'to undergo, experience; test', испытáние 'ordeal'. The root is found also in Latin, e.g. *putō* 'I think, suspect; tidy; cut' — think of *amputation* (cutting away, into 'both').

A more recent acquisition is прóбовать, non-past прóбую, etc., perf. попрóбовать 'try', probably coming through Polish *próbować*, and related to a Middle Latin form *probāre* 'to approve', derived from *probus* and thus ultimately probably related to прáвый 'right'.

4.3.55 *Turn* — ВОРОТ, ВРАТ, ВЕРТ — КРУТ ((*vort-, *vьrt- — *krǫt-)

It is good to start from a less obvious verb: завернýть, non-past завернý, завернёшь, ... завернýт, imperf. заворáчивать, non-past заворáчиваю, etc., or завёртывать, non-past завёртываю, etc. means 'to wrap up (tr.)', among much else. We can imagine closing something by turning paper behind and around it. Something is missing here. Завернýть goes quite neatly with завёртывать, if we allow for a *tn* group becoming *n*. Also, if we suspect the underlying presence of вертéть, non-past верчý, вéртишь, ... вéртят 'twirl, twist, turn (tr.)', we note a disregard for the softness of the *t* in the derivation of завёр<u>ты</u>вать. We might note too a verb завертéть 'to begin to twirl'. The picture is beginning to look very complicated. What is missing, however, is a verb заворотить, which would pair very neatly with завора́чивать. Well, заворотить does in fact exist, and does pair with завора́чивать in meanings apart from 'to wrap up' ('to turn, roll up, tuck up'), and завора́чивать has its own special (if informal), imperfective-only, meaning 'to be the boss of (+ instr.)'. Note too the epicene noun вороти́ла 'bigwig'.

What emerges from this complicated picture is that there are, so far, two roots, namely ВОРОТ and ВЕРТ, with the first suggesting pleophony and the second an original front *jer*. If the first is correct, we might expect a variant root ВРАТ. We do not have to look far: возврати́ться, non-past возвращу́сь, возврати́шься, ... возвратя́тся, imperf. возвраща́ться, non-past возвраща́юсь, etc. 'come back, return', with its Church Slavonic metathesis, jotation of *t*, and treatment of a weak *jer* in a prefix. Don't forget the alternative perfective верну́ться, demonstrating just how close the links are in this family.

We may move from here to note обрати́ться, non-past обращу́сь, обрати́шься, ... обратя́тся, imperf. обраща́ться, non-past обраща́юсь, etc. 'to treat; address' (constructed with к + dat. for the person addressed or treated, and с + instr. for how that person is treated), with the loss of *v* in the group *bv*, something we also note in the Native Russian обороти́ться, imperf. обора́чиваться 'to turn round; turn out' (plus the alternative perfective оберну́ться).[45]

Given pleophony and metathesis, we assume an earlier root *vort-*. This makes us think of *vortex*, which fits in with the idea of 'turning' — the examples are numerous: воротни́к 'collar', переворо́т 'coup d'état, revolution', развра́т 'depravity', отвраще́ние 'repulsion', воро́та 'gate', врата́рь goalkeeper'. There is a whole series of ablaut variants, e.g. a root *vert-* also seems likely, given веретено́ 'spindle' and, since time turns or revolves, вре́мя 'time' — all cognate with Latin *vertō* 'I turn'.[46] Close cognates include Lithuanian *vartaĩ* 'gate' and *veřsti*, non-past *verčiù* 'to turn, I turn'. Perhaps верёвка 'rope' comes in here too.

In крути́ться, кручу́сь, кру́тишься, ... кру́тятся 'to revolve, whirl' we note the Native Russian consonantal alternation in the first person singular and the retracting stress. The root is КРУТ and it also gives круто́й 'steep' — so this example goes against the suggestion that stress is fixed where derivation is nominal; perhaps it is a question of how ancient, and thus even obscured, the derivation is, and of complex prosodic issues. So things go round, change direction on steep slopes: 'a rolling stone gathers no moss'. We can reinforce this by mentioning Lithuanian *krañtas* 'bank (of river), edge'. Though there relationship between the Baltic languages, of which Lithuanian is one, and the Slavonic ones is ancient, the Lithuanian word reminds us that at an late stage of

---

[45]Do bear in mind that the semantic nuances here are quite complex and that there is no space to explore them.

[46]We might be tempted to bring in верх 'top' as well, given that something might turn and twist as it rises.

Common Slavonic there were two nasal vowels, the second, *ǫ, possibly comparable to French *on* in *bon*. As we've seen, the cyrillic letter designed to represent this sound was Ѫ, a letter (but not sound), which survived in Bulgarian until the spelling reform after the Second World War. This nasal vowel arose in exactly the same circumstances as the front nasal *ę (in cyrillic ѧ), namely when the nasal consonant in a nasal diphthong preceded a consonant, and when the vowel in a nasal diphthong at the end of a word was long, e.g. the у in the accusative singular of many feminine nouns: жену́, from *genām, the root in an even earlier form relatable to English *queen*, Norwegian *kvinne*, not to mention the root of *misogyny*, *gynaecology*, etc., formed on Greek *gūnē*.

Much, much more could be said about verbs of 'turning'. It would be a good exercise to list as many as possible, using conventional and reverse dictionaries. Remember to note aspect and how verbs pair, if they do.

4.3.56 *Use* — (ПО)ЛЬЗ — (ПО)ЛЬГ — ЛЬГ(ЪК) — ТЕРЕБ — ТРѢБ (*(po)lьg-, *lьg(ъk)-, *terb-)

In some verbs 'to use' there is a root ЛЬЗ (concealing a real root ЛЬГ, as in the word льго́та 'privilege') and a prefix по-, but the sequence польз itself functions more or less as a root since льз itself does not form the basis of word families, though we could argue against this by citing нельзя́, made up of не + the nominal root ЛЬГ plus a dative ending which changed the г into з by the Second Palatalization and then itself changed into я, probably as a 'restoration' of a nominative, as in стезя́ 'path', contrasted, as we have already seen, with the genitive concealed in ни зги не ви́дно 'it's pitch-black (= "one can't see the path")'. We can imagine a similarity to constructions such as быть грозе́ 'there's going to be a storm', ва́м не вида́ть таки́х бед 'you will never see such misfortunes', with a possible link with the original status of the infinitive as a noun in the dative (we find it as a noun as well as an infinitive in, for example, мочь 'power', which doesn't actually occur as a verb, знать 'the nobility', and стать 'build; points (pl., of a horse)'.

The forms with льз, with the *z* hard, however, might be seen as Third Palatalization and likely to be Church Slavonic. The verb испо́льзовать, non-past испо́льзую, etc. 'make use of; exploit' has the prefix из- and is both imperfective and perfective, hence interesting in being prefixed yet imperfective and in being biaspectual. At one stage verbs in -овать represented the potential to be derived imperfectives rivalling -ывать, but this never really happened (probably partly because they specialized in provided the morphology for borrowings and were biaspectual except where forms such as аресто́вывать 'to arrest' emerged and also because of a tendency for -овать and -ывать to be pronounced identically, viz. [əvətʲ]) and is restricted to a very few complex families, e.g, испове́доваться 'to confess' and минова́ть 'to pass by', both biaspectual (but worth checking in a good dictionary), and participial forms such as неописуемый 'indescribable', испытующий 'searching (of a look)', all corresponding to modern imperfectives in -ывать.

The verb пользоваться, пользуюсь, пользуешься, ... пользуются + instr. has perfective воспользоваться, thus with the prefix воз-/вос-. It is a quite neutral sort of 'use' word, and can be extended to phrases such as пользоваться хорошей репутацией 'to have (lit. "use") a good reputation', пользоваться случаем 'to make use of/profit from an opportunity'. Note that the noun польза means 'use, profit, benefit' and provides the adjective полезный 'useful', whence бесполезный 'useless, thus the mobile vowel making an appearance. If we reconstruct полезный as пользьный, it can be confirmed that when there are consecutive hard/soft signs in an underlying form, the last one disappears and the immediately preceding one becomes е (from a soft sign) or о (from a hard sign).

We might note that this root is linked to лёгкий 'light; easy', in which the first vowel, though historically reflecting a *jer*, never alternates with zero. In other words, we expect, but do not get, the short-form masculine льгок.

If in doubt about how to translate 'use', then употребить, non-past употреблю, употребишь, ... употребят, imperf. употреблять, non-past употребляю, употребляешь, ... употребляют + acc. might be recommended. This is a Church Slavonicism, the East Slavonic, pleophonic, form reflected in теребить, non-past тереблю, теребишь, ... теребят 'pick (at); pull (flax); pester' (there may be a link with 'rubbing', as in the verb тереть) The family may have earlier senses of clearing or clearing land, leading to working and to doing things out of need, in order to achieve something. A nominal form has given a very important modal in several Slavonic languages, e.g. Ukrainian треба and Bulgarian трябва 'it is necessary'. This verb has a double prefix and a quite regular aspectual derivation. Removing the first prefix we obtain потребить, imperf. потреблять 'to consume, use', reflected in expressions such as потребительское общество 'the consumer society', товары широкого потребления 'consumer goods'. Removing the second prefix we obtain требовать, требую, требуешь, ... требуют 'to demand', perf. потребовать, an entirely regular -ов(а)- verb.

4.3.57 *Want, wish, seek* — ХОТ — ЖЕЛ — ИСК (*xot-/*xъt-, *žel-, *isk-)

The most common word for 'want' is хотеть, non-past хочу, хочешь, хочет, хотим, хотите, хотят, perf. захотеть — note its conjugation in the singular according to the first and its plural according to the second conjugation. Its etymology is quite obscure, with the likelihood of an affective origin, given, for example, the *x* at the beginning. Some ancient origin might be reflected in a similarity to Breton *c'hoant* 'desire'. It features in the meaning 'hunt': охотиться, охочусь, охотишься, ... охотятся, with the noun охота meaning both 'hunt' and 'desire', to which we can attach охотно 'willingly'. Russian only requires a root with the vowel *o*, but other Slavonic languages require *ь, e.g. Polish *chcieć*. This verb is particularly important in South Slavonic languages, because it helps, along with other languages in the Balkans, to provide the future tense, somewhat as in English, e.g. *I'll do*.

Also common is жела́ть, non-past жела́ю, etc., perf. пожела́ть. The etymology here is even more obscure, though a link with Greek *thelō* 'I wish' is very likely. We imagine the possibility of a link with 'pain' and 'pity', i.e. жаль, and even желу́док 'stomach' might be tempting. Given a First Palatalization, there might be scope for an ancient vowel alternation, as evidenced in the Russian dialect verb га́лить 'to wish'. Wishful thinking might suggest a link with Lithuanian *galéti* 'to be able'. Associated with the problems here may be that, though the verb is attested in many Slavonic languages, in several, mainly from Serbo-Croat up to the Czech and Slovak area, a probably older form in *-ěti* is attested.

Finally, because 'seeking' and 'wanting' do go together in general and in actual lexical meaning in some Slavonic languages, we can mention иска́ть, non-past ищу́, и́щешь, ... и́щут. As we might imagine, there is no real perfective, but we can suggest найти́ 'to find' and поиска́ть 'to have a little look (for)'. Bulgarian и́скам 'I want' reflects the lexical change, and Polish *szukać* 'to look for' the tendency for several Slavonic languages to lose (the details are complex) absolute word-initial *i. We might mention an interesting semantic narrowing in Czech *vískat* 'to delouse' (a sense of running one's fingers through one's hair). For Russian, note the pronunciation reflected in the spelling when a consonant-final prefix occurs, e.g. разыска́ть 'to seek out', imperf. разы́скивать.

4.3.58 *Work* — РАБ(ОТ) — СТРАД — ТЬРП (*orb-, *strad-, *tьrp-)

In the word рабо́та the component -от- is a suffix. In East and West Slavonic and in parts of the South Slavonic area we have *rob-, as the reflex of inversion of a diphthong with falling pitch, but a Church Slavonic form has prevailed in Russian, thus ра́б 'slave' (note the word for a female slave, namely раба́, presumably with a zero-suffix and a feminine declensional ending). As we've seen already, the word itself is cognate with German *die Arbeit* 'work', Latin *orbus* 'orphaned, deprived', and the word *orphan* itself, as in Greek *orfanós*. There is the same base in ребёнок 'child', presumably with the original *o* assimilating to the original *e* of the immediately following syllable. The word itself would have started off as *orbę, a consonantal-stem noun based on *-nt-, the *n combining with the immediately preceding *e to give a front nasal, which would subsequently denasalize to give *ja*, thus ребя́та in that and many other plurals denoting the young of animals. The -ёнок- suffix is a Russian innovation; in other Slavonic languages the original structure, and neuter gender, is retained, e.g, Ukrainian теля́ 'calf' as against Russian телёнок.

In the derived verb we have рабо́тать, non-past рабо́таю, etc. 'to work', without a clear perfective. We normally go for порабо́тать, though it has a clear nuance of 'a bit of'. Possibly this structure reflects a static, general state such as we have in спать 'to sleep' (see 4.3.47), different though the non-pasts may be. By transitivizing, or 'factitivizing', the verb, we get поработи́ть, non-past порабощу́, поработи́шь, ... поработя́т, imperf. порабоща́ть, non-past порабоща́ю, etc., 'enslave; enthral', the *šč* reflex of jotated *t* revealing a Church Slavonicism. There are numerous verbs derived from рабо́тать, e.g. зарабо́тать, imperf. зараба́тывать 'to earn' and подрабо́тать, imperf. подраба́тывать 'to earn a bit extra', both exhibiting regular derivational processes.

From this we may move to страда́ 'hard work; harvest work' — note the zero suffix. This word is perhaps more familiar as страда́ть, non-past страда́ю, etc. 'suffer', with as rough perfective пострада́ть. It has an obsolete, Church-Slavonic, non-past стра́жду, стра́ждешь, ... стра́ждут. It may be that examples like this suggest that verbs now manifesting the first conjugation and having jotation throughout exhibit one important type, now much reduced by the innovation of affixation of the jot to the stem-final vowel rather than to the root-final consonant, possibly starting with verbs whose root ended in a vowel, e.g. зна́ть, with its root ЗНА. So ка́пает 'it drips' replaces (partly) ка́плет 'it drips', and many others. Of course, this is a rough approximation of a much more complex phenomenon.

Coming back to the focus of the discussion, страда́ть in dialect may have the meaning 'to harvest; get, win, earn (fig.)', the last meaning picking up an English word used to render meanings of зарабо́тать and подрабо́тать. And we have постра́да in dialect, indicating the end of the harvest time. There are indications that the initial *s* is not always present in the many attestations across Indo-European, but examples with *s* include Latin *strēnuus* 'demanding', in which we can see English *strenuous* and Greek *strēnés* 'sharp' (a closer semantic link for this will soon be seen). And, as befits 'suffering', Russian стра́сть 'passion' comes in here too, with the suffix -т- and the familiar development of **d* or **t* immediately before **t*. We may note that in Latvian *strādāt* means 'to work'.

At this point we come to терпе́ть, non-past терплю́, те́рпишь, ... те́рпят 'suffer, endure', another rather static verb, with rough perfectives потерпе́ть 'to suffer, sustain' and вы́терпеть 'to endure'. We may also mention dialectal perfective терпну́ть and the pair за-те́рпнуть, with the sense of growing numb ('falling asleep'), including figuratively, e.g. with fear. This verb is cognate with Lithuanian *tir̃pti* and Latin *torpeō* 'I become stiff', *torpidus* 'numb', thus English *torpor*, *torpid*, etc. The meanings extend to Russian те́рпкий 'astringent; tart, sharp'.

Worth mentioning in this connection, because it helps confront the complexities of verbs of motion, is imperfective-only выноси́ть 'to bear, endure', usually used in the negative and common in other forms, e.g. невыноси́мый 'unbearable'. Compare it with the expected pair вы́нести, imperf. выноси́ть 'to carry out' and perfective вы́носить, imperf. вына́шивать 'to bear, be pregnant, hatch'.

4.3.59 *Write* and *print* — ПИС — ПЕЧ(АТ) (*pis-, *peč(at)-)

In приписа́ть, non--past припишу́, припи́шешь, ... припи́шут, imperf. припи́сывать, non-past припи́сываю, etc. there is the basic verb писа́ть, on-past пишу́, пи́шешь, ... пи́шут 'write'. The derivation is straightforward. The basic verb has a root ПИС. This is historically related to English *picture*, which comes from the Latin passive participle *pictus*, from the verb *pingo, pingere, pixi*. It means 'to paint', just as can писа́ть. The Latin *c* represents an original palatal *k'*, which in Slavonic became *s*, as in сто as against Latin *centum*.[47] Now there is also a Latin verb *pinsō* 'I push, shove', with an inserted *n*; in Russian there is an identical verb пиха́ть, non-past пиха́ю, etc., perf. пихну́ть, non-past пихну́, пихнёшь, ... пихну́т 'push; shove, cram'. Here the original *s* (ignore the *n*-infix) has become x. If the palatal *k* had become *s* early enough, then 'to write' would be пиха́ть. It can't have, so it seems the *s* became x before the palatal *k'* became *s*! The *s* becoming x is something we have seen before — the *ruki*-rule (see 4.2.7.3). It happened in the Baltic languages too, with slight differences. This root might also be found in пёстрый 'multicoloured', which indicates the variant *рьs-, found in Czech *psát* 'to write'.

Печа́тать, non-past печа́таю, etc. 'print (imperf.)' (perf. напеча́тать) is a verb formed on the noun печа́ть, originally masculine and now feminine, which is probably in turn based on the root behind the verb пе́чь 'to bake', thus, as it were, 'branding'. The character of the original suffix is not entirely clear —Polish has a nasal, but the evidence of other Slavonic languages does not support this.

Just to finish off...

See what you can make of the following groups of words. Can you work out how they are related to each other, i.e. what lies behind the variation in stems? They are listed in no particular order. At this stage on the whole just try to describe, without seeking too much explanation. If you can make lateral connections, however, do. For example, don't just think about the particular group of words; think about the actual forms. For instance, in (1) we have an adjective and its short comparative form. We can see that the к has become ч. In a way, that's enough. But if you wished to go further, you could ask what caused the change of consonant, and the answer would be got by comparing гро́мкий - гро́мче with other similar pairs.

---

[47]This also applies to PIE palatal *g*, which became *z*. An good example from Russian is зуб 'tooth', which is related to English *comb*, i.e. something with 'teeth'! In Greek there is *gómphos* 'tooth, nail, stake'. The *g* is originally a palatal *g*, which became *z* in Slavonic. Compare, already encountered, знать 'to know' and *gnostic* — or even bring in *recognize, know*.

1. громкий - громче	17. дух - душа́
2. муж - му́жество	18. мочь - могу́ - мо́жешь - по́мощь
2. лицо́ - обли́к	19. стать - ста́ну
4. веду́ - вести́	20. власть - о́бласть
5. дви́гать - дви́нуть	21. медве́дь - мёд - есть
6. разгово́р - разгова́ривать	22. нача́ть - начина́ть - начну́
7. день - дня	23. сестра́ - сестёр
8. брать - беру́ - собо́р	24. слыха́ть - слы́шать
9. голова́ - глава́	25. спать - сплю
10. встре́тить - встре́чу - встреча́ть	26. стоя́щий - стоя́чий
11. пла́кать - пла́чу - пла́чешь	27. плати́ть - плачу́ - пла́тишь
12. вода́ - водяно́й - во́ды - во́дка	28. подня́ть - по́днят - поднима́ть
13. весна́ - вёсны	29. жена́ - жёны - же́нский
14. веду́ - вёл - ве́дший	30. стена́ - сте́ны
15. статья́ - стате́й	31. земля́ - земе́ль - земно́й
16. на́ция - на́ций	32. ти́хий - сухо́й

Some suggestions

1. громкий - громче: jotation, confirmed by comparison with просто́й — про́ще 'simple — simpler'.
2. муж - му́жество: the suffix -ьство, with the weak *jer* vocalized perhaps to separate the consonants.
3. лицо́ - обли́к: Third Palatalization in лицо́.
4. веду́ - вести́: underlying infinitive *vedti*, where *dt* became *tt* then *st*.
5. дви́гать - дви́нуть: simplification of consonant group *gn*.
6. разгово́р - разгова́ривать: imperfectivizing suffix and lengthening of immediately preceding (root) vowel.
7. день - дня: root ДЬН, revealing mobile vowel alternation.
8. брать - беру́ - собо́р: ablaut, with front *jer* in the root of the non-past.
9. голова́ - глава́: pleophony and metathesis/inversion.
10. встре́тить - встре́чу - встреча́ть: jotation in the first person singular of a second-conjugation verb and in the derived imperfective.
11. пла́кать - пла́чу - пла́чешь: jotation throughout the non-past of a first-conjugation verb.
12. вода́ - водяно́й - во́ды - во́дка: different pronunciations of the root vowel and the root-final consonant, but all united through the spelling. Note the suffix -ька.
13. весна́ - вёсны: like #12.
14. веду́ - вёл - ве́дший: simplification of *dl* and different pronunciations of historical *e* — probably Church Slavonic in the participle.
15. статья́ - стате́й: zero ending in the genitive plural. Underlying *-ьjь. Russian treatment of 'tense' *jer*.
16. на́ция - на́ций: as #15, but Church Slavonic treatment of 'tense' *jer*.
17. дух - душа́: jotation of root-final consonant reflecting particular declension class.
18. мочь - могу́ - мо́жешь - по́мощь: various reflexes of root МОГ, the first and last being Native Russian and Church Slavonic respectively, and the third a First Palatalization before a primary front vowel.

19. стать - ста́ну: an inserted *n*, which may be an infix to a vowel-final root СТА.

20. власть - о́бласть: simplification of the group *bv* to *b*.

21. медве́дь - мёд - есть: the в reflects the original declensional marker *w* of the *u*-stem noun медъ.

22. нача́ть - начина́ть - начну́: reflexes of a nasal dipthong, giving a nasal vowel, preconsonantally, in нача́ть and, pre-vocalically, in начина́ть (with lengthening of the root vowel in the derived imperfective) and the non-past of нача́ть.

23. сестра́ - сестёр: moble vowel by analogy in the gen./acc.pl. of сестра́, and change of *e* to *o*.

24. слыха́ть - слы́шать: different origins, the former probably iterative, with an *a* suffix, the latter probably durative, with an *ě* (its antecedent) suffix.

25. спать - сплю: unexpected non-past, given the infinitive. Possibly a combination of an iterative in the infinitive and past stem, and another verb in the non-past.

26. стоя́щий - стоя́чий: Church Slavonic and Native Russian reflexes respectively of a jotated *t*. The former is the present participle active; the latter is the same, but sidelined as an adjective or noun.

27. плати́ть - плачу́ - пла́тишь: as #10. Note the mobile stress, and look up the derived imperfective, e.g. of расплати́ться.

28. подня́ть - по́днят - поднима́ть: forms reflecting the development of a nasal diphthong, as in #22.

29. жена́ - жёны - же́нский: note the various root vowels; that of же́нский may be an inhibition of the change of stressed *e* to *o* by the suffix -ьск-.

30. стена́ - сте́ны́: note the stressed vowel. An indication of *jat'*.

31. земля́ - земе́ль - земно́й: note the analogical mobile vowel of the gpl, coming between the components of a jotation *m*, supported by the absence of *l* from земно́й.

32. ти́хий - сухо́й: evidence for the hard-adjective character of adjectives in к, г, and х. Note too the evidence from the Old Moscow pronunciation, namely of a reduced *o* in the vowel of the unstressed ending.

Appendices and Abbreviations

Appendix 1: The Common-Slavonic equivalents of the Russian vowels and consonants

What follows is expressed in very approximate terms.

The vowel phonemes of Modern Russian are usually symbolized as follows:

i/y		u
	e	o
	a	

The vowels have the following origins in Common Slavonic ('*' = hypothetical; the macron, or dash over the vowel, indicates length — absence of the macron indicates shortness; the little 'v' over the *e* is the way of indicating *jat'*; the cedilla-like hooks under *o* and *e* indicate nasality):

/i-y/:   **i* (‹ **ī/ej*), **y* (‹ **ū*): с<u>и</u>ний 'blue' / в<u>и</u>д 'view', с<u>ы</u>н 'son' respectively.

/e/:   **ě* (‹ **ē/oj-aj*), some **e* (‹ **e*), **ь* (‹ **i*): в<u>ѣ</u>ра 'faith' / цен<u>а́</u> 'price', н<u>е</u>сти 'to carry', д<u>е</u>нь 'day' respectively.

/a/:   **a* (‹ **ā/ō*), **ę* (‹ high front vowel+ nasal vowel): душ<u>а́</u> 'soul', п<u>я</u>ть 'five' respectively.

/o/:   **o* (‹ **a/o*), some **e*, **ъ*, **ь*: д<u>о</u>м 'house', л<u>ё</u>д 'ice', с<u>о</u>н 'sleep, dream', л<u>ё</u>н 'linen, flax' respectively.

/u/:   **ū₂* (‹ **aw/ow*), **ǫ* (‹ **back vowel + nasal consonant): с<u>у</u>хо́й 'dry', р<u>у</u>ка́ 'hand, arm' respectively (**ū₂* = *secondary* long **ū*, which took the place vacated by the shift forward of *primary* long **ū* — see сын above).

The very approximate schema for Late Common Slavonic would be:

Palatal		*Velar*	*Labio-velar*	
i	ь	ы	ъ	u
e				o
	ę		ǫ	
	ě	a		

Do remember that the name 'labio-velar' indicates that the lips play a role in the articulation of these vowels, i.e. the lips are 'rounded'. To the above one may add the syllabic resonants m, n, r, and l (possibly with palatal forms). The vowel *ъı is often denoted as *y. This presentation is based on Samilov 1964.

At a stage preceding jotation and the Slavonic palatalizations of velars, Common or Proto-Slavonic is likely to have had the following consonants:

		labial	*dental*	*palatal*	*velar*
stops	vss	p	t		k
	vd	b	d		g
fricatives	vss		s		x
	vd		z		
sonorants	nasal	m	n		
	glides	w/v		j	
	liquids		l		
			r		

These provided all the ingredients for the simplifications of consonantal groups, jotation, the palatalizations, and the monophthongizations of diphthongs (the diphthongs *oj, *aj led to the secondary front vowels which caused the Second Palatalization, the liquid diphthongs (= r, l, leading to metathesis and pleophony), the nasal diphthongs (leading to the rise of nasal vowels), and the diphthongs in *w, leading to *u). The development of the *jers*, their vocalization and loss, then reintroduced closed syllables and consonantal groups.

Appendix 2: A Sketch of the history of the Russian sound-system

What follows is expressed in very approximate terms, as in Appendix 1.

B.C.

The *ruki*-rule and the change in PIE palatal velars.

B.C.-A.D.

Simplifications of consonantal groups, jotation, overlapping with
the First Slavonic Palatalization of Velars, all together building up into the Open-Syllable Period and, for instance, the monophthongization of tautosyllabic diphthongs (including the beginnings of the nasal vowels and of liquid metathesis);
the Second Slavonic Palatalization of Velars;
changes in liquid diphthongs (pleophony, metathesis/inversion)...

and its passing:

the Third Slavonic Palatalization of Velars and the loss and vocalization of the *jers*.

Certain elements fitting in with the emergence of Common East Slavonic (850...)

The earliest might be:

(a) The denasalization of the nasal vowels: *ǫ* › *u*, *ę* › *a*. The difference between such words as рад and ряд comes to rest on the hard or soft quality of the *r*. Bit by bit this will extend to other positions, reinforcing the important distinctive character of soft consonants in Russian.

(b) Absolute word-initial *e-* becomes *o-* unless (arguably) there is a *jer* in the immediately following syllable.

(c) The fading of absolute word-final *ъ, ь*. Together with the denasalization of *ę*, this is an extremely important development, in that the loss of a final soft sign had the effect of the transfer of softness from the soft sign to the preceding consonant, e.g. *kost'* ‹ *kostь* 'bone'.

followed by...

(a) The fading of word-internal weak *jers*.

(b) The vocalization of 'strong' *jers*, *ь* to *e* (*ë*), *ъ* to *o*.

(c) The vowels *i* and *y* merge phonologically, but not phonetically.

(d) The vowels *e* and *ě* begin to merge phonetically.

and...

(a) The syllables *ky*, *gy*, *xy* (кы, гы, хы) become *ki*, *gi*, *xi*.

(b) The emergence of the phonemic/phonological opposition between hard and soft consonants before *o*.

(c) The sounds *š* and *ž* become hard.

(d) The sound *c* becomes hard, but only after the completion of the merger of *e* with *ě*.

(e) The emergence of *akańje* (essentially the *a*-pronunciation of *o* immediately before the stress).

(f) The emergence of *v* before absolute word-initial *o*, e.g., вот, вóсемь, держáть ýхо вострó 'to be on one's guard' (but óстрый; cf. навострúть ýши / лы́жи 'to listen with great attention' / 'to prepare to make off', where we probably have a phonetic insertion of *v* between the two vowels 'inspired' by the existence of вострó).

and...

(g)   The emergence of the phonemic opposition of hard and soft consonants before *e*.

and it continues, apace.

Appendix 3: The Russian verb and aspect

Veyrenc 1970:89-98 has been liberally drawn on here, meanings are on the whole not given, and some use is made of transliteration. Most of all to be borne in mind is that aspect is a relatively recent phenomenon so far as conventional descriptions of Russian are concerned. In the Old Rus' language such a phenomenon as the addition of a prefix to a simple verb did not automatically create a perfective verb. Such instances in the modern language are often seen as somehow alien to the spirit of the language, i.e. they may be calques. Two phenomena, which will provide the building blocks for the system, are there at the beginning and are in no way peculiar to Slavonic: (i) prefixes, as just mentioned, and (ii) the derivation of iteratives. It can be readily imagined that they help in forming the base for the opposition of perfective and imperfective verbs respectively. That aspect evolved so comprehensively in Slavonic is in great part connected to the decay of the system of tenses. Veyrenc gives the following iterative developments:

(a)   verbs derived with the suffix **i*: **nesti* — **nositi*, **idti* — **xoditi*;
(b)   verbs with the suffix **a* alongside the suffix **i* or **ě*: **skočiti* — **skakati*, **xvatiti* — **xvatati*, **stǫpiti* — **stǫpati*, **viděti* — **vidati*;
(c)   verbs with the suffix **a* alongside the semelfactive suffix **nǫ*: **tьlkati* — **tьlknǫti* (= толка́ть, толкну́ть), **prygati* — **prygnǫti*, **dvigati* — **dvignǫti* (Veyrenc mentions that the iteratives here often had the old non-past, e.g. **dvižet-*, but might move to the **znati* pattern);
(d)   verbs with the suffix **ja* alongside the suffix **i*: **proščati* — **prostiti*, **rož(d)ati* — **roditi*, **lišati* — **lišiti*, **rěšati* — **rěšiti*, **věšati* — **věsiti*, **strěljati* — **-strěliti*.

The above four types, probably reflecting the earliest types, are now completely scattered, their original rationale, whatever it precisely was, quite lost: determinate vs. indeterminate, aspectual pairs (лиша́ть - лиши́ть), transitive-intransitive pairs (ве́шать - ве́сить), lexical dissociation, and occurrence of one partner only with a prefix (вы́стрелить).

The remaining three types exemplify iteratives used as independent verbs (in the past tense) until the nineteenth century:

(e)   verbs with the suffix *a* on an adapted root: бира́ть — бра́ть, жина́ть — жа́ть, еда́ть — есть;

(f)   verbs with the suffix *va* on a vowel-final root: быва́ть — бы́ть, пива́ть — пи́ть, знава́ть — зна́ть;

(g)   verbs with the suffix *yv(a)* (*iv(a)* alongside jotation): пи́сывать — писа́ть, и́грывать — игра́ть, кри́кивать — крича́ть, си́живать — сидѣ́ть, ла́вливать — лови́ть.

Note that verbs of group (g) may overlap with verbs of groups (a)-(d). This helps account for some of the complex aspectual relationships encountered, e.g. -пры́гивать replacing пры́гать in derived imperfectives. Note further that all but one (быва́ть) of the iteratives in the pairs in groups (e)-(g) are defective; in actual fact, they do not conjugate, but are confined to the past and, on the whole, to the negative infinitive. This may be semantically justifiable, namely on account of their habitual and remote nuance.

    Given this complex base, which has a significant input into the modern verbal system and the phenomenon of aspect, what else happens to reinforce this development? First, one might mention a very important factor, the decay of the tense system, namely and specifically the loss of the imperfect, the aorist, and of the various periphrastic perfect tenses; to balance this, and perhaps assist the new development, there was no emergence until late of a clear future tense, and then only in imperfectives. Instances of imperfects formed on 'perfective' bases and, less often, aorists on 'imperfective' bases, and in particular (because it is still very present) the emergence of the imperfective future made it clear that a binary aspectual relationship had emerged in the grammar of the language.

    Here, bear in mind the great importance of prefixes (the precise term is 'preverbs'). These prefixes to a very large extent echo prepositions, and prepositions tend to grow out of spatial and temporal expressions. So their attachment to verbal roots constrains, limits, narrows the lexical character of the verb. One can imagine this being translated into aspect, specifically the perfective aspect, with the relationship between the simple verb and the prefixed verb being in the realms of *Aktionsart* 'Mode of action' rather than aspect. This limitation, for the non-past, became translated into a future sense in many verbs; one must remember that this is not in all verbs — in the Old Rus' language there was no obligatory future sense at all, in Modern Russian there are numerous such verbs which are not paired for aspect and may be either perfective (состоя́ться 'to take place') or imperfective (состоя́ть 'to consist') (they are often Church Slavonicisms or/and calques), and the perfective non-past often has a habitual sense. In other words, the keyword is 'limitation', or 'specialization'.

    From the earliest times the potential for aspect as a generally significant phenomenon was present (as were others); the aspectual possibilities in (a)-(d) above, with the increasing use of prefixes interacting with them in complex ways, gave the impetus to its development. The first four provide the semantic base, the second three provide the morphological patterns, and prefixes are added. Thus:

(i)   собра́ть — собира́ть, узна́ть — узнава́ть (stressed monosyllabic suffix);
(ii)   улови́ть — ула́вливать (unstressed bisyllabic suffix).

With this one must bear in mind the separation of the imperfective from the iterative. In other words, узнава́ть derives not from the prefix у- plus the iterative знава́ть but from the 'perfective' узна́ть. This new verb, unlike знава́ть, conjugates — it has a non-past. In other words, the iterative is defective and 'remote'; it does not conjugate. In the new pair, узнава́ть — узна́ть, the imperfective is not defective (at least eventually, once the periphrastic future has emerged), while the perfective, with its lack of a specifically future morphology (to be supplied by the synthetic non-past) is slightly defective and thus marked — it is pretty clear what it stands for. The pair is better balanced: the periphrastic future cements the opposition, and the key components of the iterative (habit and natural action) join the derived imperfectives. Over time there is an alignment of the more ancient types on the new concept, all the while bearing in mind that each verb ultimately has its own story.

And along with this one must remember that prefixed simple verbs can remain paired with their source simple verb (indeed, for many of us those were the first encountered and taught as the *real* pairs), but they are in fact rather few: с-де́лать, на-писа́ть; and one mentions with riders such pairs as по-ду́мать, у-слы́шать, у-ви́деть.

Veyrenc reports that prefixed verbs in -ать with derived imperfectives are quite rare, that those in -ить with them are far less rare, and that those in -овать with them are minimal. Non-prefixed verbs in -овать never took off as imperfective formants (-ывать, with which they to some extent coincided in pronunciation, held sway here, and their specialization in the integration of foreign borrowing further limited their grammatical scope), though one finds relics in, say, participles, e.g. неописуемый 'indescibable'. So, prefixed verbs in -овать, even non-prefixed ones, come to function as perfectives by adaptation to the system: -о́вывать. This unstressed bisyllabic suffix is the imperfectivizer which remains seriously productive. The stressed monosyllabic ones, particularly -ва-, are far less so. And at the same time one notes the fading away of the simple verbs where prefixed verbs are available, e.g. слать acquires посла́ть, and the derived посыла́ть sometimes replaces слать; ги́бнуть acquires поги́бнуть, and the derived погиба́ть tends to replace ги́бнуть. The problem, which has lasted for centuries, is that of the 'empty prefix' — above mention was made of сде́лать, etc., but the cases are infrequent and often questionable.

Retain, then, that Russian aspect is not a direct inheritance from Proto-Indo-European, though features of that system are retained in a fossilized form.[1] Thus, the PIE *durative* may be reflected in the short-long opposition of root vowels, e.g. as in брать — бира́ть (obs.) and the $*e : *o$ ablaut relation, as in нести́ —

---

[1]PIE might be said to have had a *cursive* aspect, subdivisible into *durative* (present and imperfect) and *punctual* (aorist), and a *resultative* aspect (the perfect).

носи́ть (the latter in each pair may be seen as the durative). In suffixes, the suffix *-ĕ-, as in смотре́ть and стоя́ть was durative, and the *j suffix indicated an action, as in писа́ть. The nasal infix, of which there are traces in, say, ля́гу, denoted the onset of a change, and as a suffix could denote the onset of a state (со́хнуть 'to dry') or the onset of an action (толкну́ть 'to give a push'). As Veyrenc notes, the Old Rus' language retained a set of endings for the non-past and another for the imperfect-aorist; nothing remained of the perfect endings. The aspectual system of PIE broke up and a temporal system emerged. Aspect forged itself a new place, through word-formation: prefixation and derivation; and a new character: the perfective is singled out as limiting the process — for it the process becomes less central. Aspect selection becomes less morphological, more syntactic and semantic, as all learners know to their cost. It is supremely difficult for a non-native speaker to internalize the essence and make authentic use of Russian aspect.

So, morphologically, Russian was left with one conjugated form, the non-past, and a nominal form conveying the past tense and conditional mood.[2] Aspect supplemented this morphologically impoverished inventory.

Appendix 4: Verb prefixes and suffixes

Prefixes

в-	вз-	воз-	вы-	до-	за-
из-	на-	над-	недо-	низ-	о/об-
от-	пере-	по-	под-	пре-	пред-
при-	про-	раз-	с-	у-	

For an overview of the verb, here is a summary table (Guiraud-Weber 1988:24-56) — the columns give, respectively, 'Preverb', 'Meaning', 'Biaspectual?', 'Productive?', '2 preverbs?', 'Examples'.

в/во/въ-	'in';	+	+	-	входи́ть
вз/взо/вс/взъ-	'up; more'	+	+	-	всходи́ть
					взвыть
вы-	'out; finish'	+	+	-	вы́йти
					вы́играть
до-	'reach'	+	+	+	доходи́ть
					доплати́ть
					допродава́ть
за-	'beyond'	+(-)	+	+	заходи́ть
					закры́ть
за-	'begin'	+(+)	+	-	закрича́ть

---

[2]To these one might add impersonals, non-finite forms, and various types of modals.

на-	'against'	+	+	+	наéхать
на-	'accumulation'	-	+	+	накупи́ть
о/об/обо/объ-	around'	+(-)	+	+	обходи́ть
					обду́мать
					опроверга́ть
от/ото/отъ-	'separation'	+(-)	+	-	отойти́
от/ото/отъ-	'end'	-(+)	+	-	отобéдать
пере-	'cross'	+	+	+	переходи́ть
					перере́зать
пере-	duration'	-(+)	+	-	переночева́ть

And here are a few examples of preverbs + postfixes (ibid.) — the columns represent, respectively, 'Preverbs + postfixes', 'Meaning', 'Biaspectual?', 'Productive?', 'Government', 'Examples'. The abbreviations in the second column are forced by space constraints and should be interpretable.

в-ся	'effort to achieve'	+	+	в + acc.	вду́маться
вы-ся	'ach'v'd satisfaction'	+	+	-	вы́спаться
до-ся	'ach'v't thru perseverance'	+	+	до + gen./-	доби́ться
за-ся	'go too far/lose o's'	+	+	+ instr./-	зачита́ться
					заговори́ться
из-ся	'neg ach'v'm't'	-	+	-	изолга́ться
					испья́нствоваться
на-ся	'do s'g enough'	-(+)	+	-	наговори́ться
					наéсться
о-ся	'error/accident'	+(-)	+	-	оговори́ться
					оступи́ться
от-ся	'achieve+return'	+(-)	+	-	отосла́ться
					отшути́ться
при-ся	'effort+ach'v't'	+	+	к + dat./-	прислу́шаться
					прижи́ться
про-ся	'no rush/error'	+	+	на + acc./-	пройти́сь
					просчита́ться
раз-ся	'intense start'	-	+	с + instr./-	распла́каться
					расходи́ться
с-ся	'harmony/together'	-(+)	+	с + instr./-	срабо́таться
					сжи́ться
у-ся	'feel fine'	+(-)	+	с + instr./-/	ужи́ться
					усе́сться

Remember that certain of these prefixes are subject to spelling and word-formation rules.

Suffixes

(i) Aspectual

-а́й+: отреза́ть, non-past отреза́ю, отреза́ешь, ... отреза́ют 'cut off (imperf.)'.	-ва́й+: дава́ть, non-past даю́, даёшь, ... даю́т 'give (imperf.)'.
-́-ыва́й+: прика́зывать, non-past прика́зываю, прика́зываешь, ... прика́зывают 'order, command (imperf.).	-ну+ (mainly stressed; does not drop from the past stem): рискну́ть, non-past рискну́, рискнёшь, ... рискну́т 'take the risk (perf.)'.

(ii) Others (imperfective examples unless mentioned otherwise):

-а/я+: писа́ть, non-past пишу́, пи́шешь, ... пи́шут 'write'; взять, non-past возьму́, возьмёшь, ... возьму́т 'take (perf.)'; молча́ть, non-past молчу́, молчи́шь, ... молча́т 'be silent'; стоя́ть, non-past стою́, стои́шь, ... стоя́т 'stand'.	-ай/яй+: чита́ть, non-past чита́ю, чита́ешь, ... чита́ют 'read'; отделя́ть, non-past отделя́ю, отделя́ешь, ... отделя́ют 'separate'.	-е+: смотре́ть, non-past смотрю́, смо́тришь, ... смо́трят 'look, watch'.
-ей+: боле́ть, боле́ю, боле́ешь, ... боле́ют 'be ill'.	-и+: носи́ть, non-past ношу́, но́сишь, ... но́сят 'carry, wear' (stress rules for verbs in -и́ть are difficult to define).	-(ь)ничай+: не́рвничать, non-past не́рвничаю, не́рвничаешь, ... не́рвничают 'be nervous'.
-ну+: па́хнуть, non-past па́хнет, past па́хло 'smell (of)'; до́хнуть, non-past до́хну, до́хнешь, ... до́хнут, past дох(л)- 'die'..	-о+: боро́ться, non-past борю́сь, бо́решься, ... бо́рются 'struggle'.	-ова+/-ева+: чу́вствова́ть, non-past чу́вствую, чу́вствуешь, ... чу́вствуют 'feel'; плева́ть, non-past плюю́, плюёшь, ... плюю́т 'spit'.

Abbreviations

CES	Common East Slavonic	OChS	Old Church Slavonic
ChS	Church Slavonic	OR	Old Rus' language
CS	Common Slavonic	PIE	Proto-Indo-European
CSR	Contemporary Standard Russian	PES	Proto-East Slavonic
ES	East Slavonic	RChS	Russian Church Slavonic
IE	Indo-European	SS	South Slavonic
NveR	Native Russian	WS	West Slavonic

fem. / f	feminine	prep.	prepositional
masc. / m	masculine	cond.	conditional
neut. / n	neuter	tr.	transitive
sg. / s	singular	intr.	intransitive
pl. / p	plural	clit.	clitic
1, 2, 3	first, second, third person	coll.	colloquial
nom.	nominative	obs.	obsolete
voc.	vocative	refl.	reflexive
acc.	accusative	perf.	perfective
gen.	genitive	imperf.	imperfective
dat.	dative	rhet.	rhetorical
instr.	instrumental	lit.	literally

The abbreviations, which I use sparingly (several of them not at all), have been chosen to achieve a certain consistency rather than in accord with convention. Thus, Old Church Slavonic is conventionally and affectionately known as 'OCS', but I have gone for 'OChS' here. Other, more generally known abbreviations, are assumed to be familiar.

<	'comes from', 'has its origin in' (usually a chronological statement).
>	'leads to', 'is the origin of' (usually a chronological statement).
*	placed before a hypothetical sound or form.
+	placed before an unacceptable or incorrect form.

Note that translations of verbs, in the infinitive with or without other forms, are given as either 'to X' or just 'X'.

Accent in languages other than Russian has not been given exhaustively.

References

The list is restricted to the works which I actually used in putting this book together. Many other useful works might be found in the publications mentioned in the Preface. In the entries the place of publication is given in its current English form. Names of publishers are given according to convention, thus «Русский язык» is given as 'Russky yazyk', when there seems to be a convention.

Andrews, Edna, *The Semantics of Suffixation. Agentive Substantival Suffixes in Contemporary Standard Russian* (München — Newcastle: Lincom Europa, 1996).

Arany-Makkai, Agnes, *2001 Russian and English Idioms* (New York: Barron's, 1997).

Benson, Morton and Evelyn Benson, *Russian-English Dictionary of Verbal Collocations* (Amsterdam and Philadelphia: John Benjamins, 1993).

Bethin, Christina Y, *Slavic Prosody. Language Change and Phonological Theory* (Cambridge: Cambridge University Press, 1998).

Bolla, Kálmán, Erna Páll, and Ferenc Papp, *Курс современного русского языка* (Budapest: Tankönyvkiadó, 1970).

Borras, F.M. and R. Christian, *Russian Syntax. Aspects of Modern Russian Syntax and Vocabulary* (Oxford: The Clarendon Press, 1977 (second edition)).

Brokgauz, F.A. — Efron, I.A., *Малый энциклопедическiй словарь I-IV* (Moscow: Terra - Terra, 1997 — reprint of the SPb 1907 edition).

Browning, Gary L., *Workbook to Russian Root List* (Columbus, Ohio: Slavica, 1985).

Buck, Carl Darling (with the co-operation of colleagues and assistants), *A Dictionary of Selected Synonyms in The Principal Indo-European Languages. A Contribution to the History of Ideas* (Chicago and London: The University of Chicago Press, 1988 (paperback edition) — published 1949).

Černyx, P.Ja., *Историко-этимологический словарь современного русского языка, I-II* (Moscow:Russky Yazyk, 1994).

Chvany, Catherine V., 'Strategies for Review', in Lubensky/Jarvis 1984: 54-80.

Comrie, Bernard, Gerald Stone, and Maria Polinsky, *The Russian Language in the Twentieth Century* (Oxford: The Clarendon Press, 1996. This is the second edition of Comrie and Stone's *The Russian Language since the Revolution* 1978).

Comtet, Roger, *Grammaire du russe contemporain* (Toulouse: Presses Universitaires du Mirail, 1997).

Cubberley, Paul, *Handbook of Russian Affixes* (Columbus, Ohio: Slavica, 1994).

Cyganenko, G.P., Этимологический словарь русского языка (Kiev: Radjans'ka škola, 1970).

Dal', V., Толковый словарь живого великорусскаго языка *I-IV* (St Petersburg - Moscow: M.O. Vol'f', third edition, 1903-1909).

Dunn, J.A., 'Is There a Trend Towards Analyticity in Russian?', *Slavonic and East European Review* 66/2 (1988) 169-83.

Dušenko, K.V., Словарь современных цитат (Moscow: Agraf, 1997).

Efremova, T.F., V.G. Kostomarov, Словарь грамматических трудностей русского языка (Moscow: Russky yazyk, 1993).

Felicyna, V.P. and Ju.E. Proxorov, Русские пословицы, поговорки и крылатые выражения. Лингвострановедческий словарь (Moscow: Russky yazyk, 1979).

Galkina-Fedoruk, E.M., K.V. Gorškova, and N.M. Šanskij, Современный русский язык (Moscow: Učpedgiz, 1958).

Glazunov, S.A., Новый англо-русский словарь современной разговорной лексики (Moscow: Russky yazyk, 1998).

Golub, I.B., and D.E. Rozental', Секреты хорошей речи (Moscow: Meždunarodnye otnošenija, 1993).

Gribble, Charles E., *Russian Root List. With a Sketch of Word Formation* (Columbus, Ohio: Slavica, 1973).

Groen, B.M., 'The Geminate Palatals and Affricates in CSR', *Dutch Studies in Russian Linguistics* (Amsterdam: Rodopi, 1986) 115-31.

Hamilton, W.S., *Introduction to Russian Phonology and Word Structure* (Columbus, Ohio: Slavica, 1980).

Haudressy, Dola, *Ces mots qui disent l'actualité* (Paris: Institut d'Études Slaves, 1992).

Hoad, T.F. (ed.), *Oxford Concise Dictionary of English Etymology* (Oxford and New York: Oxford University Press, 1996).

Jarancev, R.I., Русская фразеология. Словарь-справочник (Moscow: Russky yazyk, 1997).

References

Kalenčuk, M.L. (ed.), *Язык: Изменчивость и постоянство. К 70-летию Леонида Леонидовича Касаткина* (Moscow: Institut russkogo jazyka im. V.V. Vinogradova, 1998).

Kalenčuk, M.L. and Kasatkina, R.F., *Словарь трудностей русского произношения* (Moscow: Russky yazyk, 1997). (Pages 7-46 offer a valuable up-to-date survey of the phonetics of Russian.)

Kiparsky, Valentin, *Russische historische Grammatik. Band I. Die Entwicklung des Lautsystems* (Heidelberg: Carl Winter, 1965; translated by J.I. Press and updated by JIP and VK as *Russian Historical Grammar. Volume 1. The Development of the Sound System*, Ann Arbor: Ardis, 1979).

Kiparsky, Valentin, *Russische historische Grammatik. Band II. Die Entwicklung des Formensystems* (Heidelberg: Carl Winter, 1967).

Kiparsky, Valentin, *Russische historische Grammatik. Band III. Die Entwicklung des Wortschatzes* (Heidelberg: Carl Winter, 1975).

Kostomarov, V.G., *Словарь морфем русского языка* (Moscow: Russky yazyk, 1986).

Levin, M.I., *Russian Declension and Conjugation: A Structural Description with Exercises* (Columbus, Ohio: Slavica, 1978).

Lopatin, V.V. (otvetstvennyj redaktor), *Орфографический словарь русского языка* (Moscow: Russky yazyk, 1992).

Lubensky, Sophia, and Donald K. Jarvis (eds), *Teaching, Learning, Acquiring Russian* (Columbus, Ohio: Slavica Publishers, Inc., 1984). (= Lubensky/Jarvis 1984).

Lubensky, Sophia, *Russian-English Dictionary of Idioms* (New York: Random House, 1995).

Marder, Stephen, *A Supplementary Russian-English Dictionary* (Columbus, Ohio: Slavica, 1992).

Matthews, W.K., *Russian Historical Grammar* (Oxford: The University of London, The Athlone Press, 1967, reprinted 1975).

Обратный словарь русского языка (Moscow: Sovetskaja ènciklopedija, 1974).

Ožegov, S.I., *Словарь русского языка* (Moscow: Russky yazyk, 1990. Very many editions, the latest with N.Ju. Švedova).

Patrick, George Z., *Roots of the Russian Language. An Elementary Guide to Wordbuilding* (Lincolnwood, Illinois: Passport Books, 1992).

Poltoratzky, M.A., *Русская лексикология и лексикография (в очерках)* (San Francisco and Albany: Russian Language Journal, 1967).

Press, Ian, *Learn Russian* (London: Duckworth, 2000).

Pul'kina, I.M., *A Short Russian Reference Grammar* (Moscow: Progress Publishers, second edition, n.d.).

Remnĕva, M.L., *История русского литературного языка* (Moscow: Izdatel'stvo Moskovskogo gosudarstvennogo universiteta, 1995).

Rozental', D.E., I.B. Golub, M.A, Telenkova, *Современный русский язык* (Moscow: Meždunarodnye otnošenija, 1994).

Ryazanova-Clarke, Larissa and Wade, Terence, *The Russian Language Today* (London and New York: Routledge, 1999). (The *Bibliography and further reading* section, pp. 340-58, is invaluable.)

Samilov, Michael, *The Phoneme* Jat' *in Slavic* (The Hague: Mouton, 1964).

Šanskij, N.M., *Русский язык. Лексика. Словообразование* (Moscow: Prosveščenie, 1975).

Šanskij, N.M., *В мире слов* (Moscow: Prosveščenie, 1985).

Šanskij, N.M., V.I. Zimin, A.V. Filippov, 'Краткий этимологический словарь русской фразеологии', *Русский язык в школе* 1979/1-6, 1980/1-2.

Šanskij, N.M., V.V. Ivanov, T.V. Šanskaja, *Краткий этимологический словарь русского языка* (Moscow: Prosveščenie, 1971).

Šapošnikov, V. [N.], *Русская речь 1990-х. Современная Россия в языковом отображении* (Moscow: MALP, 1998).

Schenker, Alexander, *The Dawn of Slavic. An Introduction to Slavic Philology* (New Haven and London: Yale University Press, 1995).

Šeljakin, M.A., *Справочник по русской грамматике* (Moscow: Russky yazyk, 1993).

Skljarevskaja, G.N. (otvetstvennyj redaktor), *Толковый словарь русского языка конца XX века. Языковые изменения* (Saint Petersburg: Folio-Press, 1998).

Šmelev, D.N., *Архаические формы в современном русском языке* (Moscow: Gosudarstvennoe učebno-pedagogičeskoe izdatel'stvo Ministerstva prosveščenija RSFSR, 1960).

Šmelev, D.N., *Современный русский язык. Лексика* (Moscow: Prosveščenie, 1977).

References

Smirnickij, A.I., *Русско-английский словарь* (Moscow: Russky yazyk, 1985. Many editions).

Sreznevskij, I.I., *Материалы для словаря древнерусского языка I-III* (Moscow, 1958. Photoreproduction of 1893 SPb edition).

Sullivan, J., *An Intensive Russian Course. Part Four* (St Andrews: Russian Department, 1997).

Švedova, N.V. (Glavnyj redaktor), *Русская грамматика I-II* (Moscow: Nauka, 1980).

Tixonov, A.N., *Словообразовательный словарь русского языка I-II* (Moscow: Nauka, 1987).

Tixonov, A.N., *Школьный словообразовательный словарь русского языка. Пособие для учащихся* (Moscow: Prosveščenie, 1991).

Townsend, Charles E., *Russian Word Formation* (Columbus, Ohio: Slavica, 1975. Corrected reprint of 1968 edition).

Townsend, Charles E. and Laura A. Janda, *Common and Comparative Slavic: Phonology and Inflection, with special attention to Russian, Polish, Czech, Serbo-Croatian, Bulgarian* (Columbus, Ohio: Slavica, 1996).

Trask, R.L., *A Dictionary of Grammatical Terms in Linguistics* (London and New York: Routledge, 1993).

Trask, R.L., *A Dictionary of Phonetics and Phonology* (London and New York: Routledge, 1996).

Unbegaun, B., *Russian Grammar* (Oxford: Clarendon Press, 1957 and subsequent editions).

Unbegaun, B. (ed.), H.W. Ludolf, *Grammatica russica*, (Oxford; Clarendon Press, 1959).

Vakurov, V.N., L.I. Raxmanova, I.V. Tolstoj, N.I. Formanovskaja, *Трудности русского языка. Словарь-справочник. Части I-II* (Moscow: Izdatel'stvo Moskovskogo universiteta, 1993-4).

Vasmer, M., *Russisches etymologisches Wörterbuch* (Heidelberg: Carl Winter, 1950-58 — three volumes; also consulted in the four-volume translation and revision by O.N. Trubačev: Moscow: Progress, 1964-73).

Verbickaja, L.A., *Давайте говорить правильно* (Moscow: Vysšaja škola, 1993)

Veyrenc, Ch. J., *Grammaire du russe* (Paris: Presses Universitaires de France, 1968).

Veyrenc, Ch. J., *Histoire de la langue russe* (Paris: Presses Universitaires de France, 1970).

Vinogradov, V.V., *Очерки по истории русского литературного языка XVII-XIX вв.* (Leiden: E.J. Brill, 1950).

Vinokur, G., *La langue russe* (Paris: Institut d'Études Slaves de l'Université de Paris, 1947. Translated from the Russian by Yves Millet).

Vlasto, A.P., *A Linguistic History of Russia to the End of the Eighteenth Century* (Oxford: Clarendon Press, 1988. Paperback edition; original d.p 1986).

Wade, Terence, *A Comprehensive Russian Grammar* (Oxford UK and Cambridge USA: Blackwell, 1992).

Wade, Terence, *Russian Etymological Dictionary* (London: Bristol Classical Press, 1996).

Wheeler, M.C.C. (General Editor: B.O. Unbegaun), *The Oxford Russian-English Dictionary* (Oxford: The Clarendon Press, 1980. Second edition). (Several editions, the latest incorporating Falla, P.S., *The Oxford English-Russian Dictionary* (Oxford: The Clarendon Press, 1984).)

Wolkonsky, C.A. and M.A. Poltoratzky, *Russian Derivational Dictionary* (New York: Elsevier, 1970).

Word-Nest Editor (Ithaca: Exceller Software Corporation, 1987-9).

Zaliznjak, A., *Грамматический словарь русского языка. Словоизменение* (Moscow: Russky yazyk, 1987).

Zemskaja, E.A. (ed.), *Русский язык конца XX столетия (1985-1995)* (Moscow: Jazyki russkoj kul'tury, 2000).

Index

The Index is by no means exhaustive, but should be reasonably useful. Reference is to sections rather than to pages.

Index

9 781853 996153